A Regency Christmas Feast

FIVE STORIES BY

Mary Balogh

❄

Sandra Heath

❄

Edith Layton

❄

Barbara Metzger

❄

Patricia Rice

SIGNET
Published by the Penguin Group
Penguin Books USA Inc., 375 Hudson Street,
New York, New York 10014, U.S.A.
Penguin Books Ltd, 27 Wrights Lane,
London W8 5TZ, England
Penguin Books Australia Ltd, Ringwood,
Victoria, Australia
Penguin Books Canada Ltd, 10 Alcorn Avenue,
Toronto, Ontario, Canada M4V 3B2
Penguin Books (N.Z.) Ltd, 182–190 Wairau Road,
Auckland 10, New Zealand

Penguin Books Ltd, Registered Offices:
Harmondsworth, Middlesex, England

First published by Signet, an imprint of Dutton Signet,
a division of Penguin Books USA Inc.

First Printing, November, 1996
10 9 8 7 6 5 4 3

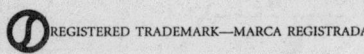

Mary Balogh was born in Swansea, South Wales. She now lives in Saskatchewan, where she taught for twenty years. She won the *Romantic Times* Award for Best New Regency Writer in 1985 and has since become the genre's most popular and bestselling author. Recently she has begun to write historicals, which have received critical acclaim as well. Her most recent Regencies are *The Famous Heroine* and *The Plumed Bonnet*.

Sandra Heath, the daughter of an officer in the Royal Air Force, spent most of her early life traveling to various European posts. She now resides in Gloucester, England, together with her husband and young daughter. Her most recent Regencies are *Lucy's Christmas Angel* and *Halloween Magic*.

Edith Layton, historical romance author, is the winner of numerous awards, including the first Romantic Times Award granted for Best Short Story Author in 1992. The mother of three grown children, she lives in Jericho, New York, with her physician husband and enormous, exuberant dog, Abraham.

Barbara Metzger, one of the stars of the genre, has written over eighteen Regencies and won numerous awards, including a Reviewer's Choice Award for Best Regency and a National Readers' Choice Award in 1995. In addition to writing, she is a professional artist/craftsperson, painting on driftwood. She lives on the end of Long Island with her little dog, Hero.

Patricia Rice was born in Newburgh, New York. She attended the University of Kentucky and now lives in Mayfield, Kentucky, in a rambling Tudor house, with her husband and her two children, Corinna and Derek. Ms. Rice has a degree in accounting, and her hobbies include history, travel, and antique collecting. Her most recent historical romances are *Paper Moon* and *Denim and Lace*, both from Topaz.

Contents

The Gingerbread Man

❄

Edith Layton

His Grace dreamed about gingerbread again.

He smelled the sweet, sharp spice of it. Pungent and heady, it filled his nose. He could feel the just-baked heat of it fresh from the oven, almost as though it were actually there, beside him on his pillow, just as if he held it in his hand and it was about to pass his lips. He licked those lips in his sleep. He could almost taste the gingery, tart sweetness of it, hear it snap as he bit down: the head, the arm, one of the little iced buttons on the gingerbread man's vest? It didn't matter. Just so long as he had some, *soon.*

His Grace swallowed—and tasted—nothing. Nothing but the promise of gingerbread. But he still smelled it and the longing for it suffused him. He moaned. His desire was so keen he turned, and then tossed, and then anguished: awoke ...

... alone and confused, to a stark white morning, absolutely devoid of gingerbread.

Which only made sense. After all, His Grace, the Duke of Blackburn, was fast approaching his thirtieth year and besides, so far as he knew, he didn't like gingerbread.

But he had dreamed of it every night for more than a week now, and had craved it desperately in every

MIMI'S GINGERBREAD PEOPLE

Dough:

3 cups sifted flour
½ teaspoon baking soda
1 teaspoon baking powder
1½ teaspoon cinnamon
1½ teaspoon ginger
½ teaspoon nutmeg

½ cup light molasses
½ cup melted butter or
    margarine
½ cup sugar
1 lightly beaten egg

Icing: 1¼ cup confectioner's sugar, ¼ cup milk

Mix together sifted flour, baking soda, baking powder, cinnamon, ginger, nutmeg. Combine and then add slowly to spice/flour mix: light molasses, melted butter or margarine, sugar.

Add lightly beaten egg and mix into batter slowly, until dough forms. Divide dough into 2 balls, flatten between sheets of waxed paper.
Refrigerate ½ hour up to overnight.

Roll dough ⅛- to ¼-inch thick, cut with cookie cutters.

Bake 350 degrees lightly greased cookie sheets 8 to 12 minutes, or until slightly brown—with cookies still soft on top. Remove carefully, cool on rack. Decorate when cool.

Icing: Mix confectioner's sugar and milk—add food coloring as desired.

Makes approximately 18 to 20 big burly Gingerbread men or hefty Gingerbread wenches or 3 to 4 dozen charming little gingerbread boys or girls.

---

dream, and now he was becoming concerned. Owen Whitley, the seventh Duke of Blackburn, was no stranger to lust. But this kind of lust was absurd, he thought as he sat up and ran a hand over the morning stubble on his lean cheeks. He hadn't felt so ashamed of a dream since he'd been thirteen. But the tasty treats he had dreamed of then were of a much different sort.

Gingerbread, His Grace thought with a snort of disgust. He swung his long legs over the side of his high bed, and as if on cue, but merely because of years of finely trained instinct, his valet, Krupper, came into the room, pushing a small trolley full of shaving equipment before him. Krupper saw the opened window, sighed, and with a great show of world-weary patience, closed it firmly before he approached his master. Sleeping with opened windows was bad for the health and bizarre besides, but Krupper knew his master's idiosyncrasies too well to argue over it. And his master knew Krupper's preferences too well to comment.

Evil miasmas might flourish in the air, but His Grace had been raised in the countryside, and felt even London air was better than none. Besides though London was raucous at any hour, he was lucky enough to have his bedroom window facing his own courtyard, and his nearest neighbors were two sweet old sisters who went to bed with the sparrows and never made a sound to disturb him in the night. Owen took a deep breath now, before the footman who had followed Krupper into the room could relight the fire in his hearth. The air was still cold, scented with the usual London mixture: woodsmoke, horse, and morning mist ... and gingerbread—at least, Owen could still scent it in his mind. He frowned. Krupper saw it, and quietly raised the window sash an inch.

"No," Owen grumbled, "it's not the window. It's

... Tell me, Krupper, do you smell anything ... ah, sweet?"

Krupper raised his thin nose and sniffed. "Shaving soap, but it is your usual, my lord: sandalwood. And ah—bay rum, I suppose, though the bottle is as yet unopened."

"Not anything ... gingery?" Owen asked.

"Heavens, no! Woody, with perhaps a trace of violet, but I have not changed my own toilette in years; we don't wear such scents, Your Grace, and never have." He looked an accusation at the footman, who turned scarlet and said with dignity, "Ain't me. Used plenty of soap on me hands, but it ain't Sunday. Dint use nothing else neither, I swear."

"Bother," Owen said, and frowned, and then seeing how his servants were looking at him, he smiled. It was such a generous smile, so warm and absolutely genuine, that they relaxed. Anyone would have.

His Grace had the most astonishing smile. He was a fine-looking man, tall and lean, with even features and a strong jaw. But he was fair-haired and ice-eyed, with such high cheekbones that he could look a little cold when his face was calm, and actually menacing when he brooded. But his smile transformed him. It made him look young and friendly, and in Krupper's private opinion, perhaps even a shade too accessible, for a man of such high degree.

"It's nothing," the duke told his servants, "never mind." But it was something, and he couldn't stop thinking of his night as he washed and dressed and prepared to go out and begin his day. Ten nights of unrelenting gingerbread was taking its toll. Owen was beginning to worry about himself, a thing that he couldn't recall ever doing before.

"And that's what's so strange," he told his hostess a few hours later as he sat in her parlor, taking a cup of tea with her. "I mean, a man may worry about his life, which I did when I was in the Peninsula; or he might worry about his fortune—which I promise you I do when I go to White's or somesuch gaming place and am lured into a high stakes game. But I'm unused to worrying about my sanity!"

Unfair, his hostess thought, seeing the smile he flashed at her, manifestly unfair that he could smile like that and not realize what it did to a female's heart, and stomach ... and lower locales. But she could never be the one to tell him.

So she simply acted as she always had, as though she didn't notice a thing but the words he said. "Stark raving mad," she said airily, addressing her teacup, "such a pity. Comes from such a fine family too. But His Grace had to be taken off to Bedlam, raving about pastries, and frothing at the mouth for gingerbread ... Oh, I don't think so, Owen, I really do not," she said, laughing.

"Not quite that bad," he admitted, grinning at her. Trust Elizabeth to find the humor in it. That might have been why she was the person he'd told about his problem. She always saw the funnier side, and had since they'd been children. Younger sister of his best friend, growing up in the same shire, and half the time the same house, Miss Elizabeth Lloyd could be counted on to josh a fellow out of his sullens, then and now.

Perhaps it came from her being a younger sister, a tagalong suffered by her brother and his friends if she promised not to cry. And one who soon found herself included in their sport, because she not only never cried, but always made them laugh. Always—when they were young, as well as when they were older and considered themselves dashing blades, and found to their chagrin and delight that Elizabeth could still take them down a notch or two.

Garrett was wed now, with brats of his own. But Elizabeth had never married, and was still his good friend, Owen thought with pleasure. Odd that she never wed, he thought fleetingly, as he often did, for she was youthful looking, still very pretty in a gamin-like way, with her russet curls and bright blue eyes. Even at—Gad! he realized with a little shock: seven and twenty.

Already? he could scarcely believe it. She'd been pursued by many likely lads in her day. ... *In her day?* Owen thought uncomfortably—that made it sound like she was a confirmed spinster. That couldn't be. He, after all, was a full three years her senior. But seven and twenty was considered beyond mature for a woman, and she did live alone in London, with only her elderly cousin as a companion, which was a thing no young girl could do. ...

"Well," Owen said, refusing to think of such dire things as time passing on such a fine morning, "I thought I'd ask you about it, Elizabeth, because it occurred to me that maybe there was something about gingerbread when we were young, something I'd forgot, that was troubling me. Dreams are often conscience calling. I know it sounds odd, but you shared my childhood, do you recall—did we ever do anything particularly significant with gingerbread? Did I?"

"Nothing I can remember," she answered, her head to the side as she considered it. "Except for leaving it over most of the time, for in fact, as I recall, you never cared for it. Now, hedgehogs—the kind our cook used to make—you remember: ladyfingers covered with whipped cream, shaped like a hedgehog, studded all over almonds? Those you positively drooled over. Don't make such a face, you know you did."

"You forgot the whiskey she used to flavor it with," he put in.

She grinned and said, "Hardly—I knew why you boys loved it. But, gingerbread . . . Do you know," she said thoughtfully, "I think it's only the Season. Scents are very powerful things, and all of London seems redolent of gingerbread with Christmas coming. Such wonderful scents are coming out of every bakeshop that I vow I put on a stone every time I pass one."

"As if you had to worry," he said, eyeing her. Because she was still trim, if a bit full breasted, he thought, and then looked away, because as fine a sight as it was, it seemed somehow wrong to ogle *Elizabeth's* bosom.

"Oh, but I do have trouble with sweets—" she began.

But before she could elaborate, he interrupted her. Females could go on for hours about the supposed defects in their figures, whatever a fellow said. "There you are," he said quickly, "London reeks of Christmas these days. That must be it."

"Well, it might be," she mused, "but it may be more, at that. Do you know? Scent's a powerful provoker of memories. I can't get a whiff of eau de cologne—you know, that stuff Napoleon is supposed to adore—without thinking of Monsieur Regardez—you remember our music teacher?"

"Lord, yes!" he said, his gray eyes sparkling, "Garrett and I made him despair, but he doted on you. I haven't thought of him in years, but now I think on it, I smell that cologne, and there he is before me as though no time had passed at all."

She smiled. "Just so. And gin always reminds me of Bream—your undergardener, remember? Gin and mint, that is, because he was always chewing it in hopes no one would know...." They laughed, remembering.

"So," she went on, her head tilted, trying to put the notion into words, "although they say dreams are brought about by late dinners or guilty consciences, I shouldn't be surprised if sometimes they're only memories trying to surface. Perhaps gingerbread reminds you of something important you did one Christmas, something you need to think or talk about. Or perhaps, it's something that's about to happen that you ought to think about. It could even be something someone else is concerned about that's troubling you.

"Were I you"—she went on eagerly—"I'd ask everyone I know intimately, about gingerbread. Don't smile. Maybe it's something someone said in passing that's bothering you, something you can't remember that's the problem. Bring up the subject in conversation and see what happens. No one has to know you're plagued by dreams of it. Maybe something someone will say will jog the memory free, and you'll be able to deal with it, and be done with it.

"Truthfully, thinking about gingerbread only makes me hungry," she admitted, "Mind, I don't like the stuff, but I can never resist eating it. It always looks as though it should taste good, and never does—like drinking vanilla."

Now he laughed. She saw his fair head go back, his

white teeth flash, and she sighed to herself when he subsided and said with a wry look, "Hmm. And now, why does the scent of vanilla always remind me of a certain young person who wasn't old enough for perfume, and so doused herself in vanilla, like any farm girl would? Except she must have used the entire bottle. Gad! You must have had half the boys in Kent following you around licking their lips that day."

"And for all the wrong reasons," she said with an exaggerated sigh of sorrow.

"But it was innovative." He grinned. "But then you always were. Poor tyke, I suppose you had to be, because if you didn't amuse us we didn't let you come with us on our adventures. What brutes we were!"

"Were?" she asked slyly.

He nodded to acknowledge the hit, then asked suddenly, "As to that—are you going home for Christmas?' '

Her eyes widened, "Of course," she said in surprise, "aren't you?"

"Don't know," he said truthfully. "I always do but ... I'm .. truth to tell," he said, leaning forward, elbows on knees, "I'm in the way of, ah, courting now. So, much as I love Kent and the manor, I may have to skip a homecoming this Christmas. Since my intentions are leaning in that direction, I may have to do the pretty and stay here in London with the lady for the holiday."

"Oh," she said, and blinked. "Oh," she said recovering, "then am I to wish you happy?"

"Lord, no!" he said, startled, sitting back abruptly. "Not yet, at least. I said I'm considering the matter."

"You never said that before," she persisted.

"No, but you shouldn't be so surprised, I *am* nearly thirty, my dear."

"Who is she?" Elizabeth asked, "Lady Mary? But no, it can't be. . . . That Davis chit? The little one, all blond, like you?"

"Not like me in the least, Gad! What a horrible thought," he said, laughing. "No, her hair's much lighter than mine, and she's got brown eyes, besides—you know her."

"Actually, no, I don't," she said softly.

"Why, she's the Incomparable this Season," he said, "of course you do."

"Of course, I don't," she said too brightly. "I know *of* her, but I don't know her. How could I? The girl is seventeen, Duke. I am seven and twenty: a vast gap separates us, my dear. I'm old enough to be her mother."

"That you are not! You were never that precocious," he said with a teasing smile. "I remember well—in fact, you were almost sixteen before that would have been . . ." he paused, unsure of how to say it.

But now that he thought of it, he remembered very well the day he'd realized she'd become a woman. It had been on a Christmas vacation, actually, he recalled now. He'd stopped off at his house, said hello to his family, and then headed out, on a horse, to get to his best friend Garrett's house as quickly as he could. He'd found his friend, but there'd been a strange, lovely woman with him. He'd automatically straightened his neckcloth. . . . And then Garrett had laughed at him for it and for the suddenly intent expression on his face.

Still, even so, it had taken a moment for Owen to

realize that the shyly smiling young beauty was his old friend Elizabeth, grown to a splendid nubility: high breasted and curvaceous. Owen had been stunned. He'd had to look away and readjust his sight before he looked back to see his old playmate the way he had to see her.

"Almost sixteen before it—or I—would have been ... if you'll forgive the pun—conceivable?" she asked gently.

"Just so, you little wretch," he said, putting down his teacup. "Well, charming as this may have been, taking tea with you, telling you about a lady I wish to court and being subtly told I might be old enough to be her father—no, no it's true, I suppose, but it's the way of the world, so you shan't shame me this time, witch. I really do have things to be done today," he said as he uncoiled his long body from his chair. "I think I will take your advice, though. Gingerbread memories—yes, I think I'll be off to actively seek some out."

They walked to her door together.

"Shall I see you tonight at the Swanson's party?" he asked, pausing after her footman had helped him shrug into his greatcoat and handed him his high beaver hat.

She tilted her head again. "I don't think so," she said slowly, "I've been asked to a musicale. I believe I'll go there, instead."

"Somewhere, Monsieur Regardez must be smiling," Owen said. He laid the tip of his gloved fingers alongside her cheek, and smiled down at her. Then he left.

Elizabeth went into the parlor and stood by the window, resting her hot forehead against the cool windowpane, watching until the tall, straight figure was long out of sight. She was not weeping just yet, because she had got so used to yearning, after all, that finally being told it no longer mattered, that it was already too late, hurt far too much for simple tears.

He had only to mention gingerbread, Owen thought. But it was not so simple. After all, although it seemed like the most innocuous topic in the world, it was not so easy for a gentleman known as a Corinthian to slip such a word into everyday discussion. The first place he went after he left Elizabeth was to Mantons, to practice his shooting. But although he had many friends there, all they wanted to talk about was guns, their scores at shooting, and their plans for shooting better next time. There was no way he could think to slip the subject of gingerbread into their conversation.

"Don't need to look so pained, old man," one of his friends commented, seeing his impatience with their chatter, "not everyone's got an eagle eye, like you. No, most of us have to work to even wing a target, so we talk it up and down and try to find a better way. Well, I can see you're bored to flinders. Me too. Hey! I'm off to Tatt's, they've got in some beauties, I hear. Care to tag along?"

Ordinarily, Owen would have. He never missed a chance to see some new horseflesh, and Tattersall's had the finest in London. But the duke's ready smile flattened. All they would talk about there would be horses. Damned if a fellow could slip a comment about gingerbread into that either. *"Fine hocks, good chest, but do you know, it's the oddest thing but the color reminds me of gingerbr—"* No. It could be done, but it wouldn't do. He didn't want to ask in such a way as to make a point of it.

He was vaguely ashamed of his recurrent dream. It was really so childish. If he'd been troubled by terrifying nightmares or visited by obscene dreams, he might not feel that way. It might even be amusing to share such things. But the truth was that it was embarrassing for a grown man to be dreaming about gingerbread, and even more so because he couldn't stop doing it. Elizabeth understood, but few others would. But then, Elizabeth was a remarkable girl.

Owen sighed. He was determined to get to the bottom of his dreams before they disturbed another night. So he declined the invitation to view horses, and walked off alone. No sense going for a bout of fencing at Monsieur Perrot's Fencing Academy either, as he'd planned, he thought glumly, though that was always fine sport. No, the one place he might be able to talk about whatever he chose with his friends could only be at his club at this hour.

His Grace, the Duke of Blackburn passed a pleasant moment deciding on which club to visit, and then strode off down the street. He stopped only once, at a bakeshop. He hesitated at the doorway, his nose slightly elevated, sniffing. He went in, and soon came out with his purchase. When he thought no one was looking, he took a tiny bite, and then sighed and slipped the small brown figure of a man into his greatcoat pocket. It tasted like wood. He wasn't surprised. It had smelled reminiscent, but not like the gingerbread of his dreams: rich and spicy, and wholly delectable.

When he entered the sunny dining room at his favorite club, he saw several of his friends at luncheon.

They waved at him, and called him to their tables. He chose the one that had called to him first. Owen was a popular man: known to be witty, and yet kind enough to have many friends, even so. Many gentlemen in London were pleased to call the tall, slender soft-spoken duke "friend."

"Hey, Duke," Rupert Alden, an old school friend said, when Owen had seated himself and ordered his luncheon, "we were just talking about Christmas. Going to be in town this year? Or are you off to the countryside as usual?"

"Town," Owen answered absently, sipping at his wine.

"Aha"—Rupert winked at the others—"put me down for a guinea then," he told them. "If Blackburn's staying here for Christmas, instead of going to his beloved manor, then I say the deed is done by the New Year."

"What deed?" Owen asked.

"Your engagement to the Davis chit," Rupert answered readily. "Now, don't blast me," he said, pushing back his chair and holding up his hands, "we've a bet going, and you know how it is."

Owen bit back what he was going to say, because he did know. London gentlemen bet on everything from the length of a rainstorm to a lady's virtue. The best thing to do was to divert their interest. "I was going home, but I'm feeling lazy this year," he said.

They all hooted, "Lazy? You? Pull the other," George Harris said with a laugh, "you're a dervish, my boy. No, it's the yaller-haired chit, all right: double *my* bet, gentlemen!"

"Don't be so sure," Owen said softly, "after all, there's no one at home for me this year, you know."

They stilled at that and looked at each other, abashed. It was too true, and they'd forgotten, but the duke's aged father had died early in the year. And they all knew that his mother had been gone for years. They looked at each other guiltily, at a loss for words, because they realized the new duke's wounds must indeed be raw. Well, so they were, but so they'd always be, Owen thought. But that was exactly why he was staying in town. He needed a warm family Christmas more than ever, only this year he'd decided it was time to begin his own family.

The table was silent, with everyone applying themselves to their meal with too much gusto. Owen relented. "No, the manor will be quiet this year and that's how I prefer it," he said. "I've family feelings, but no desire to be up to my chin in children."

A few of the men chuckled, and Owen added wryly, "My oldest sister has too many brats to haul down from the North, five at last count—and my other sister's increasing. And though it's early days, I hear she's complaining about walking so far as the dinner table. Yes, you all remember Georgette; she wanted a sedan chair to get to the carriage whenever we had to go anywhere. She was the toast of the Season, because everyone said she was so 'restful.' " As they all laughed, he added, "Brother John's with Wellington, in my stead, now that Father's gone and the duke considers me too vital to the name to be of any use to him. Brother Tom is sailing at His Majesty's command, and brother James is visiting with a friend in Hampshire. No, it must be London for me this year. I mean, can you see me dandling babes on my knee or fetching for Georgette?"

They laughed, relieved. And while all of that was

true, none of it was, because Owen knew that if he asked, any of his siblings would be happy join him at the manor. But he was in the market for a wife; and the marketplace was in London, he thought wryly. Still, it wouldn't do for anyone to know that.

"Don't feel sorry for me," Owen said, and then on sudden inspiration added, "I won't miss much—except . . . except my cook in Kent makes the most wonderful gingerbread. I shall miss that."

They roared with laughter.

Owen looked hurt. "No," he said, "I meant that. Don't any of you remember how good gingerbread was when you were young?"

"D'ja know?" Henry Caldicott, a plumpish young gentleman, commented, "Always loved the *thought* of it, but it didn't taste like nothing. I mean, now, Christmastime, give me a pudding or a mince tart, or a—"

"Or a syllabub or a trifle or a plum pie or a bucket of sweet cream—never met a dessert you didn't like," one of his friends hooted, and they all laughed.

"Ain't so," Henry said stubbornly, "I always looked forward to gingerbread. My mouth was all set for it, it looked and smelled so good. But when I had it, it wasn't nothing like what I expected."

"Are we discussing desserts, or females?" Lord Daventry asked with an uplifted eyebrow, which made them all laugh harder. "But now you've mentioned it," that gentleman added, "I find myself actually wanting a taste of gingerbread, at that. Ho! Philips!" he called to their waiter. "Is there any *gingerbread* in the larder?"

Of course there wasn't, it was an exclusive gentleman's club in the heart of London. But because it was, the waiter nodded, and said, "Of course, gentlemen," and scurried out of the room to find a footman to send to the nearest bakeshop.

"There is something about gingerbread"—Owen spoke in what he hoped was a casual tone—"something that stays in the mind, isn't there? It's like it's all of childhood in one simple sweet."

They were considering that when the waiter came hurrying back, looking threatened. "Gentlemen," he said quickly, "would that be gingerbread *cake*?" Or gingerbread *men*?"

"Both, I suppose," said Lord Daventry with a wave of his slender hand. Then he told Owen with a smile, "There. A decision to make right off. Not so simple then, is it?"

"I liked the little manikins with raisin eyes," the Viscount Rockingham said suddenly, and they all turned to stare at him because he sounded so serious, and yet they all knew him to be a cynical and close-mouthed man. "I looked forward to Christmas because of them—I saw them in the shops and always wanted one. I wondered what one tasted like. Yes, I'd like to try one now."

"*'Wondered'?*" one of the men asked with a frown. "Gads, Rockingham, they were a ha'penny or some-such trifle. Cheap as they could be. Never say you never had the blunt to buy one?"

"I didn't," the dark-faced lord said simply, "my father didn't believe in worldly excesses. Money was one of the things he denied us. Christmas was another. I thought I had indulged myself in everything I had been deprived of when I came into the title," he said with a wry smile. "Seems I forgot something. Yes, I should like to try a gingerbread man today, I think."

Owen had known the Viscount Rockingham for

years, and yet now realized he'd never known much more about him than the fact that he was good company: a rakish fellow with a mordant wit. From the expressions on the faces of the other men he supposed they had not known more than that either. He made a note to actually talk with Rockingham more often in the future; he regretted that he never had before, because the man seemed to have depths he hadn't known.

"Funny, that," one of the other gentlemen mused, "my father was a strict and humorless man too, always awkward with us children. But now I recall he'd buy gingerbread men at the holiday for us, saying they were traditional and educational—for the story I suppose. You know, '... *run and run fast as you can, you'll never catch me, I'm the gingerbread man* ...' At any rate, he'd bring us some. Aye, and tell us the story, very seriously, and then hand us the gingerbread men as though he was giving out edifying tracts. But then he'd always nibble a bit of ours, saying he was testing to see if they were sound. Poor fellow, I imagine now it was the only way he could excuse his pleasure in them."

"My father dotes on Christmas," another gentleman said. "It's my mother who does the nibbling though. She's always saying this is too rich and that's too sugary, and what about my form? So she never took a dessert when we were young, but always finished ours! Yes, but now I recall, she never turned down a gingerbread man, because it wasn't a sweet to her, so much as a toy, I think. She'd nibble a head, and an arm, and when she got to a leg my father would shout: 'Hey, easy there, my love, the children are watching.' Lud! I never knew what that meant until now!" he said in amazement as they all laughed with him.

Soon, they were all telling gingerbread tales: stories

from their childhood, both sweet and sad to hear, exposing themselves and their pasts as they'd never done before. Owen was astonished, it seemed gingerbread was the very key to a man's memories. But although he laughed as he listened to them, or grew silent with compassion, he realized he'd never heard any of the stories before. And so, no matter how warm or chilling they were, none of them could have been the reason for his own dreams.

As a cap on their storytelling, footmen arrived with trays of gingerbread men, and gingerbread cakes. The men fell on them with cries of delight, as though they were children and not some of the most influential statesmen, bravest bucks, finest dandies, and most rakish lords in all England. Seeing their delight, other tables clamored for gingerbread as well, as the roomful of men began to swap childhood reminiscences of gingerbread. None of which helped Owen at all.

He did, however, discover—as he told them all— that he found gingerbread cake a waste of chewing, and the gingerbread men, more to the taste of a termite than himself. Most agreed.

"Yes," Lord Rockingham announced sadly, "even so. Such tempting shapes and aromas, leading to disappointment, after all. Gingerbread is very like most of the dreams we pursue—whether they are of females, or horses, or other such awaited promises: stale at the edges and bland at the center when we finally get them. The idea is all. Because the waiting is far more enjoyable than the outcome."

And so was that what his dreams were telling him? Owen wondered as he strolled home to change his clothes for the evening. That he wouldn't find pleasure in his marriage to the Davis girl? What did he expect from that alliance, anyway? An accommodating wife, a good hostess, and a good mother to his children. She seemed to be capable of providing all those things for him. She was pretty, charming, well born and bred; the Toast of the Season, in fact. But adorable as she was, he didn't lust for her. At least not with the kind of longing the gingerbread dreams signified. But then, he didn't expect lust as a factor in choosing a wife. The women he desired in that way became his mistresses.

He'd liked a great many females, but never loved one. He kept seeking for that elusive emotion, and had come up with passion, appreciation, and admiration—but each for a different woman—instead. He wasn't a rake, but enjoyed sensual pleasures, and found them more pleasurable with a woman he knew. So he kept mistresses, from time to time. Women well up to snuff, who enjoyed the same pleasures, and pleased themselves by supporting themselves by so doing. Owen felt his blood quicken, thinking of the woman he now had in his keeping.

He decided he wouldn't go to the Swanson party tonight. He was promised to see the Davis chit the next night anyway, and Elizabeth wouldn't be there, so there wouldn't be much fun for him in it. Elizabeth made the dullest London soirees sparkle, or at least, her whimsical humor always did. But failing that ... there were other, easier forms of amusement, other ways to pleasantly pass a wearisome night.

Owen remembered that it was high time he paid a call on his mistress ... after all, it might be one of the last times he could. He supposed he'd give that up when he wed.

Or would he? If he loved Caro Davis, certainly. It

would go against the grain to take another female in his arms if he loved his wife. But would he? And did she expect that? It was as well that he intended to accompany her everywhere this Christmas; there'd be many answers for him. But as to the question of those plaguey dreams of his ... he thought, and frowned.

"My dear Duke," a thin voice intruded on his thoughts. He looked down, to see his neighbors, Miss Araminta Fortesque and Mrs. DeWitt, gazing up anxiously at him. They were of a size, two diminutive ladies. But Miss Araminta was thin as a wraith, Mrs. DeWitt, plump as an old tabby. Both sisters were elderly, gray as geese, and had been since he could remember. Because they'd lived together since then too, Owen sometimes wondered if Mr. DeWitt had expired on his wedding day. They always dressed in drab, and invariably in clothing that had no fashion, but were neat as a pair of pins, and bright eyed as children.

"Ladies," he said, sketching a bow.

"Your Grace," they said, and curtsied. "Happy Christmas," Mrs. DeWitt said promptly, her sister echoing her greeting.

"Since it's likely you'll soon be gone from London"—Mrs. DeWitt went on in her gruff tones—"we think it best to offer you felicitations of the Season now."

"But I plan to be in town this Season," he said. The ladies exchanged a significant glance. "Business matters," he lied quickly, finding himself strangely uncomfortable with the thought of all London knowing his matrimonial plans.

He bowed, they curtsied again, and then he walked on toward his town house.

"A lovely gentleman is our duke," Miss Araminta breathed to her sister as they continued down the street.

"Deuced fine gentleman, I wonder what sort of a neighbor the Davis chit shall be?" Mrs. DeWitt answered.

"Oh dear," Miss Araminta said, "do you think there will be a problem?"

"One never knows," Mrs. DeWitt said darkly, "with new brides."

"Oh my," Miss Araminta sighed, glancing back at the tall straight figure of the duke as he strode toward his town house.

"Well, we shall see," Mrs. DeWitt said. "Don't fuss, Araminta. She may be as good a neighbor as he. Only time will tell. Speaking of time, come along, we've more errands than hours, you know. Christmas won't come any slower because we haven't the time!"

Her sister bowed her head, and the two hurried into the last of the short winter's afternoon.

Owen walked on. He made a mental note to ask his secretary to be sure the ladies got an extra large basket from him this Christmas. He had many elderly neighbors, now he came to think on it, and he remembered them all at Christmastime. But he always took particular care to send the two sisters an especially fine parcel as a greeting of the Season, and they always returned the sentiment by sending some quaint home-made, totally useless object as a gift for him. But now it also occurred to him that although they were always groomed, they also wore the same clothing, year in and out. He hoped they weren't in financial straits. They were excellent neighbors, after all.

His Grace dressed for dinner, told his valet not to wait up for him, and strolled off into the night. He wasn't going far. The lady he was visiting didn't live in as exclusive a neighborhood as he did, but she did live in a good part of town. He paid enough to ensure she did. He—as well as all her past protectors—he reminded himself.

It was a neat arrangement, she was as exclusive as she was professional. She had her apartments, he funded her for so long as he availed himself of her services. As much as he enjoyed her company, he never deceived himself about that. It was a business arrangement for pleasure. He wasn't a boy anymore, he could deal with that.

After all, he couldn't very well make love to a "good" woman without marrying her. And although it was unusual for a man of his station, tastes, and times, neither did he like getting that close to a stranger. He'd decided long ago that it must be because he liked so many women for their own sakes. He'd loved his mother, doted on his sisters, and enjoyed the friendship of Elizabeth, for example. So when it came to sexual matters, it was only natural that he should also need to at least *like* his partner. It was hard to feel greedy and alone at the height of passion. Or so he told himself. But as things were in his world, he really had little choice. Most women of pleasure were not women who gave him much pleasure out of bed.

It was as well, he thought now, as he approached his mistress's flat, that he would soon be married.

"You look wonderfully well," he told his mistress when she greeted him at the door with her slow catlike smile. But so she did. She was not a beautiful woman. But she was attractive and very seductive. Dark haired and dark eyed, with a good form, and a provocative smile that hinted at secret pleasures. She looked as though she were just exactly as good at the things she did as she was. And she was not stupid. Women of her caste, class, and expensive upkeep seldom were.

He admired how she looked in her sheer gown, but however seductive she looked, he didn't take her into his arms and tumble into bed with her. His was not that kind of emotion toward her, and theirs was not that kind of arrangement. They appreciated each other but they were intimate strangers, and both would have been shocked at such a show of impetuous passion. Instead, he helped her on with her cape and they left her house. They went to dinner at a restaurant in the Strand. It was an elegant place, famous for catering to gentlemen bent on dalliance. There was no risk of Owen meeting any respectable female he knew there. Or at least, he thought with amusement, he wouldn't see them. Couples dined in private rooms in such discreet establishments.

"My lord," his companion purred, when the last remnants of their dinner had been cleared, and the waiter stood waiting for their dessert order, "let us skip this last course. I know a quiet place where the sweets available are said to be ... sensational. Shall we go?"

"Hmm?" he said distractedly, because he was studying the card the waiter had given him. "In a moment, my dear. Ah—have you any gingerbread, I wonder?" he asked the waiter.

His companion's eyes widened, but the waiter was too well trained to blink. "To be sure, my lord," the waiter said. "And for you, madame?"

"Coffee," she said absently as she stared at her escort. She was too wise to ask why he'd refused her offer. But also too aware of her own attractions to doubt them. She decided he hadn't heard her. When the waiter left, she spoke. *"Gingerbread?"* she asked curiously.

Such a man would never look flustered. She'd never seen the duke lose control even at the height of passion. But now, he looked a little sheepish. Her interest piqued, she leaned forward, and not only to offer him a better glimpse of her fine high breasts.

"Christmas is coming, my dear," he said with a shrug of his wide shoulders. "I suppose that's it. I happened to see a rack of gingerbread men in a shop window this morning, and it triggered memories. Surely you remember such treats? But I imagine I'll be disappointed. This is a fine restaurant, but nothing ever lives up to childhood reminiscences—things never do taste as good as memory serves"—he smiled at his pun—"do they?"

"I don't like gingerbread," she said flatly, her voice cool and her eyes bleak, as though she were seeing something far off. This was so unlike her that he stared. Because now he realized that her every word and action was always cued to his reaction, and the difference—this abstraction of hers in his presence, was startling. It robbed her face of animation and color.

"I used to want gingerbread," she said absently, "well, what child would not? I remember"—her voice grew colder still—"it was my father who used to bring it home. Such a good man, so doting to his daughter. And she not even his, but only a stepdaughter. And yet see how he indulged her! Gingerbread and Christmas presents: new frocks and toys and hugs and kisses. But mostly I remember the little brown men with their white-buttoned vests and their foolish grins. He'd give them to me with a flourish. And how my mother would smile at him for it. But I did not. I knew the price he'd ask me to pay for it later, when she wasn't there, when he stole into my room, while she lay sleeping, and I wished to God that I were ...

"But that was then," she said, recovering herself and looking back at him. She saw his expression.

"Oh, Lud!" she said gaily. "What was I going on about? You're right about the stuff, it does take one back to childhood ..."

He didn't speak, but everything he had to say was there in the gravity of his expression and the horror and pity in his eyes.

"I shouldn't have mentioned it," she said sadly.

"I'd no idea ..." he said, and heard himself. How foolish. Of course, there was no way he could have known. He felt worse, wondering if he should have. But now he realized that he never discussed such things as childhood, or memories, with his mistresses. And now that seemed brutal to him. He felt as bad as he did confused; all he did know was that anything he might say now would be inadequate, and so he fell still. She bowed her dark head, and smiled to herself. It was a different smile than any he'd ever seen her wear: weary and self-mocking. It made her look much less desirable, and far more likable. He felt terrible.

"Well, that's done it, hasn't it?" she asked the air, "But then, I sensed our relationship was drawing to an end, anyway. I mean: to prefer gingerbread to me?" she laughed to herself. She was insulted and yet no fool. The thing had been winding down and she knew it. She'd miss him. Who knew if she'd find his like again? He was elegant, handsome, clean and clever, and had always treated her with consideration. And too—he was one of the few who had ever managed to stir something in her body. That was so rare she decided to reward him. He'd pay her well for their past times together. She owed him honesty as a parting present.

"Why is it, do you suppose," she mused aloud, "that the gentlemen always want to hear about the terrors of your childhood, but are so selective about it? They don't mind hearing you were impoverished. They positively love hearing about the horrors of the slums you crawled up from. Or so the other girls in my profession tell me. But other terrors? Those less random, and less specific to class? I did not, nor will I lie—nor would I have told the truth either, if the gingerbread hadn't loosened my tongue." She laughed.

"We had money, my lord," she said, holding her head up and looking at him directly. "Not a fortune, like yours, but my stepfather was an apothecary, we lived well. Not well enough for me, of course. No amount of money could ever pay for what he expected from it. Don't look so, my dear," she said, and there may have been bittersweet mockery in her voice. "Why do you think I went into this profession, after all?"

"Not for love, and all for money. I know that," he said quietly. "Its only that we gentlemen choose not to. Well, can you blame us?"

He met her gaze steadily, and she was the first to look away. "No," she said softly, "I don't blame you. I liked you very well, Your Grace. There's truth, and no need for it now, so you know it's true. Lud!" she said in more normal accents, as the waiter entered the parlor again. "You were right! Gingerbread does nudge the memory, doesn't it? But look—all my honesty for nothing: there are no evil little men here, only a fine cake."

"I'm so sorry," Owen said, covering her hand with his, knowing that was all of her he could ever cover again. He wasn't the sort of man who wanted to feel like an oppressor. The illusion of free will and equal desire was everything in an arrangement like theirs, and they both knew it.

"Sorry? Why, do you know," she said honestly, "so am I." She looked at the cake with loathing. "One more thing for me to hate about gingerbread, I suppose."

What was there about gingerbread, after all? Owen wondered as he prepared himself for his lonely bed that night. Such a simple thing, a child's treat, an adult's indulgence, but it seemed the portal to childhood was made of the damned stuff. He felt sorry for his mistress, but sighed as he laid his head down on his pillow. It was for the best. Now he could go to his marriage bed unencumbered: mind, heart, and body. He'd see the lady of his choice tomorrow night, and tell her he'd be requesting an audience with her father. He'd be engaged by the end of the year, married soon into the new one. That was that, and so it would be done, he thought, and closed his eyes, and slept.

... And dreamed about gingerbread again: spicy, sweet, tart and moist, melting in his mouth, surrounding him, tormenting him, filling his nostrils with the hot exotic scent of pleasures lost and found and so near and yet so far ...

He woke in a sweat and sat straight up and stared into the dawn light: confused—alone and lost—an adult in a child's world, a child in a man's body, alone and longing for something he didn't have and never wanted and couldn't be without.

"More gingerbread?" she asked when he paid her a call the next morning. Owen nodded. Elizabeth sighed. It had only been a day since she'd seen him, only a day since she'd first learned about his problem, but to her critical eye he already looked thinner, the planes of his face sharper; his light eyes held a disquiet she hated to see there. He was self-contained, a man of strong will and emotions, held hard. But his weariness spoke all that he would not.

A dream about gingerbread disturbing his rest? It was a foolish thing to beset him, but she knew him too well to laugh and cared too deeply to tease him for it now. He constantly dreamed about something he couldn't have. Well, she thought sadly, she knew that kind of dream too well to even think of laughing about it. The only difference was that hers was a waking dream, and his came only when he slept.

"I've asked everyone I know about it," the duke told her as he sat in her parlor in the morning sunlight, his expression bland, but his lean face still bearing traces of his restless night. "You were right," he said. "I've heard some astonishing things because of my questions. Both good and bad. Amazing how such a simple thing stirs so many stories from the recesses of people's minds. I've gotten to know many people much better. That's good, I imagine. But none of it helps me in this. The dream continues.

"I've stuffed myself with the demned stuff too," he said bleakly, "but it does no good. I hate gingerbread. But there I am, like a greedy boy, devouring it everywhere I find it in London. But it's never the stuff of my dreams. Am I losing my mind, Elizabeth?''

He gazed at her steadily, his gray eyes imploring. "You've known me since we were babes, you'd tell me, wouldn't you?"

"Since *we* were babes!" she said, her eyes widening, trying to make a jest of it. "But I am a full three years younger, my dear."

He didn't laugh. She didn't know if he even heard her. "Gad!" He shook his head. "What a ridiculous question. But it's one I ask myself daily. Am I mad? I haven't forgotten anyone's name, I don't have any other bizarre urges; I remember everything I have to do each day—but I dream the same damned dream each night! Be honest with me, Elizabeth, do you think I'm in a decline?"

Her heart broke to see him suffer so, but before she could speak, he went on, a little desperately, "Who else can I ask, after all? I'd horrify my family with such a question, and amuse my friends. But you're like a sister and a friend to me. And after all, who else knows me so well and is always so honest with me? So continue to be my friend, and tell me straightly please, will you?"

"Of course you're not mad," she said harshly, because he had called her sister and friend and she knew she was both to him, and so much as that was so, still it hurt even so, because that was all she was to him. "You're having a dream. It's persistent. Since it can't be a portent of things to come—because you've already gone and eaten some gingerbread, it surely means there's something you're supposed to know. When you find out, it will cease, I'm sure. It's not gingerbread itself, clearly. So then—*Christmas*," she said in sudden triumph. "It has to be rooted in the holiday, because, as you say: everyone remembers gingerbread as a Christmas treat."

"Not everyone," he answered softly, his high cheekbones flushing slightly, though she didn't know why. He hadn't told her about all the responses to his question. She might be a friend, but he never forgot that she was a female.

"Anyway, it's a relief to find out that you don't think me mad," he said on a long sigh, "it may be you're right. The holiday will pass, and the dream may go with it. If not, there are worse things to dream about, I suppose. Thank you, Elizabeth," he said more heartily, putting down his teacup and rising, "I think you're right. I'll ask 'round some more, but I won't let it bedevil me. Nor let it change my plans in the least. Past time I was wed, after all. Best buy some dancing slippers, my dear, you may well be dancing at my wedding come springtime. But be sure, there'll be no gingerbread at my wedding feast!"

He laughed. She did not. It seemed to her that her heart stopped. She seemed to see him in a mist, and hear him through a buzzing in her ears.

"Elizabeth, are you all right?" he asked suddenly, reaching out to hold her steady. Because she had stood when he had, but now seemed to sway on her feet, and her face had grown pale—so pale he could see the ghost of a few freckles high on the bridge of her little nose. Her skin was so pure and fair, he'd forgotten how the sun had dappled her cheeks with them when she'd been a girl. He hadn't seen them for so long, he'd forgotten that with her russet hair and dusting of freckles, she'd always seemed like a young fawn to him in those days. Now he wished she had more of the little gingery specks on her cheeks, so she could be his little Elizabeth again.

He held her shoulders, and she brushed against him for a moment before she regained her balance. It was disconcerting. She felt light and fragile as a child, but also soft and inviting as a woman—instinctively he wanted to draw her close. . . . So he held her upright instead. He knew her face as well as his own, but now he couldn't really see her. It was as though he were seeing two people in one: the adorable child—a lovely young woman, wavering back and forth before his eyes. He blinked. Perhaps he *was* going mad, he thought in alarm.

"I'm all right, much better," she said, stepping back abruptly. He dropped his hands, guilty for no reason he could think of. That damned gingerbread story his mistress had told him. It made a man feel like a lecher with any young girl he cared about, he thought ruefully.

"Don't worry, it's only—a problem of a—female nature," she said before he could ask about her health again.

"Ah," he said, because he knew what she meant, but didn't know what else to say. A woman's biology wasn't the sort of thing a gentleman discussed with a girl, even a girl who was a close friend.

"So," she said brightly, "it's to be the Davis chit, is it? Lud! Forgive me, but in light of what you said, I can't keep calling her that, can I? What is her first name again?"

Her monthly time must be giving her pain, he thought, watching her uneasily, because her large blue eyes were dazzling with unshed tears. Soft, flowery blue, the blue of wild flags, or the wild bluebells in the springtime meadows of home ... "Her name?" he said foolishly. "I, um, yes—Caro—Caroline, that's it!"

"Well, congratulations," she said bluntly.

"Hold!" he said. "Not so fast. It's not gone that far ... yet. I haven't even put the question to her, though half of London thinks I have."

"As if you don't know the answer, as well as most of London already does," she said with a brief laugh. "Well, good luck, my dear, not that you need it. And do let me know when it is fait accompli, will you not?"

"Oh, that won't be until after the holidays, in any case," he said quickly. "But speaking of things to come, I'll see you tonight at her ball, won't I?"

"No," she said softly, "I won't be there."

"But I thought you were going."

"I am not. No, you're not losing your mind," she said, seeing his expression, "I was going. But something came up."

"Then tomorrow," he said, "I'll tell you about the ball. Feel better, my dear."

They said good-bye, and she watched him leave. This time she didn't watch him from the window, because she had to rush up the stairs to the privacy of her own room to weep. *A female thing,* she had said, she thought as she wept: indeed, so it was. He loved another female. Or at least, he wanted to marry one. She'd always known the day would come—but like knowing the day of one's death, that didn't make it any easier to bear.

She'd loved him from the day she'd met him, and she couldn't remember when that had been, she'd known him since she could remember. But she could clearly remember that first Season she'd come to London, that first dance he'd had with her as an adult.

That had been a dream fulfilled. He'd gazed at her with admiration. He'd smiled, and bowed low, and offered her his hand into the dance. He'd danced with her. At last, he'd seen her as a woman grown. She'd waited for the rest of the dream to come true.

It had not.

A dozen worthy men had asked for her hand that Season, and she'd politely declined, waiting patiently for him to come and ask. He had not. But he had come to ride with her, to walk with her, to talk with her. And so, of course, he'd known of her popularity. He'd congratulated her on her success, and so she'd clung to her hopes. He was not unaware of her. He was yet young. His father had married late. He was clearly waiting for her to mature too.

Another Season came and went, and yet she waited. He had to serve his country, and she admired him for it. But she worried and waited for him to return to her. He did. He returned. Not to her specifically, but to her locality. They remained friends.

Another Season, another reason: and another and another and another. Now she was seven and twenty, and could see another decade looming. All her friends were wed; most were mothers. Her parents despaired, and then gave up their hopes, thinking she had none. They were indulgent enough to let her have her way and let her set up a spinster's establishment. But then, they'd three other daughters, after all, as well as two sons and many grandchildren, and more coming every year.

Elizabeth was very clever, and very careful. Because she was also very afraid of her good friend the Duke of Blackburn ever knowing her hopes. Precisely because he was a good man and a close friend, she knew he might offer for her if he thought he was breaking her heart by not doing so. But knowing that was why he offered would certainly break her heart.

And so they none of them knew—neither parents nor sisters nor brothers, nor the man she loved—how much she wanted her own home and children. But only *his* home and only *his* children.

He loved no other. She was sure of that. He had mistresses in his time, true. Not many, he was no rake, and he never took any who were not thoroughly professional, and he had, after all, never given his name or his heart to any other woman. It dismayed her, even so. But he was a man, and he didn't love them and so though it hurt, it did not kill her. *This,* she was sure, as she wept, would. Him—and that foolish Davis chit! Pretty and silly and popular because of it. But not for him, surely not for a man like him. He was no longer a childish dream of hers. Elizabeth knew him too well to adore him. She loved him, instead.

He had flaws, of course, she knew he did. She loved him the more because of them, because his virtues outweighed them. He was a man of action who liked a good day of riding, a thoughtful man who liked a good evening of reading. He was a true nobleman, kind to the powerless he didn't have to be kind to, with the courage to be cruel to the powerful who could hurt him—if he thought they deserved it. He was a gentleman in every construction of the word, and a man whose presence sent shivers of desire through her. There was no man she'd ever thought more attractive. Was he tall, lean, strong, and ice-eyed? Then that was exactly how the best-looking man in the world should look. He was the measure by which she judged all other men, and none had ever come close to him, much less topped him in her eyes.

And he was going to marry some silly little fribble of a chit because it was time for him to be wed? He wasn't perfect, but that was beyond foolish of him. Even so, he deserved so much better. Elizabeth wasn't sure she was that much better, but she knew him, she knew what would please him and she'd devote her life to that, if she could. She made him laugh, she made him happy—she could make him happiest.

But ... she sat up in her bed now, and wiped her eyes. But, in a way, she'd begun to realize this day was coming for a long time. Other men may have praised her looks as well as her allure, but he never had. Why should he, after all, if he didn't think it? Honesty was one of his virtues. What was it young Marston had called her once, because of her hair? ... *a perfect autumn rose.* But even if so, what good was it being a perfect rose, if a gentleman preferred lilies? Or daffodils, or daisies? When a man had a taste for peaches, what use were apples? Even perfect ones. Elizabeth took a steadying breath. She was simply not to his taste, she could wait forever, and would never be.

Well, and what was she to do? Wither and die, because he did not find her to his taste?

He wanted gingerbread, she thought with a sniff, as she sat up straighter, and she—she was some other flavor. What should she do, grow stale because of it? Elizabeth gave a watery giggle, thinking about how tangled and silly her thoughts were becoming. And found herself smiling because she actually could giggle. But why not? She'd feared and yet anticipated this for so long that now that she really knew it was almost a relief, in spite of the pain.

Well, then, she thought. She rose to wash her face. Well, then, she would go on. She wouldn't get what she wanted, but she would learn to want what she could get. Dreams were one thing. Reality was another. She wouldn't waste her days and nights pining for what she could sense and smell but never taste— the way he did in his dreams these nights. She had not too many nights and days left to dream, after all, she thought. She was a spinster: a girl who had waited too long at the fair.

In a curious way, his dreams had served her purposes. They were a lesson to her. She wouldn't let her recurrent dream make her sick, and she wouldn't worry about losing her mind. She'd find it. And a new life.

Time, Elizabeth thought as she dashed cold water on her face and her dreams, *past time* to get on with living and wake from all her foolish dreams.

"You look very fine this evening, Your Grace," Miss Araminta told Owen, greeting him as they chanced to meet when he stepped from his house to the street.

"Up to all the rigs," Mrs. DeWitt concurred heartily, eyeing what she could see of her neighbor's formal garb in the dimming twilight: from his high beaver hat to his silk breeches and white hose, nodding her approval as though she knew every nuance of masculine fashion.

Owen bowed, and wished he could return the compliment, but the sisters were dressed in their usual non-fashion. Tonight they carried several packages, and had an air of bustling purpose about them.

"I see you're off to paint the town," Mrs. DeWitt

said. "Come along, Araminta, time's wasting," she
told her sister, and then added, "good night, Duke.
It's a new day for you, and a good night for us. Your
time to rise and greet the fashionable world, but our
time to prepare for bed."

Miss Araminta tittered at this weak sally, Mrs. De-
Witt gave a bark of a laugh, and the two sisters curt-
sied, then hurried to the front stair of their own house.
Owen waited until they were safely in, and then strode
on, frowning. Women of property should have had
footmen to carry their purchases. He considered the
pair. Old clothes, carrying their own parcels, rushing
through the cold London streets by themselves each
evening? Poverty was a shame as well as a crime in
his world, and he knew all the rigs men went to in
order to hide it. Pawning the family heirlooms, mort-
gaging their estates, living in debt, increasing that debt
by high wagering in a mad attempt to win it back. And
then if that failed: fleeing the country or life itself, by
going home to put a period to their existences.

But these two? What could they do? What was left
to pawn, what did they have to sell? He doubted they
would wager. He knew they couldn't begin a new life
on the Continent. Owen hated to think of the two odd
sisters as destitute, and resolved to have his man at
law look into their finances. If he had to make an
anonymous contribution, he would. It was worth it to
keep such good neighbors—and Christmas was com-
ing, and they were part of his childhood, as well. Gad!
he thought, this Christmas: with its phantom ginger-
bread and thoughts of childhood, marriage, and
children!

But that was exactly what he was thinking about as

he strode through the streets toward the Davis town house.

The Davises were wealthy, and Miss Caroline's father was wise. He had a daughter who was a gem of a girl, the toast of the Season: pretty and personable, and he presented her in a sparkling setting to accent her charms. The town house was brilliant with light, light enough to show that everything in and about the house was first-rate. The furnishings, the uniforms on the household staff, the portraits staring down at the guests from the silk-covered walls, all proclaimed it: the chit this ball was being given for was well-born, well-bred, of good family with considerable fortune, and she was up for bids.

In a manner of speaking, of course, Owen thought with a wry grin, as he gave his coat to a footman and prepared to join the throng in the ballroom. He waited to be announced. From the way Caro's bright head shot up when she heard his name, he knew she'd been waiting for just such an announcement. And from the way her mama and papa looked up, he knew they were eager for yet another pronouncement—from him. And why not? he thought. He didn't give himself airs. But a *duke,* and in her first Season? If she were his daughter, he'd be anxious too. A curious thought, and not one he liked, he thought as he went forward to greet her.

No matter what Elizabeth had said, Owen thought as he approached the Davises, Caro Davis was of age, after all. It wasn't as if he were leagues older. Only thirteen years, a trifle, not exceptional at all these days. But still: *thirteen,* he thought now, a little shocked in spite of himself. Still, it was common to marry a younger woman—everyone did it. He was only thirty, it wasn't as if he were a lecherous old man—the way he felt this afternoon, when he'd touched Elizabeth. Odd that—

He stopped thinking as he took Caro's little hand. That was, after all, the best way to deal with thoughts of marriage. Once, he'd thought to love. Once, he'd thought he would someday declare himself to his beloved in a welter of romantic passion. But it hadn't happened. It just had not. Still, marriage did have to happen. It was time. Now, he had to think about the children. Yes, the children.

"Good evening, my dear," he said and winced, inwardly; *"my dear"*? Suddenly that sounded so—avuncular. And yet he said it all the time and it sounded right. With Elizabeth, for example. But then, Elizabeth was nearly of an age with him. "You look lovely tonight," he added, in truth. For she did.

She was justly called the Incomparable this Season. Petite, with a fine rounded little figure, a mass of blond curls, fair skin, luminous violet eyes, a tiny dimpled chin. He was a tall man, and the contrast between them had seemed pleasing to him before, but now he was nagged at the realization that in all things she was somehow less than himself: height and age ... Well, but he hadn't offered for her yet, he told himself, silencing his doubts. Although why he had not, he couldn't say, he was the envy of all the other men because she seemed to favor his suit.

"Why thank you for your compliment, Your Grace," she said softly, lowering her violet eyes. Then she peeped up at him through her lovely long eyelashes. He was enchanted. The music struck up. She looked her question at him. He smiled, but remained silent. She laughed, shrugged one shapely little shoulder, and let her father lead her out for the first dance. Owen could not have without as much as declaring himself utterly in the face of the *ton*.

But it was not really presumptuous of her to have waited for him to ask. He'd heard the speculation about his increasing interest in her, she must have too. He'd taken her for a drive, danced with her most particularly at every ball they'd been to together; he was hanging after her, and they both knew it. But he wasn't yet snared, and she knew that too. Clever little lady, he thought, feeling much better about everything as he watched her dance.

When the next set formed, they danced together. She was graceful and silent, charmingly shy with him, as always. He did the pretty by other ladies he knew after that, biding his time until he could take Caro in to dinner. Then he'd have a chance to speak with her. With all the idle pretty chatter a man might engage a society maiden in, there was little chance to really talk together. They had exchanged pleasantries but never actually discussed anything with each other. It was high time. She seemed perhaps a little in awe of him. That wouldn't do. But as the time for the supper dance drew near, Owen found himself nonplussed, wondering what to talk about.

Still, there was, after all, Owen thought with a certain grimness, the matter of gingerbread, after all. He'd quizzed everyone he knew in London about it; it was time to sound her out. And yet, he thought suddenly, his spirits rising, wouldn't it be delightful if it had been something *she'd* said that had spawned all his dreams?

"... *Gingerbread?*" she said when he broached the subject, when they were finally seated together at a little table, apart from the others. She dimpled. She was primed for this moment. Her parents were getting uneasy. Others had offered, His Grace had not, and yet he continued to—hover. *Time to pour on your charm,* Mama had said. *Show him the stuff you're made of,* Papa had said. So she would, and so she would have him, Caro thought: the cap to her glorious Season—nabbing the catch of the Season. His Grace was rich and attractive, and *hers,* Caro thought smugly.

He was perhaps a trifle cool, compared with the other beaux who flocked around her, and older than most of them too. But richer and more distinguished, and he really looked yards younger when he smiled. Which was seldom. But then, Caro thought, she could go elsewhere for smiles after they were wed, a married woman had such freedom, and the duke didn't look as though he would care. She wondered if such a cool fellow ever would. He was very up to all the rigs, after all, or so everyone said. And so why not that one too?

But now he seemed disposed to really chat with her. It was about time. But about *gingerbread*? What nonsense. It must mean he was in a frolicsome frame of mind. That was a relief. Talking about anything more difficult was too trying, and so whenever he had, she'd smiled and been peacefully sweet with him. He'd liked that. But now he wanted some drollery? Wonderful. She was just the girl for it. Time to turn on the charm, indeed, and wouldn't he be pleased!

"Gingerbread?" Caro cooed, "Oooh, she loves gingerbread, Your Grace!"

"Who?" he asked, confused.

"*Her,* she just loves it,' she said with a giggle, "but she's sooo sorry! Gingerbread mans are too, too naughty for her, for they make her look like a little dumpling, you see, but she does love them even so."

He looked at her blankly. She pursed her plump pink lips, and pouted. He was almost enchanted by the sight. "*She* does, wicked man," she whispered with a charming show of mock sulkiness.

He simply stared at her as though she'd lost her wits.

"*Her*—I mean me!" Caro said, "Oh, bother! It's the way people talk when they are friends, silly."

He was appalled. "I do not talk that way, Caro," he said firmly.

"Wicked fellow," she said sunnily, "but all of us do. 'Tis the latest thing!"

"It is?" he asked, his gray eyes wide.

She nodded, and then proceeded to tell him what else was. The Duke of Blackburn sat, transfixed, as the Incomparable of the Season finally revealed herself to him in her full splendor: prattling on, chattily acquainting him with all the fun and roundaboution her set was up to these days. Baby talk was the least of it. Lisping and riddles were prime.

"But *she* refuses to lisp," Caro said with a show of hauteur, "because it is too too popular, and it wouldn't do for her to be common, would it? I mean, every shop girl is lisping, and it ith tho tho tedious, ith it not?" She giggled and batted her astonishing eyes. "But she need not lisp, everyone adores baby talk, it is too charming. The gentlemen all send poetry to her too," she added, and rapped his knuckles with her fan. "Naughty fellow to have not penned one poem to her!" she said merrily. "But she will forgive you, if you ask her very sweetly."

The gentlemen sent flowers and poetry and sweets,

and really clever lads sent kittens; it was the newest rage. "So there!" she said triumphantly, when she was done with her recital. "See how nice her is to still be speaking with you when you've neglected her so! She forgives you though."

"Indeed," he said, aghast.

Owen went to sleep near dawn, so troubled by his thoughts he was hardly aware of getting into bed. He had left the ball early and paced London's streets, gone to his club and drunk himself even more morose. Exhaustion, and all the brandy, finally put him to sleep . . .

. . . to dream of gingerbread again. Stifling sweet, pungent fumes of gingerbread suffused his dreams. He groaned with longing and despair and felt as though he were suffocating and gasped for air—and woke to a bleak morning, with nothing sweet in sight, and all his dreams dashed.

He looked haggard when he called on Elizabeth. She looked weary as well, her blue eyes shadowed with blue, her face pale. Still, she mustered a surprised smile for him.

"A call every morning this week, Duke?" she asked as they sat in her parlor again, and she poured tea. "We're friends, to be sure, but take care. You've never been so attentive before. The *ton* will think you're courting me, and what shall Miss Caro say to that?"

"Much I care," he grumbled. "Gad, I tell you—and only you, Elizabeth, because we're such old friends, but the girl is a clothhead! It's over, so far as I'm concerned, and I wonder that it was ever begun! All she's got in her head is those eyes, which are remarkable, true. But I need more in a wife than that. She has the conversation of a three-year-old! She says it's on purpose because it's the fashion but I wonder ... and don't want to find out, I assure you! I left the ball early, as a matter of fact. Doubtless she'll have Chudley, or Harrington, or some other of her besotted beaux. And much luck to them! They'll need it."

Elizabeth didn't seem to be particularly surprised. Rather, she seemed to him to be abstracted. Distant and preoccupied, and strained. But she had complained of some "female problem" the day before, so Owen made no comment about her distraction, nor asked how she felt. It would only have embarrassed her. Poor girl, he thought, nothing he or she could do about her discomfort but wait for her time to pass and time itself to cure her: females had a hard row to hoe in this world, Nature herself saw to that.

"So, anyway," Owen said heartily, looking at the purity of her profile as she gazed out the window, "this means that I'll be going home for Christmas after all. Just what I need, I think. Once I'm there, maybe these foolish dreams will cease. The fresh air—there'll certainly be enough to distract me there too. I made sure of it. I asked my secretary to send invitations by messenger, first thing this morning. And so doubtless all our neighbors and our kin who can be will be there: my sisters, their husbands, our old friends and theirs as well, and all the children. Gad! I'd best bring buckets of gingerbread at that! How many nephews and nieces are there now, anyway? I'd thought to add to their number soon, but as it stands, maybe it's best I don't. We've a legion of children as relatives between us now, don't we?"

"Indeed," she said softly, "indeed we do."

"So!" He slapped his hands on his knees. "Done

then. Well, Christmas is coming, and the New Year won't wait for us. I was thinking of leaving for the manor as soon as Wednesday. When shall I come get you, my dear?"

"Oh," she said, turning to face him, a strained smile on her face, "ah—well, as it happens—you need not bother. Not this time, at least. For I won't be going home this year, after all."

"What?"

"I'm not going home," she explained. "I'm going to . . . to Henry Murcer's house, instead."

"Murcer's house?" Owen blurted in astonishment. "But why?"

"Come, that's not very flattering," she said. "He asked me, is the why of it. And I thought it wise to go, so we could get to know each other better. I'm— I'm by the way of considering his offer, you see."

"Murcer?" Owen asked again, dumbfounded. "But you—he—you've been friends for years, old Murcer and you."

"*Very* flattering . . ." she said with the trace of a real smile. " 'Old,' indeed. He's our age—your age actually, Owen. And yes, we've been friends for years, since I came to London, in fact. But he's always made his intentions clear, should I choose to see them. And now, I think I do."

"But Murcer . . ." Owen said, stunned. He fell still, thinking of their mutual friend. There was nothing he could say against the man, because he liked him, actually, but it seemed bizarre. Elizabeth and Lord Murcer? The fellow was a good man, true, a worthy chap, in all, but so ordinary. Neither strikingly handsome nor clever. Somehow, he'd thought that Elizabeth, when she decided to wed . . .

No, he thought in surprise, he had not. He had never thought of Elizabeth actually marrying at all. She'd never seemed taken with any man before. He hadn't heard that she was favoring Murcer's suit, or anyone's. It bothered as much as stunned him. "A very good fellow," was all he could mutter now, "but to marry him? Are you sure, Elizabeth? Friendship's easy. Marriage is a lifetime affair."

It seemed to him she squared her slender shoulders. "Yes," she said with more spirit, her blue eyes blazing, "so it is. Exactly. Friendship is very easy. Marriage is not. But I'm of a mind to think of my future now. You're not the only one to think about children at Christmastime, Owen. I'm not getting younger, either. And you were contemplating marriage, weren't you? A wise idea. It set me thinking. Murcer says his parents would like to meet me, and as for me? I—I should like to see what may be my future home, as well."

"But—but do you love him?" Owen asked.

She leveled a cool blue penetrating stare at him. "Love? Is that necessary, do you think, my dear?" she asked in chill tones. "Think on your plans with the Davis chit, before she overwhelmed you with her nonsense. Hmmm? And then rethink your question, if you please."

It seemed she actually waited for him to do just that. But he was too confused to attempt it. After a few seconds of silence, her chin went up. "So," she said with resolve, "there it is. I'll won't be going with you. But I'll see you in the New Year, my old friend. And perhaps then—I'll have some news for you."

"Oh," was all Owen could think to say. He felt strangely insulted, and even more than a little angry.

He couldn't say why, because she'd every right to do as she pleased, of course. She wasn't accountable to him, after all. But she might have consulted him before taking such a huge step.

"Of course," he said, rising to his feet, drawing himself up to every inch of his full six feet of icy nobility, "I wish you well. You are indeed doing what I was about to do. Very wise of you. However, I remind you, *I* chose to tell you of my doings, every step of the way. Odd, that you didn't think to mention a word to me."

"Oh, come now," she said, with forced laughter, "you're not my father, Owen. Only three years between us, after all. And you were never that—*precocious*—is that the word you used for me when last we discussed age?"

"So it was," he said icily. "Gad! Look at the time," he said, fumbling for his fob, scarcely glancing at his watch. "I'm late already."

"But, what about your dreams?" she asked with real concern as she rose to see him out.

"What of them?" he asked coldly as he strode to the hall and her front door, because he couldn't remember what she was talking about.

He remembered later, of course. When he discovered himself trying to drown his unease in gingerbread. Because he'd turned in at Gunthers' tea shop instead of his club, and had ordered a cup of tea and a bit of gingerbread before he fully realized what he was doing.

Fine, he thought in dismay, as the waiter brought him a plate and he stared down at a brace of wickedly grinning gingerbread men, *you lose your mind, and she gets a husband. Lovely way to pass your declining years, in Bedlam. Babbling about gingerbread boys, while she dandles real babies on her knee. . . . Little russet-haired girls with peacock blue eyes,* he thought, vacantly staring at the brown, currant-eyed ginger-bread boy before him.

He absently took a bite. And then sat up and stared at the fractured piece he still held in his hand.

"Waiter!" he shouted. The waiter appeared instantly, looking perturbed. The gentleman had a strange and wild look in his eye.

"Is anything amiss?" the waiter asked anxiously.

"No, but, tell me, have you always had such ginger-bread?" the duke demanded.

The waiter relaxed. "Indeed, sir, we always attempt to purvey the finest for our clientele. But if it isn't to your taste, we can always get you something else. A plum tart, perhaps? A seed cake? No? Then perhaps some gingerbread of the cake variety. These are more of a novelty, for the Season, you see."

"No, no, never mind. This is fine. It's more than that, it's excellent, the best I've ever had, actually," Owen mumbled, shamed at the attention he'd drawn to himself, because other diners were staring, "There's no problem. The reverse, in fact. I—er—called you to wrap it up for me, please, for I find I've got to leave." *Before* I *make a complete cake of myself,* he thought bitterly.

He strode from the shop with the gingerbread in his coat pocket. It was the same, he'd swear to it. This was exactly what had haunted him through so many nights. He was sure. The scent and taste matched the treat of his dreams: redolent of ginger, sweet but tart, soft and chewy and utterly delicious. . . . And so what?

So he'd solved the mystery about the origin of his

dreams. The place served delicious gingerbread. That was scarcely news. It was London's most popular and exclusive pastry shop, famous for its wedding cakes and ices, and other delicious treats. Of course, they'd have tasty cakes of any sort. He'd thought he'd never liked gingerbread but obviously he'd eaten such before and enjoyed it, sometime in the past. It made sense.

So did the obvious solution to his sudden obsession with the stuff, as well as his dreams of it. He passed the shop often in his daily rounds, and the scent of it had obviously triggered his memories, setting up a desire for more. Elizabeth was wrong in more ways than one.

Gingerbread simply signified: gingerbread.

And so? He had larger problems now. But he could not, for the life of him, decide what they were. All he knew was that they sat on his back like a weight, and oppressed his heart. *Truly mad now,* he thought as he strode on through the winter afternoon, his spirits low as the gray clouds above him, and twice as cold.

His Grace, the Duke of Blackburn, went home and dressed for the evening. He went to dinner at his club. He kept to himself, though he kept himself in constant company all evening. And yet he could never remember being lonelier. In fact, he could never remember being lonely before. That troubled him. He resolved not to let it. She was not the only female in London, there were dozens of young women who would be only too pleased to bear him company; although, actually, he preferred the company of his own sex, after all, he decided. He understood men. And why not? They were explicable.

He left dinner and went to another club, and then another, and then to a gaming hell and then to a tavern and then to a rout and then to a friend's house for a cordial and then back to a tavern and then went reeling into bed near to dawn.

And woke in a sweat, dreaming of gingerbread again. He punched his pillow and groaned, and buried his head in his arms, and slept again. And dreamed of sweetness and tartness and delicious scents .. of a faint reminiscent perfume ...

He was dancing to the strains of a wonderful waltz. The woman in his arms was graceful, her perfume delicious, sweet as vanilla, spicy as ginger. It seemed he couldn't hold her close enough. He was no boy, he'd had many women, but there was something overwhelming about this one. Her hair was soft and scented and her firm breasts peaked against his chest, the skin of her cheek was like satin and he nuzzled it as he drew her closer still as they swayed, locked together as longing rose in him ... He glanced down.

He couldn't see her face clearly, but she wore white, the color a young girl might wear in her first Season. That gave him pause, he was tempted to step back, curiously ashamed. But then he reassured himself. There was nothing girlish about this wondrous, sensuous female he waltzed with. Her breasts were high and full, he could see down into the shadowed valley between them, and for a moment he wanted to quit the dance and bury his face there ... but the music swelled even as his desire did, and they turned and turned to the music. The dance was like a prelude to love, and she danced with him as though they were already one.

It seemed to him, in the curious way one knows things in dreams, that they'd danced thus before, long, long ago. But then, for some reason, he'd not been bold enough to take what he wanted, the way he knew he would now. Because now he knew he had to hold her even closer and move with her in a different sort of dance, one that promised pleasure beyond any he'd ever felt before.

He could feel his skin growing heated as his desire rose and his body rose to hers. But suddenly she pulled away.

He paused, filled with frustration and yearning.

He was dimly aware of people watching, and realized he shouldn't have held a female so close, even in a waltz, so he shrugged an apology and bowed. She returned to his arms, they danced again, but the scent of her, the warmth of her and the absolute pleasure of holding such a slim, curved, and beautiful body so close overpowered him and he dragged her close again. She broke away.

His desire was so keen he forgot about propriety and went to snatch her back into his grasp—but then he saw her clearly. And stopped. Because it was Elizabeth standing there, in the gown she'd worn at her come-out all those years ago, and she was looking at him ruefully, a slight smile on her lovely mouth.

He felt shame and remorse, but even so, he couldn't resist her, and as shocked at himself as he was aroused, he reached for her again.

She held out her hand. But not to take his. Only to show him what she held in hers: a gingerbread boy. He stared. She sighed, and showed him that she held three of them—three little gingerbread boys with piped-on icing eyes and foolishly smiling mouths. As he watched, they grew to real boy size. Then they stood at Elizabeth's side, grinning at him. He recoiled in horror, because he suddenly saw that they all had Henry Murcer's face. . . . Elizabeth took their hands, gave him a sad smile, shrugged, and turned away . . .

He woke.

It was not yet dawn. The winter sparrows had not yet woken to squabble outside his windows, the sky was still black with icy night fog. But the Duke of Blackburn shot out of bed. He rummaged in his wardrobe like a wild man, and then pulled on a shirt and stuffed it into a pair of hastily donned britches, tugged on boots, and struggled with a neckcloth. It was too early to wake his valet, too late to rouse a footman to let him out, so he dressed in some disorder and slid from his town house, and took to his heels when he reached the pavement and ran full out down the empty streets, frightening a few lamplighters, making a few drunken bucks reeling home sing out: "Go get 'em" without knowing what they were cheering about.

And then he hammered on Elizabeth's door.

A white-faced footman appeared, and then another, and then her butler came to see what caused the commotion, his own vest half-buttoned over his nightshirt, his hair still wild from sleep. They sniffed at the duke's breath when he demanded to see their mistress, and bit their lips. Then they lit some more lamps and saw the look in the duke's wild icy eyes. They led him to the salon and left him there to pace.

"Owen!" Elizabeth cried when she opened the door. She raced into the room to see him. Her hair was still in a night braid, she wore a wrapper buttoned to her chin, and one cheek—the one that had obviously just been resting on her pillow, was rosy, while the other was white as the rest of her face was—with fear. "My dear," she said tremulously, coming up to him and reaching up one trembling hand to lightly touch his cold, cold face, "whatever is the matter!"

"Nothing now," he murmured, and pulled her into his arms, and kissed her.

At first, she stiffened in shock. Then, she relaxed, and her hands went to his shoulders and she murmured something to him; then she sighed and opened her lips against his, and drank as deeply of him as he did of her.

They clung together. When he finally had to breathe other, less sweet air than her own breath, he raised his lips. He laid his head alongside hers. But he didn't loosen his grip. And neither did she.

"No!" he whispered fiercely into her hair. "No, you shall not! You shall not marry anyone but me. Never, I won't have it! You are mine, and have always been, and so it shall be. Do you hear?"

"I hear," she said, but he heard her voice shake, and drawing back, saw her eyes were filling with tears.

And so he had to kiss her again, and again, and then go to a chair with her, and take her on his lap and kiss her yet again.

"So," he said at last, lifting his lips from hers, but refusing to remove his hand from her breast, because there was only so much he could bear to deprive himself of now, after so long a hunger. "So. There it is. I've been a fool, Elizabeth. All the while, there you were, and I could not—would not, see what was before me. Because, I suppose, so long ago, I was shamed at wanting you. Because," he said, when she attempted to speak, "you were my best friend's sister, and in those days, that most lamentable of creatures— a girl."

He smiled with her, but it was a smile that almost

broke her heart. "I guarded myself against it then," he said. "My guard remained even when I'd no use for it any longer. What a fool I was. Please, Elizabeth," he said seriously, touching his hand to her chin, her cheek, her hair, "listen. Murcer's a good man. Maybe better than me," he added with a hint of his old pride to give the lie to that claim, "but he'll never love you as I do. Or as I can. I want to marry you and give you that parcel of children. I need you more than he does, to be sure. You must marry me, for I do love you, and always have. And somehow, I must have known it without knowing until I thought I might lose you. Then I went quite mad, to be sure.

"But think," he insisted, his eyes on hers, "why else have I never loved anyone else? I never have, you know. There never was, nor ever will be anyone else for me. I know that now. I only wish I'd known it before. We're wasting valuable time, my love. No. *I've* wasted it. Tell me that it's only me. I can't be that wrong. Foolish and blind, in the past, yes. But I can't have misread your lips. Your kisses can't have lied. You never have. Don't start now. Will you have me? Will you love me? Will you forgive me?"

She touched his face as a blind woman might, trying to make herself believe what she saw in the rising dawn light.

"Say you can come to love me," he insisted, his eyes searching hers.

"I do, I have, I always shall," she finally said.

When he raised his lips from hers again, he sighed. "I'll go slower, but not much," he said with a crooked smile. "for we'll marry soon, though never soon enough for me."

It wasn't until the sun was well up and they were

laughing at the way he'd dressed himself, and he was smiling to himself at how he'd almost succeeded in undressing her and himself again, that she thought to ask.

"And what of the gingerbread dreams?" she asked with sudden concern.

"What of them?" he asked, shrugging one shoulder as she tried to tie his neckcloth for him. "I found the gingerbread at Gunthers'. Did I tell you? No? I must have had more important things on my mind," he said with a tender smile. "But the same stuff, I'd swear it. I was wrong. Some gingerbread is delicious. Not the kind from our childhood. Gunthers'. In any event, I couldn't rest because something was disturbing my sleep, and I doubt it was gingerbread, after all. Still, you were right. Something *was* trying to work through my thick head, and come into the light."

He gazed down at her, and stilled her hands by holding them tightly in his. "It's clear," he said, "I missed sweetness and spice, tartness and savor in my life. I've found it now. Gingerbread? No. I doubt I'll ever dream of it again. It's not as sweet as your lips, you see," he explained, bending his head to hers.

"Owen—" she managed to whisper before their lips met, because there was nothing else for her to say. There never had been, for her. She couldn't remember ever being happier. She never had been. But she had the delicious feeling she would be even happier soon.

It was a long time before the Duke of Blackburn found himself in his own bedroom at last. And then it was not to sleep, but only to dress again. Because he had so much to see to before Christmas. Because he was simply too happy to seek the oblivion of sleep.

The Duke of Blackburn raced around town like a man possessed in the days before he and his promised bride were to leave for his home in the countryside. But there was so much for him to do. Presents to buy, Elizabeth to get alone for a moment so he could kiss her; gifts to give, a dark corner to find so he could kiss Elizabeth; farewells to make, and Elizabeth to hug. He passed most of his last night in town in Elizabeth's arms, and only left her when he realized he was almost at the end of his self-control. *Soon,* he promised her, as he left.

Soon, he told himself, as he stood in his own bed-chamber, preparing for bed alone, *soon.* He flung open his window, as was his wont, and then finally went to bed, thinking of Elizabeth. And slept at last, and smiled as he did.

A few hours later, as dawn crept across London's sky, far beneath his window, and a little to the side, in the adjoining house, another window snapped closed.

"There!" Miss Araminta said, giggling. "Done, at last!"

"And well done," Mrs. DeWitt agreed, taking the last of the lot from the oven.

"We sold every bit," Miss Araminta exclaimed, "and they said that they want more."

"They'll have to wait until next season," Mrs. DeWitt said firmly. "The holiday is almost upon us, and so our work is done. This batch is for the duke. You saw the lovely basket he sent, did you? Well, I admit, I peeked. Two hams, a goose, cakes, liquors, and fruit as well. You'd think the man was feeding an army! So this batch is entirely for him. Not Gunthers'. They'll have to wait until next year."

"But we will make more, next year?" Miss Araminta asked fearfully.

"Indeed, we shall," her sister informed her. "No one complained, and we made quite a tidy profit."

"Well, who could complain?" Miss Araminta said. "We baked by night, when all were sleeping, and shut the windows at dawn before they awoke. And after all, even so, who would complain about such a lovely scent as freshly baking gingerbread?"

"One never knows," her sister said astutely, "the thing is that persons think that people of our degree should toil not, neither should we spin. Lucky that the duke is our nearest neighbor, or at least our oven's nearest neighbor. He never spoke a word of complaint though his rooms must have smelled like a bakeshop each midnight."

"Well, such a gentleman is never home at night, anyway," Miss Araminta said, "but now that he's to wed, I suppose he'll be keeping regular hours. Do you think that will be a problem for next year?"

"I doubt it," her sister said, smiling, "for I hear Miss Elizabeth prefers the countryside anyway, and so I don't doubt they'll be there next year at this time. Perhaps they will even have a babe by then—ah, well. Such a nice young woman. Far more suitable for our duke than that Davis chit. That's his good fortune. Now, about ours. Do you know how much profit we have made this year?"

"I think so," Miss Araminta tittered, "and just think! If we fashion houses as well as men next year, for I hear it is the coming thing—so cunning: little houses made of gingerbread—we can have twice as much profit!"

"Houses?" Mrs. DeWitt said contemplatively, "Perhaps. Perhaps not. But speaking of houses ... I've more news for you, Sister. I have figured it out. We can put the monies we earned from the gingerbread to good use as usual. We shall use some to buy presents for the family. Handkerchiefs and scent and such for the men and women, and books—improving texts, for the children. And we can give some to our favorite charities, as ever at this time of year, of course.

"And then, *for us*," she said with an air of great import, her bosom swelling with pride, "if I use just the interest from poor Reginald's investments, and you put in the interest from poor Papa's legacy—we can do the last house this very year!"

"No!" Miss Araminta breathed.

"Yes," her sister said with satisfaction, "for some anonymous donor has made a contribution to our welfare as well. I don't know who it is, but I shall not question Providence."

"Perhaps some of our good works have come back to us?"

"It may be so," Mrs. DeWitt observed, "but however it happened, we have enough without touching our capital: this year, we can buy the last house."

"And then we shall own every house on this street, shall we not?" Miss Araminta asked anxiously.

"So we shall," her sister said with pleasure, "anonymously, of course, as we keep all our financial dealings secret, just as Papa always cautioned us, for it isn't right to flaunt success. And as he always said: the appearance of frugality is good for the mind, soul, and one's neighbors. But speaking of neighbors, we shall have our choice of them entirely now. For we shall own every house on this street—save for the dear duke's, of course."

"And it's lovely that he has his, for he's such a good neighbor. And one must have *some* young people in the vicinity, after all," Miss Araminta said.

"Indeed. Well then: Happy Christmas," Mrs. De-Witt said, raising her glass of sherry.

"Happy Christmas," her sister echoed, raising her glass. She peered at her sister over the top of it, "And, next year? A new year, perhaps new houses? And not just of the gingerbread variety? There are streets full of houses in London, houses that would be perfect for our friends and purposes ... not to mention the rents that come due."

"Why, Araminta, you have grown greedy," Mrs. DeWitt said, "but do you know? I believe I shall drink to that!"

The sisters clicked glasses and giggled. But the window was closed and so no one heard them.

Especially not the Duke of Blackburn, cozy in his bed. He slept on, undisturbed, smiling in his sleep, dreaming of his lady and her warm fragrant kisses that tasted so sweet and spicy—even better than the fading scent of gingerbread.

Sophie's Syllabub

❄

Sandra Heath

The Comte and Comtesse de la Palitaine held their winter ball four days before Christmas. It was 1814, and the moonlit night was frosty as the cream of Brussels society arrived at the brilliantly illuminated house in rue Ducale, which formed the western boundary of the park in the sought-after upper part of the city. But as the guests moved to a quadrille beneath the crystal chandeliers, in the nursery another quadrille was taking place as the comte and comtesse's two young daughters danced with one of the maids and their new English governess, Miss Sophie Greenwood, whose dark-green velvet gown looked particularly seasonal.

The nursery was a cozy room, where firelight flickered, and seasonal garlands were festooned over the picture rails and pelmets. Pride of place was given to one of the comtesse's German Christmas trees, of which there were five throughout the house. There was much merriment as the unofficial quadrille became more and more disorganized, ending with everyone falling on the polished parquet floor in a helpless heap of laughter, including Miss Greenwood.

Sophie was twenty-seven years old, and something of a mystery. With her lighthearted manner, soft

SYLLABUB

1 lemon	1¼ cups heavy cream
½ cup + 2 tablespoons sherry	5–7 tablespoons wine
	¼ cup powdered sugar

Chill 4 or 6 champagne glasses. Grate half the lemon peel, and pare off the rest in strips. Place the sherry, grated peel, lemon juice, and sugar in a bowl, and leave for 2–3 hours.

Whip the cream until semistiff, then add the sherry mixture gradually while whipping. Whip until the mixture stands in soft peaks.

Divide the wine between the glasses, and spoon the sherry and lemon cream over it. Cut the pared peel into "matchsticks" and use to decorate the cream. Serve chilled.

---

brown curls, and big hazel eyes, she was considered far too attractive to still be single, but no amount of subtle questioning had elicited much information about her private life. All that was known was that she'd been companion to the elderly Duchess of Roxwell, who'd decided to travel in Europe, which was at last open because of Napoleon's downfall. Sophie admitted that under normal circumstances her financial situation would not have required her to seek a position, for she had a private income that was payable once yearly, but she had decided to do so because it offered her a wonderful opportunity to travel, and, like the duchess, she'd always wanted to see Europe. She also happened to like the old duchess, who was an eccentric but kindly soul with whom she got on well.

However, it all went wrong when the duchess died suddenly in Vienna, leaving Sophie unpaid and obliged to use her own funds to travel home to England. Then, in Brussels, burglars stole her money and most of her belongings, leaving her with two choices: go to the British consul for assistance, or seek further employment until sufficient funds had been saved to complete the journey. She decided upon the latter course, and when the post of governess at the house in rue Ducale became unexpectedly available, she applied and was accepted immediately.

If Sophie's new employer had realized then that on the night of the ball, the governess would catch the womanizing eye of the dissolute young Prince of Orange, she would never have been taken on, for the prince was the comtesse's lover! But as the ball got under way, the comtesse's world was completely rosy, for not only was the prince dancing flattering attendance, but there was also Captain Owen Lassiter, a particularly handsome and enigmatic young British naval captain who'd caught her interest.

It was to be this latter idle interest that commenced the ruination of the comtesse's grand night, for when she saw the dashing captain slip out to enjoy a Spanish cigar on the lanternlit terrace, where no one else had yet ventured because the starry December night was cold, she decided to join him. But first she spent a few minutes flirting with the prince, so that he would not feel in the least neglected.

During those few minutes, Owen sensed nothing of his hostess's predatory intentions as he drew upon the cigar and gazed over the garden toward the city's great fourteenth-century ramparts. If he'd glanced up to his right, he'd have observed the exuberant scene in the nursery, but he was too deep in thought to observe anything in particular. The dismal state of his private life over the past year had changed him. He'd always been a dedicated sailor, but now the navy and the sea were all he ever thought of. Indeed, as far as he was concerned, what else was there to think of? This being the case, he really didn't know what had possessed him to visit landlocked Brussels. He loathed being on-shore, but after a nine-month stint in the Caribbean was on leave until the New Year, when he was due to take command of the frigate *Piper,* one of the swift-est vessels of her class in the Royal Navy, and famous because of the number of prizes she'd taken under her previous captain. She was being completely re-fitted, and he had no option but to wait until she was ready. He'd gone to great lengths to gain the orders that took him to the Caribbean, for he had much from which he wished to escape. But then, wasn't escape the usual resort when one had a guilty conscience?

He was thirty-five years old, tall, elegant, and darkly handsome, with thick coal-black hair, keen blue eyes, and a complexion that was still suntanned from his recent service in the seas around Jamaica. His lean body was ideal for the gold-braided navy-blue and white uniform that was reckoned by some to be the most attractive military uniform of all, and if he'd cho-sen, he wouldn't have lacked ladies to partner him, but he was seldom in the mood to be a social animal. He'd only been invited to the ball by accident, because he'd been in a group of army and navy officers who'd been asked to make up numbers. He'd thought it might do him good, but he was bored.

God, how he wished Christmas were over and done with, that the *Piper* were ready to sail, and he could kick the dust of land off his shoes again. He pulled a wry face, watching the smoke of his cigar curl up into the icy night air. There'd been a time when he'd have reveled in a ball such as this, but that had been before He sighed, for times had changed, *he'd* changed, and if he was alone now, he had no one to blame but himself.

He was just pondering slipping away to his room at the Hôtel d'Angleterre in the rue de la Madeleine, when he heard the laughter from the nursery. At first he couldn't make out where it was coming from, but then noticed the brightly lit room in the wing to his right. As he looked, the two de la Palitaine girls, Marie-Claire and Monique, eight and ten respectively, came to the window to gaze eagerly out. He knew they were hoping to see snow, and he smiled, for children weren't concerned with the logic that to have snow, one first required snow clouds, whereas tonight's sky was starlit from one horizon to the other.

He was about to extinguish his cigar when another figure appeared at the nursery window. Dumbfounded, he stared up at the young woman in the dark-green gown. Surely it was ... ! No, that was impossible, she was in England! At that moment the cigar burned his fingers, and with a curse he dropped and stamped on it. When he looked at the window again the curtains had been drawn and he could see nothing.

The comtesse chose this moment to come on to the terrace. Petite, dark-haired, and dark-eyed, she was very beautiful indeed, and her frilled peach taffeta gown rustled busily as she hastened over to him. "Ah, there you are, Captain Lassiter," she said, her diamonds glittering in the moonlight. She shivered because it was so cold. *"Dieu, c'est froid, n'est-ce pas?"*

"Cold? Er, yes, I suppose it is," he agreed.

She looked quizzically at him. "Is something wrong, Captain?"

He pulled himself together. "No, I was just miles away."

She looked blankly at him. "Miles away?" Then her eyes cleared. "Ah, yes, you mean in your head, *oui*?"

He smiled. "Yes." He glanced at the nursery window. "You have two very pretty daughters, Comtesse, they clearly take after their mother."

She went pink with pleasure. "You are a flatterer, Captain."

"Indeed not," he replied earnestly, for he shared the view that the comtesse was one of the most handsome women in Brussels. He also shared the view that her morals were not as they might be, but that was by the by. Besides, who was *he* to pass judgment on the morals of others? In the past, his own hadn't borne close inspection, and it had cost him dear, just as, he suspected, it would one day cost the comtesse dear too.

She eyed him, tapping his arm with her closed fan., *"Eh, bien, Capitaine,* how long do you mean to honor Brussels with your presence?"

"I haven't made up my mind, but I should hear of my new vessel some time in January, so I suspect I'll remain until then."

"Good, for I intend to take you under my wing," she declared coquettishly.

His heart sank as he recognized the look in her eyes. "You do?"

"Why, yes, sir, for it is not right that a gentleman like you should be on his own." She searched his face in the moonlight. "Is there a lady in your life, Captain?"

"No." But his glance flickered momentarily toward the nursery window.

The comtesse didn't notice. "Ah, how emphatic you are, some might say too emphatic."

"I assure you, Comtesse, there is no lady in my life, nor has there been for a year now."

She couldn't hide her astonishment. "A year? *Dieu,* that is a long time."

"A lifetime," he murmured, glancing at the nursery window again. "Tell me, Comtesse, did I see a governess with your daughters a short while ago?"

The apparent change of subject surprised her. "A governess? Why, yes, of course, does not everyone have a governess for their children?"

"What is her name?"

"Greenwood. Mademoiselle Greenwood. English, of course, for the best governesses are English. Or maybe Scottish . . ." Her voice died away as she saw the expression on his face. "Captain?"

"Greenwood?" he repeated slowly.

"That is what I said."

He stared toward the curtained window. "Her first name wouldn't be Sophie, by any chance?" he asked.

"Why, yes, Captain, it would indeed." A new light entered the comtesse's eyes as she studied him. "Do you know her?"

"I, er, believe so." It *was* Sophie! He was so shaken he didn't know what to say next, for his estranged wife was the *last* person he'd expected to find in Brussels! He struggled to recover his poise. "Comtesse, would it be possible to speak to her?" he asked then.

A jealous spark flitted through the comtesse's heart. How *dared* he ask after a mere governess, when he had the belle of Brussels society showing an interest in him! "That I do not know, Captain. Perhaps if you could explain a little more . . . ?"

He hesitated, and then thought better of confiding anything in a known intrigant. Besides, now he knew where Sophie was, it surely wouldn't be all that difficult to waylay her. "Oh, it's of no consequence, Comtesse. Miss Greenwood and I haven't seen each other for so long, there's probably no point in renewing the acquaintance."

She gave a thin smile, for she knew what he was really thinking. No matter what he *said,* Sophie Greenwood *was* still of interest to him. Of considerable interest. The knowledge piqued her, for she wasn't used to taking second place to someone as inconsequential as an upper servant! Spite spurred her in that moment, and she determined to thwart him by dispatching the girls to their grandmother in Aix-la-Chapelle, in the care of their governess! Let the brave Captain get around *that!*

With a false smile, she tapped his gold-braided sleeve again with her fan. *"Eh bien,* it is far too cold to stay out here, so I *insist* we go back inside."

"Of course." He offered her his arm, and they went back toward the ballroom, but as the master-of-ceremonies announced a *ländler,* and he was obliged to whirl the comtesse on to the crowded floor, his thoughts were of Sophie.

*   *   *

A little later that same night, when the girls were asleep, Sophie slipped alone to the gallery above the ballroom. She went quietly to the greenery-decked balustrade, and peeped down into the beautiful vaulted chamber. It had walls that were hung alternately with costly Brussels tapestries and tall gilt-framed mirrors that added to the sense of spaciousness, the parquet floor was sanded, and there were German Christmas trees in the corners, each one ablaze with candles. She didn't see Owen among the guests.

She'd been on the gallery for a few moments, when the Prince of Orange noticed her. He guessed who she was, for who else but a governess would be dressed in a velvet gown, live in the house, and yet be excluded from a ball? His glance moved speculatively over her. After the hothouse charms of the Comtesse de la Palitaine, the governess's freshness was most beguiling.

A footman passed with a tray of champagne, and the prince reached out absently to take a glass, his gaze still upon the dainty figure in dark green, but unknown to him, his mistress had noticed his absorption in Sophie. The comtesse's eyes flashed with jealous fury as she rightly interpreted the expression on his face. It was bad enough that the captain should be interested in the vapid little creature, but that the *prince* should be so as well was *insupportable!* Aix-la-Chapelle was no longer a solution. The governess would have to go altogether!

Snapping her fan open, the comtesse swept toward the prince, her face tightening into another of her brittle smiles as she linked his arm and drew him to a part of the ballroom from where he couldn't ogle anyone he shouldn't. A few moments later she beckoned a footman, and instructed him to order the governess to her room. He did so, and within seconds Sophie had fled from the gallery.

It was four in the morning when Owen returned to his hotel in the rue de la Madeleine, but although he was tired, he couldn't sleep. He lay there in the warmth of the huge four-poster bed, staring up at the hangings and recalling the past, when Sophie and he had been so much to each other. He'd met her through her brother William, a fellow officer who'd also been his closest friend. William had invited him home two Christmases ago to the modest manor house home of the Greenwood family. What a wonderful time it had been, for it had brought Sophie into his life. He remembered walking hand-in-hand with her through the snow at the Greenwoods', and could recall even now the color on her cheeks, and the sparkle in her beautiful hazel eyes. When he'd kissed her, her lips had been cold at first, but had swiftly warmed beneath his. She was a creature of passion, coming sensuously into his arms with an instinctive readiness for the delights of love.

That evening, while carolers entertained the rest of the family in the snow outside the house, he and Sophie had slipped away to the drawing room, where the cook had already set out the traditional syllabub that was always served in the Greenwood household on Christmas Eve. The room had been lit by the flickering light of the fire, and the little pearls in Sophie's favorite earrings had shone as she turned to face him. How lovely she'd looked in her sapphire dimity gown, and how innocently enticing. There was something about her that drew him like a pin to a magnet, something that had haunted his existence ever since.

He smiled as he remembered how playfully she'd taken a spoon and dipped it into one of the glasses of syllabub. She'd held the spoon out to him, and he'd tasted the thick, creamy richness of the sweet that he would ever after associate with that magical moment. She'd tasted some as well, and then put the spoon down to come into his arms. His body stirred even now when he recalled how she'd pressed against him. He'd known she could feel the hardness of his masculinity, a hardness she'd never experienced before, and that it excited her. The lips she'd raised to his had tasted of syllabub, and she'd melted into his embrace as if she too were a confection of wine and cream.

Never had a kiss been so arousing. He'd felt her responding to the new emotions that swept through her, and his own arousal had intensified. His fingers had twined in her hair, and when his palm had brushed against her breast, he'd felt her nipple through the soft stuff of her gown. Their mouths had moved together, and their tongues touched briefly as her lips parted. The temptation to go further had been almost unendurable. His masculinity had pounded in his breeches, longing to be freed to find the haven of her femininity. He'd wanted her so much that in that single moment he'd known she'd always be the only woman for him.

The sweet images faded as other memories took over, memories of his own foolish male arrogance. He'd taken it for granted that her heart was his to do with as he pleased. He'd spent the night with a woman he knew was Sophie's enemy, and as a consequence had lost Sophie forever. To this day he didn't know why he'd been so damned stupid. He didn't *like* Serena Hetherington, let alone want to make love to her, and yet it had happened. It was, as men were wont to say, one of those things. Well, he'd made sure he steered well clear of those things since then! But it was too late. Too late by far.

It hadn't even been a simple matter of knowing Sophie was safely with her family, for she'd left there too, and no one would tell him where she'd gone. He was persona non grata with the Greenwoods. Sophie's parents wouldn't speak to him at all, and William had almost gone so far as to call him out over what he'd done. It hadn't come to that, thank goodness, but he'd deservedly forfeited William's friendship forever.

Now, out of the blue, he'd found Sophie again. She was the only woman who could ever melt the ice that encased his heart, the only woman who could make him live properly again, and he wanted her back. He intended to speak to her somehow, in the hope that she'd relent now that a whole year had passed. But in his heart of hearts he feared she'd *never* relent.

The comte and comtesse slept very late after the ball, so Sophie as yet knew nothing of her impending dismissal as she took Marie-Claire and Monique for an airing in the Allée Verte, a public walk in the lower city, beside the important canal that led north to Antwerp. The canal was a favorite method of transport for people as well as goods, and the girls spent some time on the bank watching the *coches à l'eau*, or water stagecoaches. The imminence of Christmas was evident in the passengers' glowing faces, and the abundance of seasonal fare they were taking home. There was carol singing on one boat, and the merry sound echoed glowingly over the cold scene as Sophie ushered her two young charges back to the rank of fiacres waiting at the end of the walk.

Sophie returned to rue Ducale to find three things awaiting her. The first was a letter from her mother, the second was news of Owen's reappearance in her life, and the third was her dismissal. They occurred in that order. On receiving the letter, which had been collected for her from the *Poste Restante* by the comte's man, Henri, with whom she'd become quite friendly, she adjourned to the quiet of the blue drawing room to read it. She wasn't supposed to enter the elegant room with its five large windows, but didn't think anyone would know for the few brief minutes she intended to be there.

The *Poste Restante* in Brussels was all the address she'd given her family, since she had no desire for them to learn she was now a lowly governess. She hadn't even told them about the Duchess of Roxwell's death, and they were consequently still under the impression she was sharing the old lady's travels. Her reticence was due to a recent calamity in her father's financial circumstances. He'd suffered because of the collapse of a company in which he had a large interest, and she knew he was finding it difficult to keep even the manor house going. The last thing he and her mother needed to know was that their daughter, whose decision to go abroad as a companion had bothered them a great deal, was now financially embarrassed as well. It was Sophie's philosophy that what they didn't know wouldn't worry them.

December, 5th 1814.

My dearest Sophie,

Forgive the scribble, but I have wonderful news. Your brother William is this day arrived home from the Mediterranean, and will be staying until the end of January, when I fear his ship departs again, this time for Australia. I beg of you that you come home if at all possible, for it may be many a long year before we are all able to spend Christmas together again. I realize that the duchess may not wish to part with you at this season, but I ask you nevertheless. Please come home for Christmas, my dear, so that we may once again sit around the fire and eat syllabub, just as we did when you and William were children. And please rest assured that your presence will not be a burden, for your dear father and I would be pleased if you came home, not only for Christmas, but to stay. Please give this your urgent consideration, my dear, for it is not right that you should be a companion, nor was it ever necessary, but you were ever an unconscionably independent and unnaturally spirited creature. What other daughter but you would choose to skip off to the Continent as a paid servant, when she could be comfortable at home?

Your loving,
Mother.

Sophie gazed at the letter, which had for some reason been delayed at Ostende. William had come home! Oh, if only she *could* be there too, to give her Christmas presents in person, instead of sending them, but she'd undertaken to remain with the comte and comtesse for six months, and so far had only been there for three. As for releasing her for a while, especially at Christmas, when they had such a full social diary, well, it was unthinkable. Besides, the whole thing was academic, for Christmas was in three days' time, so although the letter had been written at the beginning of the month, its delay in transit had left her with hardly any time to prepare and travel. She rose sadly from her seat by the fire, and adjusted the lace ruff of her simple blue woolen gown, but as she turned to leave the room, to her dismay, the comtesse came in.

Sophie dropped an apologetic curtsy. "Forgive me, madam, I know I shouldn't be in here, but—"

The comtesse said nothing as she went to lie wearily on a blue-and-silver Turkish couch, of which there were several in the room. She arranged her elegant rose velvet skirts, and then surveyed the governess. Memories of the previous night swept over her, and her eyes darkened with renewed resentment. What was it about this simpering English spinster that so attracted men? First the handsome captain, and then the prince. "No, you should not be in here, Mademoiselle Greenwood," she said coldly.

Sophie curtsied, and turned to withdraw, but the comtesse halted her. "I have often wondered about you, mademoiselle."

Sophie turned in puzzlement. "I—I beg your pardon?"

"You are a dark horse, Mademoiselle Greenwood. Here was I thinking you were a little innocent, when all the time you have an admirer."

Sophie looked blankly at her. "I—I don't understand," she said

"The handsome naval captain."

Sophie drew back slightly. "Naval captain?"

"Captain Owen Lassiter."

Sophie's breath caught. "Owen?" she repeated faintly.

The comtesse's brown eyes were bright with curiosity. "What is he to you?"

"Nothing, madam."

"I know a lie when I hear it, mademoiselle."

Sophie became anxious. "Please, madam, he is nothing to me. I haven't seen him for a year, and have no desire to see him now."

The comtesse's lips pursed. "With all due respect, mademoiselle, the gentleman concerned does not seem the sort who would ever mean *nothing* to a woman."

Sophie lowered her eyes. "He is in the past, madam."

"Really?" The comtesse murmured dryly, as she smoothed her skirts again.

Sophie knew the moment probably wasn't opportune to ask about Christmas, so she curtsied and hastened to the door, but the comtesse spoke again.

"I fear I will have to let you go, mademoiselle."

Sophie paused, and turned. "Madam?"

The comtesse rearranged her skirts. "Your employment here is terminated, mademoiselle."

Sophie was stunned. "Terminated? M—may I ask why?"

"You have not given satisfaction."

"But—but that cannot be so," Sophie stammered, unable to believe this was happening.

"Don't presume to tell me whether or not you have been satisfactory, mademoiselle! I fear it *is* so; you are dismissed, and I cannot with any honesty recommend you to anyone else, so I will not be giving you a reference." The comtesse gave a cold smile. "I presume you will wish to return to England, and since I realize that you only took this position in order to finance the remainder of your journey home, your passage will be paid and a post chaise will be hired, at my expense, to convey you to Ostende in the morning. Will that be in order?"

Sophie was still numb. "Yes, madam," she whispered.

"Do not tell the children of your departure, for I have a headache, and do not wish to have their cater-wauling to contend with."

"As you wish, madam."

Too shaken to even think clearly, Sophie went out and closed the door quietly behind her.

The comtesse drew a long, satisfied breath. That was the end of it. The prince would not cast his lustful gaze on Sophie Greenwood again, and the handsome captain would not be reunited with her either!

But not even the comtesse could take precautions against fate, and that afternoon Sophie was destined to come face-to-face with Owen after all. It occurred because the girls had been promised a walk in the park, and he happened to be watching the house when they set out.

Sophie was still thunderstruck by the suddenness of her dismissal. There hadn't been any warning at all, no hint that the comtesse was displeased with her, indeed there hadn't been anything for the comtesse to be displeased about. It wasn't even as if the comte had begun to show any interest, for it wouldn't bother his wayward wife if he did! So *why* had it happened?

She watched as Marie-Claire and Monique ran ahead, their cheeks rosy in the chill air. The park was almost deserted as they played hide-and-seek among the many statues that were hidden now beneath straw coverings to protect them from the worst of the winter frost and snow. She'd obeyed the comtesse's instructions, and hadn't told them yet that she was leaving in the morning, but she knew there'd be tears when they learned, for although she hadn't been their governess for long, they'd already become very fond of "Woody." And she of them.

She leaned back against a tree trunk to watch them playing. She wore a wine-red cloak that was trimmed with fur, and the hood was raised over her head, but still the Brussels chill cut through to her skin, for it was very exposed up here on the slope above the rest of the city. She glanced toward the royal palace, which formed the southern boundary of the park, and as she did, she was dismayed to see a familiar figure in naval uniform walking toward her. Slowly she straightened, for she knew it was Owen, and that he intended to speak to her.

She raised her chin a little defiantly as he halted a few feet away, and for a moment neither of them spoke, but then he sketched a bow. "Hello, Sophie."

"I have no desire to speak to you, sir," she said in a tone that offered no encouragement whatsoever.

His gaze swept over her, taking in the little curls around her face, and even the glint of the little pearl earrings he remembered so well. "You're still very beautiful, Sophie," he said after a moment, hardly able to believe that they were face-to-face again. It was only twelve months, and yet it seemed a lifetime. To him, it *was* a lifetime. The Owen Lassiter who looked at her now was a *very* different man from the one she'd seen before.

"I have no interest in your compliments, Owen," she replied, glancing toward the girls, who were still chasing each other around the statues.

"Sophie, can't we at least *try* to settle our differences?"

"I have no wish to settle anything with you, Owen.

You're now part of the past as far as I'm concerned, and that is how I wish things to remain."

"But it isn't how *I* wish things to remain. For three months I hunted high and low for you, Sophie. I humbled myself before your family, *begging* them to let me see you, but they turned me away."

"Can you blame them? Besides, I told them I didn't want you to find me."

"That much is clear, but what *isn't* so clear is why you're a governess so far away from home. Such posts are usually the resort of ladies in delicate financial circumstances, but you have a generous allowance."

She looked away. "I didn't set out to become a governess, rather it was forced upon me by circumstance. The late Duchess of Roxwell invited me to be her companion on a tour of Europe, and I accepted because it was an excellent opportunity, but she unfortunately died in Vienna. I was then robbed on my way home, and had to find a position in order to finance the remainder of the journey."

"I realize that your allowance only falls due once a year, but if you'd sent word to my lawyers, you *know* you would have been forwarded the necessary funds," he pointed out, for at the time of the separation he'd left instructions that any requests from her were to be treated favorably.

She met his eyes. "You *must* know that I have never touched my allowance."

He was taken aback. "Never touched it? No, I didn't know, I haven't been in contact with my lawyers since my return from the Caribbean." He looked at her in bewilderment. "Why haven't you used it, Sophie? You're my wife, so it's yours by right."

"I have more self-respect than to take anything from you, Owen."

"Do you still hate me so much?"

"I feel nothing for you," she answered.

"I don't believe that. Whatever you may feel toward me, it cannot possibly be indifference."

"You flatter yourself, Owen."

"I'm so sorry for what I did, Sophie. If I could turn the clock back, I would," he said quietly, reaching out to touch her.

She backed away. "All this comes far too late. What you did, and your cruel words to me afterward, cannot be forgotten or forgiven."

He stretched forward suddenly to catch her hand. His fingers were so tight over hers as he pulled her toward him, that she could feel the wedding ring on his finger. She tried to wrest herself away, but he was far too strong. When he had her so close she could feel his breath on her cheek, he gazed intently down into her eyes. "Despise me if you will, Sophie, but my feelings will never change. I loved you then, and I love you now."

"No, Owen, for if you loved me then, you wouldn't have done what you did!"

Her closeness affected him. Suddenly he was conscious of a tumult of feelings racing through his entire body. "Oh, Sophie, is one small error of judgment to be held against me for the rest of my life?" he cried.

She tried to pull away. "What would you say if *I'd* been the guilty one? What if *I'd* made that one small error of judgment? Well, Owen? Would *you* forgive and forget?"

"I pray I would," he breathed, releasing her.

She rubbed her wrist. "No, Owen, you'd have called

me a whore, and turned your back on me. Well, *I* had that much pride too, so I turned my back on you. Vows are vows, and you broke yours."

"Don't you think I haven't regretted it every day since?"

"I neither know nor care whether you do or not, Owen. You hurt me more than you'll ever know, and now I want nothing more to do with you. Please go."

"Damn it, Sophie, you're my wife!" he cried.

She looked at him. "And you're my husband, Owen, but you chose to ignore the fact when you went to Serena Hetherington's bed."

"Sophie—"

"Please go," she interrupted.

He gazed at her for a long moment, then, before she knew what was happening, he seized her in his arms. He pressed her to him, forcing his lips down on hers in a kiss that was so full of raw pain and passion that it overwhelmed him completely. His senses carried him away, his body responded, and he felt weak with desire as he crushed her against the virility that cried out for her. A year of hopeless yearning pounded at his loins as suddenly the sweetness of her perfume was in his nostrils again. Lilacs, always she smelled of lilacs, even in the depths of winter . . .

She struggled, but was helpless against his superior strength. She felt his arousal, tasted the need in his kiss, and remembered the nights of unremitting delight she'd once spent in his bed. Echoes of her own desires sounded hollowly through her, and for a breathless moment she almost succumbed. But then she remembered how he'd betrayed their marriage, how he'd come to her still warm from another woman's embrace, and her heart hardened again. She couldn't forgive him his unfaithfulness, or the humiliation he'd dealt her.

With a huge effort she dragged herself from his arms, and struck his face so ferociously that her fingers left weals on his cheek. His head jerked from the force of the blow, and for a long moment he gazed into her overbright eyes. Then, without another word, he walked away.

She stared after him with tears in her eyes. She'd loved him so very much, but he'd thrown her love back in her face, and for twelve long months she'd tried to forget him; now, suddenly, she'd been confronted again with the feelings she'd striven to vanquish. She wanted to be as indifferent to him as she claimed, oh, how she wanted it, but it was impossible. In that the comtesse was right. Captain Owen Lassiter was a man for whom no woman could feel indifference.

The girls ran back to her at that moment, and she forced an animated smile to her lips as they each took one of her hands to continue the walk. She glanced back over her shoulder, but Owen had gone.

That night, completely by chance, the Comte de la Palitaine dined at the Hôtel d'Angleterre in rue de la Madeleine. The comtesse was with the Prince of Orange, but the time had long since passed when her husband would have called anyone out for cuckolding him. The list of meetings at dawn in the Fôrest de Soignes just outside the city would be so embarrassingly long that he'd be obliged to get up early every morning for a month, and that wouldn't suit a man of his natural languor. Besides, why attempt to defend the indefensible? A lady's honor had to exist in the first place if it was to be championed. So tonight he happened to be with two friends, one of whom had recommended the hotel's cuisine, so they decided to sample it.

Afterward, when his friends had gone and he lingered in the smoking room over cognac and a cigar, he found himself seated next to Owen, who was doing the same while reading the English language newspaper, the *Brussels Gazette*. The comte recognized him. "Ah, good evening, Captain, I trust you enjoyed the ball last night?"

Hearing himself addressed, Owen looked up from the newspaper in some surprise. "Why, good evening, Comte. Forgive me, I didn't realize you were there."

Always ready for a little postprandial conversation, the comte moved a little closer. "How are you enjoying Brussels?"

Owen set the newspaper aside, and picked up his glass of cognac. "Very much. Well, perhaps that's not strictly true, although my reservations are no reflection on your city," he added quickly. "I fear I'm a man of the sea, and begin to fret for a deck beneath my feet."

"You will leave us soon?"

"Yes. Very soon." Owen glanced down at his cognac. "Tomorrow, in fact," he said suddenly, his mind made up on the spur of the moment.

The comte smiled sympathetically. "I perceive you are an unhappy man, sir, and not necessarily just because Brussels is far from the sea. Am I right?"

"You are, sir."

"Come, we will share another cognac together, and you will tell me all about it."

"I, er—"

"I insist." The comte snapped his fingers to a waiter, and when two large glasses were placed before them, he lit another cigar, and sat back comfortably. *"Eh, bien, Capitaine, dites-moi votre histoire."*

Tell his story? Owen didn't know where to begin, except perhaps with that other Christmas, and the syllabub taste on Sophie's sweet lips ... He began to talk, and the comte listened incredulously, only speaking when Owen had finished.

"My dear fellow, are you really telling me that you and Mademoiselle Greenwood are man and wife?" he exclaimed in astonishment.

"We are."

"Mon dieu!" The comte sat back in amazement. "I had no idea, no, er, inkling at all that my daughters' governess was a married woman."

Owen feared he might have jeopardized Sophie's position. "Er, Comte, maybe I should not have divulged such information, for as I've just told you, my wife has good reason for wishing to forget I am her husband."

"My dear sir, you were a little unfaithful, that is all. *C'est la vie, n'est-ce pas?*"

"You may think so, sir, indeed most people here may agree with you, but Sophie neither agrees nor forgives."

"And you wish to be reconciled with such a—a *puritaine*?" To the comte, this seemed the height of lunacy.

"Oh, believe me, sir, Sophie is far from being a puritan," Owen murmured, recalling the nights of passion he'd spent with her.

The comte glanced at him. "I begin to see there is much more to little Mademoiselle Greenwood than meets the eye," he observed with a faint smile.

"Much more," Owen nodded.

"Well, I confess there are times when I cannot imagine anything more agreeable than to be separated from one's wife," he went on dryly. "However, I happen to like Mademoiselle Greenwood—er, forgive me, for she is Madame Lassiter, is she not? Well, whatever her title, I happen to like her, and I am somewhat incensed that my tiresome wife has so summarily and unfairly dismissed her."

"Sophie's been dismissed?" Owen sat forward in concern. "When did this happen?"

"This morning."

"But I spoke to Sophie in the park this afternoon, and she didn't say anything."

"Nevertheless, it is so. She leaves for England first thing tomorrow." The comte paused thoughtfully, and then gave Owen a knowing smile. "And since, my heartsick friend, that is what you intend to do as well, I have a little suggestion to make, although it grieves me to assist a fellow in the madness of recovering a wife." The comte smiled, and raised an inquiring eyebrow. "Shall I go on?"

Owen's interest was piqued. "By all means, sir."

"Do you have a carriage?"

"Me? Yes, of course."

"Well, a post chaise has been hired to convey her to Ostende, but it occurs to me that if it were to be canceled, and *your* vehicle were to replace it, with you in it as well, of course ..." The comte spread his hands expressively.

Owen stared at him, and then shook his head. "Sophie would never get into my carriage, she'd take one look at me and walk away."

"Then she must not see you until it is too late. Instruct your coachman to pick you up somewhere on the way, and then to drive and drive until you have had time to persuade the lady to favor you again. It be, well . . ." There was another meaningful spreading of aristocratic hands.

A new light began to shine in Owen's eyes. "I do believe it might work," he breathed.

"My dear captain, of course it will work."

Owen hesitated, then his glance moved to the doorway, through which he could see the waiters scurrying to and from the dining room. One passed at that very moment, carrying a tray upon which stood a dessert that looked very like a syllabub. It was a sign, Owen thought, and gave the comte a quick smile. "Very well, I'll do it," he declared.

The comte beamed, and clapped him heartily on the back. "Excellent! Shall we drink to it?" He raised a hand to summon more cognac.

Owen quickly shook his head. "Not for me, Comte, I need to be sober." he said.

The comte laughed. "I quite understand, although to be sure, *I* would have to be quite in my cups in order to chase after the comtesse!"

Owen smiled, and got up. "At what time should my carriage be at the rue Ducale?"

The comte rose as well. "First light."

Owen held out his hand. "I'll be eternally grateful to you, sir."

The comte accepted the hand. "Well, I confess *I'll* be eternally bemused that any man should wish to reacquire a wife, but it takes all sorts. I wish you and Madame Lassiter the very best of happiness, Captain."

As Owen left, the comte resumed his seat and called for another cognac. Then he gazed at Owen's discarded copy of the *Brussels Gazette*. He had always thought it, but now he knew for certain—the English *were* crazy. He smiled, but then his sharp eye caught two names in the column of *on dits*. The Prince of Orange and Comtesse de la Palitaine ... Slowly he leaned across to take the paper and read. His brow darkened, for the salacious tone of the article was unmistakable. He sighed, and tossed the paper down again. Well, the captain might want to have his wife back, but Henri Francois Maximilian, Comte de la Palitaine, saw the time had come to cast *his* off forever!

Sophie slept restlessly that last night in Brussels. She'd broken the news of her departure to the distraught children, and had hugged them tightly as they clung to her, sobbing. The comtesse was impervious to their pleas, indeed she waved them unfeelingly away when they went to beg her to let their governess stay. She'd become rash over the past day or so, and was impatient to keep an assignation with the Prince of Orange at his lodge in the Fôrest de Soignes. It didn't enter her vain, selfish head that she might do better to give her marriage a little attention, and that showing compassion toward her heartbroken children might be a good place to begin.

By bedtime, Sophie had packed her belongings. After such a day, it was perhaps not surprising that it was some time before she relaxed enough to sleep, but when slumber did arrive, her dreams were as unsettling as everything else over the past twenty-four hours, because they concerned Owen. She relived her wedding night, spent at his town house in Piccadilly. She remembered her apprehension as she'd gone down to dinner, for now that true womanhood was almost upon her, she felt suddenly nervous, as if all the tender kisses and excitement of courtship had never been. But the dinner had been exquisite, and

Owen had been so natural, caring, and understanding, that her fears evaporated. The dessert had been syllabub, but then what else could it possibly have been on their wedding night? She knew he must have asked her mother's cook for the recipe, for it tasted exactly the same as the one they'd shared for those few stolen moments the previous Christmas.

Even in her dreams she saw how naive she'd been, for all the syllabub proved was that Owen Lassiter was a practiced seducer, a lothario who'd graced so many beds he knew *exactly* how to gull a fool like her. But, when he'd come to her that night, she'd adored him so much she would never have believed that within two short months he was to show callous disregard for the vows they'd made, vows that meant everything to her. No, that night was magical, and she believed him to be everything any woman could ever want in a husband—kind, gentle, handsome, warm, witty, experienced, and passionate. A paragon.

Maybe in many ways he was. He'd taught her so much about pleasure. Oh, he knew so well how to awaken her senses to the joys of lovemaking. He'd kissed her lips, her throat, her breasts, and her belly, he'd stroked parts of her that had never been stroked before, and he'd whispered things that should have made her blush, but which excited her. His caresses aroused a hunger she hadn't known before, drawing her on and on toward a fulfillment and complete satiety.

He knew so much, so very much and with hindsight she could see only too well that such sexual accomplishment was the result of having taken many women to his bed. Such a man was bound to find just one woman a little boring, even if that woman was his new bride. Oh, yes, she could see it now, but at the time . . .

Tears welled from her closed eyes as she turned restlessly in her sleep. On their wedding night everything had been so beautiful she thought the rest of their lives would be the same. She'd lain cherished and satisfied in his arms, and they'd made love several more times before dawn.

She'd continued to live in a fool's paradise when a few weeks later they left London to take up residence at Lassiter Park, his country estate near Canterbury. Then, one fateful day, a "friend" had informed her that Owen hadn't gone to the Admiralty in London when he said he had, but had only gone as far as Canterbury, where he'd been seen at dawn leaving the home of Serena Hetherington, the one woman in all Kent who'd gone out of her way to make the new Mrs. Lassiter feel unwelcome, a woman whose spiteful tittle-tattling had spread all manner of untrue rumors about Owen's bride, and whose own hopes of marrying him had been dashed by Sophie's appearance on the scene. Serena had sworn to win him back, and she'd succeeded, as was proved when Owen had been confronted with what his distraught wife had learned. He'd denied it at first, but when she continued to press for the truth, at last he admitted adultery.

"Very well, if the truth is so damned important, yes, I've been unfaithful! Will that do? Or would you like me to write it down in blood? I, Owen Lassiter, have broken the Seventh Commandment, and I chose to do it with Serena Hetherington!"

Serena Hetherington . . . Serena Hetherington . . . Serena Hetherington . . . The name rang so loudly in Sophie's ears that she awoke, sitting up sharply in her darkened room as she realized the maid was tapping at her door.

"Mademoiselle, il est sept heures! Dépêchez vous!"

The dream fled into the shadows, and Sophie glanced toward the window, where she could just see the faint light of dawn beyond the curtains. It was seven o'clock. Within an hour she'd be on her way, leaving Brussels and Owen Lassiter behind. She threw back the bedclothes, and got up.

Marie-Claire and Monique peeped tearfully over the balustrade as their beloved governess departed. A footman had already carried her luggage out to the waiting carriage, and there was no one else to say good-bye as Sophie left the house in rue Ducale. The comte had gone on to a gaming club after speaking to Owen and was still there, and the comtesse was with the Prince of Orange in his lodge in the Fôrest de Soignes. Sophie was struggling not to cry herself, because she'd become very fond of the two girls, and didn't want to leave them like this. She was therefore too upset to notice that the vehicle she climbed into was unmistakably English, and that the coachman wore a caped benjamin coat that was also quite clearly from the other side of the Channel. As the whip cracked, she glanced up at the house for the last time, then the carriage jolted forward along the damp cobbles.

Sophie shivered a little as she was conveyed down from the aristocratic heights into the main city, for the dawn was very cold. Beneath her fur-trimmed cloak she wore her warmest clothes, a blue woolen pelisse over her matching gown, and her hands were pushed into a muff, but still it seemed that the continental chill seeped through to her skin. The skies were lowering and the wind gusted dismally over the streets and squares. She saw the magnificent Grand' Place, which was perhaps the most splendid square in Europe, the shops with their Christmas wares, the evergreen garlands on the doors of the colorfully ornamented and painted houses that proliferated through the city, and occasionally, if a room was lit, she saw the festive leaves and ribbons inside as well. And everywhere there were Christmas trees, which were becoming so much the fashion here she supposed it would soon become so in England too.

It began to rain as the carriage rattled out of the capital and then west along the paved highway toward Ghent, Bruges, and Ostende, which was some sixty-four miles away. The wind buffeted the vehicle, and water sluiced dismally down the glass. It was fitting weather for her mood, she reflected, gazing out at the distorted view of flat countryside, intersected with dikes and rows of limes, willows, and tall poplars.

Suddenly the carriage jolted to a standstill, and with the cessation of rattle of wheels on the pavé, the noise of the rain became much louder. She sat forward in concern. What had happened? But as she reached for the door, it opened, and a cloaked man with a tricorn hat pulled low over his forehead began to climb in.

She drew back in alarm. "Who—who are you?" she cried.

He didn't answer, and the raindrops from his cloak scattered over her as he turned to slam the door again.

Anger spurted through her. "How *dare* you force your way in like this, Sirrah! I *demand* to know your name!" she cried in French.

Still he didn't reply, except to produce a cane from beneath his cloak, and rap it peremptorily on the roof of the carriage. The coachman's whip cracked, and the carriage lurched forward again, coming up swiftly to as smart a pace as was wise in such a torrential downpour.

Sophie was frightened, but faced the interloper with bravado. "I demand to know your name, sir!" she cried, still in French.

At last he removed his tricorn, and her breath caught as she found herself staring at Owen.

"You!" she whispered.

"Good morning, Sophie," he murmured, tossing his hat aside and beginning to unfasten his cloak. "I confess I'm all admiration for your French accent. You speak without a trace of perfidious Albion."

"I leave the perfidy to you."

His eyes flickered. "Yes, I realize that."

She recovered a little from the shock of finding herself confronted by him again. "You have no business forcing your way into—"

"I have every business, since this is my carriage," he replied, standing to remove the cloak and toss that aside as well. He wore his naval uniform beneath.

She pressed back into her seat. "*Your* carriage?" she repeated confusedly. "But, the comte hired a post chaise for me, I heard him dispatch a footman—"

He broke in. "The comte was persuaded that you'd be in safe hands if I escorted you home to England."

She stared at him. "You surely don't imagine that I intend to allow *you* to escort me?"

"Well, you can get out and walk if you wish," he offered, rapping the roof with his cane again.

The carriage halted, and he flung the door open. The wind and rain blustered in, and she stared out in dismay at the swaying trees, and the rippled water of a nearby dike. There didn't seem to be a village anywhere nearby, and the closest farm was a least a quarter of a mile away across fields.

Owen looked at her. "Do you wish to walk, Sophie?"

She colored angrily, and sat back again. "No doubt you find this amusing," she breathed.

"No, Sophie, I happen to find it most providential that the weather is aiding and abetting my purpose," he said quietly, closing the door again, and once more rapping the cane on the ceiling.

Her eyes flew to his again. "Your purpose?"

"To win you back," he said as the carriage moved on again, the wheels clattering on the cobbles.

Her lips parted in disbelief. "I would as soon be reconciled with the devil," she said stiffly.

"Do you really mean that, in your heart of hearts?"

"Oh, yes, you have my word, which, unlike yours, can be trusted implicitly."

The retort found a mark, for he flushed slightly. "How acid, to be sure," he murmured.

"You surely don't expect anything else? You treated me shabbily when we were together, and now you've found me again, you seem set on continuing to treat me shabbily. If you hope that I'm going to be gullible and misty-eyed again just because you choose to reemploy your so-called charm upon me, you're very much mistaken! I learned my lesson at your hands, and do not intend to repeat such an unpleasant exercise."

"You learned many lessons at my hands," he reminded her softly.

Color stained her cheeks. "That I do not deny."

"Nor can you deny how good it was."

"Not good enough to prevent you from straying,"

she pointed out coolly. "How long did it take you? Two months? Oh, yes, you were faithful for that length of time at least. Or were you? How many other times did you visit dear Serena?"

"I did it once, that's all."

"So you say." That was perhaps the most painful aspect of it all, not knowing if he'd told her the full truth. He'd admitted to one fall from grace, but she feared his liaison with Serena had involved many more occasions than that. It was the possibility that he may have constantly slipped between her bed and Serena's that was so humiliating, and hardened her heart so very much. She'd fallen in love with him so completely, that the hurt he'd dealt her had been almost unendurable.

For a moment he said nothing, but then held her gaze again. "Why do you think I am going to these lengths now, Sophie?"

"I really have no idea." Her voice was as flat as the Belgian countryside, for Serena Hetherington was still in her mind.

"It's because I still love you. I know I failed you before, but you're the only woman for me, Sophie, and somehow I'm going to make you realize it too."

"It's too late, Owen. I can look at you now and feel nothing."

"I cannot and will not accept those words," he replied, his voice so soft it was almost lost in the noise of the carriage.

"You have to, for they are final."

The carriage rattled on, and nothing more was said.

The paved road may have been noisy and uncomfortable, but it allowed easy travel, even in such atrocious weather, and in the hope of catching the tide the following morning, they traveled overnight. Sophie tried to stay awake, for finding herself ensconced with an estranged husband who declared he wished to be estranged no more, was unsettling in the extreme. But with the onset of darkness, the rhythmic motion of the vehicle soon began to take effect, and as she leaned her head back, her eyes began to close as she sank into a deep sleep. She didn't even stir when the horses were changed.

She awoke at dawn when the road passed over a bridge and the coachman shouted a warning to a drover whose cattle were blocking the way ahead. Her eyes flew open, and for a moment she didn't know where she was. It was still raining outside, and the wind had increased so that from time to time it made the carriage shudder. With a start she remembered, and at the same moment realized that not only was her head resting on Owen's shoulder, but his arm was around her! She sat up with an accusing gasp, but he spoke before she could say anything.

"Please don't fear for your virtue, for I promise I have not been guilty of a single transgression, in spite of the temptation."

She hastily got up to move to where she had been when she'd fallen asleep. "You should *not* have—" she began.

He interrupted. "Well, I suppose I *could* have left you to slide inelegantly on to the floor, but I thought it more gallant to present you with a shoulder and steadying arm. I'll be sure to leave you to fall next time," he said dryly.

"There won't *be* a next time," she retorted. Her cheeks felt a little warm, and she was glad the dawn light was so poor. "I—I suppose I should thank you," she added then, not wanting to sound churlish in case he *had* saved her from falling to the floor.

The belated acknowledgment fell on stony ground. "Please don't, for if there's one thing I abhor, it's insincerity."

She held his gaze in the gray light. "Well, it seems leopards *do* change their spots, for there was a time when insincerity was your stock in trade," she said tersely.

"Sleep evidently doesn't improve your disposition these days," he replied, bringing the brief conversation to an end by putting on his tricorn, tilting it forward over his face, and seeming to go to sleep, although whether or not he really was, she couldn't tell.

An hour later they reached Ostende, and after the Belgian customs had thoroughly inspected the luggage, the carriage was loaded on the deck of the packet *Nymph*. The sea was steel-gray in color, with alarming waves that were white-topped as far as the eye could see. Even in good weather it was a seven-hour voyage to Dover, so Owen secured a cabin for her, intending to remain in the carriage himself. However, the wind increased to gale force, and the *Nymph's* master, Captain Boxer, decided to wait for the next tide, and hope the weather would abate in the meantime. Some of the passengers were incensed, for that meant they wouldn't arrive in England until Christmas Eve, but the master pointed out sagely that it was better to arrive late than not at all.

As it happened, the gale did abate sufficiently, and after nightfall the packet was at last able to put out. While Owen made certain that the ropes holding the carriage on deck were as firm as they should be, Sophie stood alone at the stern, watching the coastline slip away into the spume-flecked December night. But it soon seemed the drop in the wind had been Mother Nature's trick, for as the vessel reached open water, the gale increased once more, and mountainous waves surged on all sides. The air was filled with spray, and she could taste salt on her lips as she held her hood over her damp hair.

Sophie shivered as she remained at the stern, for the air was bitterly cold. Her cloak billowed around her like a wild thing, and she could hear the wind whining through the rigging and cracking the canvas of the sails. The *Nymph* heaved on the swell, and she gripped the wet railing, staring back as the last lights of Ostende vanished.

"You didn't belong in Brussels, you know," Owen said behind her, his voice almost lost in the racket of the weather.

"I liked it well enough," she replied, not looking around at him.

"You shouldn't have stooped to being a servant to others, Sophie. It was foolish pride, inverted pride, that made you ignore the allowance I have always made for you."

"I suppose you'll say next that I shouldn't have left you."

"We *could* have solved it all, you know, if only you'd stayed."

"Well, when I *was* with you, unfortunately, *you* were with Serena Hetherington," she said, then gasped as the vessel plunged into a sudden trough between waves.

Owen put a swift arm around her waist, and as she angrily tried to push him away, the packet surged sickeningly up out of the trough again. It was terrifying, and in spite of herself she clung to him, hiding her face against his salt-sprayed cloak.

"It's all right, now," he said reassuringly.

As the vessel righted again, Sophie began to pull self-consciously away, but he held her a moment longer. "I'm not the monster you think," he said, looking intently into her eyes. "I betrayed you once, that's all."

"Once was enough, can't you see that?" she replied, twisting free and then turning to make her unsteady way along the wet deck toward the ladderway that led belowdeck.

In the little cabin, which was lit by a gimbal-mounted candle, she took off her cloak and shoes, and lay fully dressed on the narrow bed. She glanced around. The furniture was fixed to the floor to prevent it moving in just such a storm as this, and the ill-fitting porthole shutter was closed. The waves dashed against the vessel, and water trickled down inside. Timbers creaked and groaned as the *Nymph* shuddered, and suddenly there was a loud crash on the deck immediately overhead. Then she heard running footsteps, and men shouting. What had happened? She was frightened.

At that moment Owen knocked at the cabin door. "Sophie? Are you all right?"

Gladly she hurried to let him in.

"Are you all right?" he asked again, the gold braid on his uniform glittering in the candlelight.

"Yes," she said in a small voice.

He saw how pale and anxious her face was, and came in, closing the door behind him. "Don't worry, this isn't really much of a storm," he said reassuringly.

"The *Nymph* has weathered far worse, and Captain Boxer is a very experienced seaman."

"I—I'm sure you're right, but I heard a terrible crash, and—"

"It was only a few crates that hadn't been sufficiently secured. Try to sleep, if you can."

"That's easier said than done."

He smiled a little. "Well, try anyway," he said, turning to go.

"Please stay," she said quickly.

He looked at her. "Of course, if that is what you wish."

"I don't want to be on my own," she confessed, glancing uneasily toward the porthole as more seawater dripped from beneath the shutter.

He made sure the door was firmly closed, and nodded toward the bed. "As I said before, I suggest you try to sleep," he said, sitting down on the chair by the table.

But suddenly the cabin was engulfed in darkness as the candle went out. Never had the night seemed more fearsome and impenetrable than in that moment, and Sophie reached out instinctively toward him. "Owen?" she cried.

Such darkness or conditions were nothing to him, and he stepped quickly over to her, catching her hand as if he had the eyes of a cat. "It's as well the Royal Navy doesn't enlist the fair sex, or few vessels would put to sea," he murmured, maneuvering her to the bed and ushering her to sit down. Then he sat down with her, and felt in his pockets for his luminaries. He took one out, held it up until it flared into life, then he leaned across to light the candle again.

The ship pitched, seeming to plunge forever before

surging up again. Sophie's hand returned nervously to his, and his fingers closed firmly over it. "I won't let anything happen to you," he said, smiling a little at the anxiety in her eyes.

"I—I'm sure that not even a captain in His Majesty's Royal Navy can promise to hold back the sea," she replied, looking toward the porthole.

"No, but his experience can render him fairly accurate in his predictions. I've been in far worse seas than this, and in one or two vessels that could only be described as leaking tubs, and I've spent hours on deck watching wave after wave in endless tedium. I know the sea and ships, and can tell you that the shutter will hold, and we'll reach Dover safely, if in a little discomfort."

She managed a smile of sorts. "I—I know you're right, but it still doesn't stop me feeling like I do."

The storm heaved the vessel from side to side, and the noise was tremendous. Her heart pounded, and she realized her fingers were digging into his, but she couldn't help herself. She needed to talk. But what about? She searched for something to say. "Are—are you still in command of the *Fabulous*?"

"Are you really interested?"

"Yes," she replied, realizing she was. In spite of everything, she wanted to know about him.

"As it happens, I'm between commands. In the new year I take over the frigate *Piper*."

"*Piper*? But isn't she considered one of the best?" She knew the name because it had figured prominently in the newspapers for taking prizes during the recent hostilities.

He smiled. "You sound surprised. Don't you think my naval talents warrant such a vessel? Perhaps I should have remained with sloops for the rest of my career?"

"I think very highly of your naval talents, you know that."

"Yes, I suppose I do. Whatever other faults you considered me to have, incompetence at sea wasn't one of them. To answer your question, yes, *Piper* is one of the best. She's being refitted at the moment, and I'm to report at Portsmouth some time in January. I'll be notified."

"I believe her record regarding prizes is second to none."

"Yes. She never lacks eager volunteers ready to serve on her. I've been the object of much envy among my fellow officers."

"Do you know where you'll be sent once you take command? Or is it classified information?"

He hesitated. "My orders are to cruise the Mediterranean in search of pirates."

She knew how dangerous such an assignment would be, for pirates knew no rules of war, or offers of clemency, and those in the Mediterranean were more ruthless and bloodthirsty than most. Her glance encompassed him for a moment, before she lowered it again. "You know I wish you every good fortune, don't you? And that I trust you'll return not only triumphantly, but safely too?"

"I have my good luck charm," he replied quietly, taking a small golden snuffbox from his pocket.

She looked at it in puzzlement, for he didn't use snuff.

He opened it, and inside she saw a lock of her hair. She stared at it. "Oh, Owen . . ."

"It's held me in good stead until now, well, at sea

anyway, so I have faith that it will continue to do so," he murmured, taking the curl of light-brown hair out, and parting the strands gently between his fingers.

She glanced in the snuffbox again, for there was a tiny piece of folded paper there as well. "What's that?" she asked.

He held the box toward her. "See for yourself."

She reached for the paper, and unfolded it. To her astonishment, she saw her mother's handwriting. It was the recipe for syllabub, which her mother called "Sophie's Syllabub."

Owen smiled. "I know it by heart now, of course, and whenever I'm in port, and fresh cream is on hand, I have it made for me. It, er, brings back good memories." His eyes swung briefly to hers, then away again.

She refolded it, and put it back in the box. He replaced the lock of hair as well, snapped the box lid down, then pushed it back in his pocket.

The fact that he still carried two such mementos with him affected her, and she suddenly found herself wishing he'd take her in his arms again. It was such a strong feeling that her lips almost parted to put it into words, but she stopped herself in time. Being with him again like this was weakening her resolve and clouding her memory. No matter how she might feel at this precise moment, the truth was that she could *never* trust him again. He'd been as easy to talk to and pleasant to be with all the time before, but behind her back he'd seen Serena Hetherington, and that was something she must not forget.

He got up suddenly. "Look, it really would be best if you could manage to sleep. I promise to stay here. I'll sit in the chair, but you must rest."

"I won't be able to sleep."

"I'm sure you thought that last night in the carriage as well. So do as I say, and try now. When you awaken, it will be Christmas Eve."

Without another word she made herself as comfortable as she could, and closed her eyes. He went to the chair and sat down. Outside, the storm continued, lashing the waves against the vessel, and howling through the rigging like a thing demented. Sophie kept her eyes closed, trying to think of anything and everything but the fact that she was on a ship that was bobbing like a cork on waves that were far too high for comfort. The candle went out again, and she heard Owen's low curse, but he didn't get up to relight it, and as the minutes passed, the darkness became almost soothing. She found that the sounds of the storm were drifting farther and farther away, and at last she fell asleep.

Owen rested his head on his arms on the table, and snatched a few hours sleep as well, and when he awoke on Christmas Eve morning, the gale had fallen away to a fresh wind. He rose quietly from the chair, and tiptoed from the cabin. Once on deck, he saw that it was first light, and the packet was cutting cleanly toward the Kent shore. The white cliffs of Dover were just visible through the haze, and he could see the light on the South Foreland. He checked that the carriage was secure, then stretched his legs by taking a turn around the deck. After that he returned to the cabin, where Sophie was still fast asleep.

He stood looking down at her for a moment, then sat on the edge of the bed, reaching out to push a stray brown curl away from her face. If only he hadn't been such a fool, if only he'd remained faithful, she'd still be his now. He put his hand to her cheek, drawing his thumb softly over her lips. How he'd always adored making love to her first thing in the morning, when she'd still been drowsy and warm from sleep.

She began to stir, and he quickly got up again. He was seated in the chair when her eyes opened. She smiled with relief as she realized the storm was over. "Are we near Dover?"

"Yes. Another half an hour should see us in port."

She got up and found her brush and comb in her overnight valise. Her brown curls crackled in spite of the salt spray that had dampened them the day before. She thought of something then, and turned toward him.

"If—if you will just take me to the Ship Inn, I'll engage a post chaise to take me to Oxford."

"There's no need. I'll take you to Oxford."

"I'd rather you didn't."

"And I'd rather I did," he replied, a little more sharply than he'd intended. Somehow her request had caught him on the raw, and his tongue responded accordingly. He tried to modify his tone. "Look, Sophie, I may not be the light of your life anymore, but I'm still your husband, and I'm still concerned for your safety and well-being. Dishonorable conduct in the past does not preclude me from displaying *honorable* conduct now. I cannot and will not permit you to travel alone."

"But I've been traveling alone since the duchess died—I've had to."

"And whose fault is that?" he snapped.

She drew back slightly. "Very well, escort me to Oxford if you insist . . ."

"I do."

She said nothing more, but continued to comb and pin her hair as best she could.

He turned away. Damn! The last thing he'd wanted was to fall out at all, but he was cut to the quick by her intention to part at the Ship Inn. He couldn't bear to let her go again, but had to face the unpalatable fact that *she* didn't want to stay with *him*. If he'd learned one thing from the stupid interlude with Serena Hetherington, it was that women like Sophie did not regard the physical act of making love in the same light as men. A man could feel the urge to make love with any woman who caught his eye, and he could satisfy that urge without it meaning any more than a passing fancy, but the Sophies of this world only made love when they were *in* love, and that made all the difference in the world. Too late he knew how much his thoughtless night with Serena had hurt her, too late he *understood* her; now he had to accept that it was also too late to save the marriage that mattered so much. Everything was too late.

The Christmas Eve sun broke through and the wind died away as the *Nymph* waited for the tide and the pilot. Neither took long, and soon the vessel came alongside at the quay. The white cliffs towered above the town, and the houses, with their comfortably English facades, spread up a long valley from the shore. Christmas was evident everywhere, from the piles of holly on the cobbles, to the flock of geese that made a great noise as they were driven to market. Everywhere there was bustle and noise, and some musicians by a tavern were playing and singing a Christmas carol. "*Good King Wenceslas looked out, on the feast* of Stephen, When the snow lay round about, deep, and crisp, and even ..."

The customs officers came aboard, and it was some time before they were satisfied there was no contraband aboard, then Owen escorted Sophie ashore, but as they went across the gangway, something happened. She stumbled, and as he bent quickly to catch her, the snuffbox slipped from his pocket into the water between the ship and the quay. "Owen! The snuffbox!" she cried.

Dismay colored his eyes. "Well, no doubt Dame Fortune will still smile on me," he murmured, and continued to help her ashore.

The loss of the snuffbox bothered her, and as he sent a man to hire horses at the Ship Inn, then returned on board to keep a close eye on the unloading of the carriage, she stood at the edge of the quay, gazing down at the shining water. Superstitious anxiety suddenly seized her. Without his amulet, he might be in more danger ... She said nothing as he rejoined her, and they walked to the Ship Inn for a much needed breakfast.

The sun had vanished behind clouds a little later as they entered the carriage again and commenced the long climb out of Dover on the London road. It was the Canterbury road too, and would take them past the gates of Lassiter Park, a fact that was on both their minds, but which neither of them mentioned. As she recognized the distant silhouette of the estate's seventeenth-century prospect tower on its hilltop two miles ahead, a thousand and one emotions cascaded through her. Sweet memories vied with unhappiness, the joys of love with the pains of betrayal, and the braveness of her new independence with the vulnerability of fearing for the life of the only man who'd ever meant anything to her. The loss of the lock seemed a terrible omen, a warning that he and the *Piper* would sail out of Portsmouth into the gravest of hazards.

Suddenly she opened her reticule and took out her little pair of scissors. She snipped a lock of her hair, then held it out to him. "Take it, please," she said quietly.

He gazed at it, knowing full well why she wanted him to have it. "Sophie, I—"

"Please, Owen. You cannot leave England without a talisman, and if you carried my hair before, you must carry it again now." She pressed it into his palm. "Keep it with you, for I hope with all my heart that it will protect you. And—and if you wish, I will *make* my mother write out the syllabub recipe again, so everything will be as it was ..."

"If only everything really could be as it was," he murmured. Then suddenly he caught her hand, and pulled her toward him to kiss her softly on the lips.

She was taken by surprise, and for a moment didn't resist. The touch of his lips was tender and loving, and found a response that came from deep within her. For that heartstopping second, the past melted away, and there was just love.

His fingers tightened over her hand, and she was conscious of the desire that ached through his kiss, for it began to yearn through her too. She mustn't succumb! This was the path to fresh hurt! She pulled abruptly away. "No!"

"Sophie, how can you deny—"

"Deny what? That you can still cause me pain? That to be with you is to rake over things that I wish to put behind me? We were so happy, but you callously ruined everything. Why did you do it? And why with Serena Hetherington, of *all* women?"

Desire still washed confusingly through him as he leaned back in his seat. "Oh, Sophie, don't you think I haven't asked myself the same questions over and over again? I can't say anything in my own defense. It just happened, and that's all there is to say. I was on my way to the Admiralty. It wasn't an urgent summons, just a request that I call there soon. I stopped at a Canterbury inn because one of the horses' shoes needed attention, and Serena came up to speak to me. She was tearful because she'd received bad news, I don't even recall what it was now, but I felt obliged to comfort her a little. But she was very upset, and I didn't think I should leave her, so I decided to stay until she'd recovered. But one thing led to another, she was crying, I put my arms around her, and ..." He paused wretchedly. "That's all there was to it, Sophie, I *swear* it. I was a fool, I gave in to my base male nature, and woke up the next morning wishing with all my heart that I'd driven straight through Canterbury the day before. If it's any consolation, I wasn't the most ardent lover she'd ever had."

"But was *she* the most ardent lover *you'd* ever had?"

"No."

"So you'd have me believe it was as insignificant a thing as anyone could possibly imagine? A mere trifle?" She twirled her hand in the air like a maiden aunt speaking of a child's faux pas, but if her tone was light, her glance was not.

"Yes, Sophie, as insignificant as anyone could possibly imagine," he repeated quietly.

Her deep bitterness sounded then. "You thought so

little of me, and how I'd feel, that you simply fell between the sheets with her because the urge took you. Can you imagine how that makes me feel, even now?"

He tied a knot in the lock of hair, and put it in his pocket, then sat forward, holding her gaze earnestly. "But that's just it, Sophie, I *do* know now how my conduct affected you. I know, I understand, and I despise myself for what I did."

Tears suddenly filled her eyes. "I could *never* have done such a thing to you, Owen. When I made my vows to you, I meant them, every word."

He seized both her hands. "And I meant mine! I was a fool to end all fools to betray them, and now I crave the chance to put matters right. Will you give me a chance, Sophie?"

"No. Please, don't ask." But she thought of the contents of the snuffbox, and of how she'd felt when she'd given him another lock of hair only a few moments before. And of how she'd felt too when he kissed her afterward . . .

He could see indecision in her eyes. Her words said one thing, but her gaze told him quite another, so he didn't let go of her hands. "Come home with me now, Sophie. No one at Greenwood Place knows you're coming home, so no one will ever be any the wiser. Come with me now to Lassiter Park, we could not only spend the rest of this Christmas Eve together, but if you stayed tonight, we could be together on Christmas Day too—"

"No," she interrupted quietly. "It wouldn't be right."

"Why not? What rule would we be breaking?"

She didn't say anything.

He smoothed her palms with his thumbs. "Spend a little time with me, Sophie, proper time, not hurried, stressful hours traveling, and if after that, you still wish to go, I will not put any obstacles in your way. All I ask is that you grant me one more chance to prove my love. We're still man and wife, and at liberty to do as we please." He paused to look shrewdly into her eyes. "Or are you afraid your heart might overrule your head?" he challenged quietly.

'I just don't want to be hurt anymore, Owen. You *sound* in earnest, but then you did before too. How do I know you aren't merely intent upon seducing me again? Maybe you're so bored waiting to take over your new command, that I'm a handy diversion?"

"Is that what you really think of me?"

"I don't know, Owen. I trusted you before, but you let me down most cruelly. I'm just afraid you'll do the same again. You've always known so well how to brush my defenses aside, how to allay my fears so I'm exposed to your wiles."

"You make me sound like a calculating monster!" he protested.

"Maybe you are. Maybe all men are when it comes to luring a woman between the sheets. On our wedding night, when I was so nervous and uncertain, you knew exactly what to do to make me smile and feel at ease."

He was puzzled. "I—I don't understand . . ."

"The syllabub."

He stared at her. "The syllabub?" he repeated blankly.

"You knew it would make me think how warm, tender, loving, and thoughtful you were, and that . . ."

"And that it would make you relax sufficiently to

do as I wished when I got you to the marriage bed?"
He gave an incredulous laugh.

She blushed, and looked away. "Laugh at me if you
will, but when I look back now, and remember all that
happened afterward, that simple gesture of yours
looks far too knowing to be loving, so don't try to
make me feel foolish, for I do already, foolish for ever
giving you my heart."

His hands tightened over hers. "Sophie, that sylla-
bub *was* a simple gesture, a gesture of love. I wanted
that particular dish to always mean something special
to us, something we'd think of every time we ate it,
something that would make our eyes meet in that pri-
vate way only lovers have. I wasn't being calculating,
I swear." He released her hands. "Maybe if that's
what you think of me, it really is too late for us, but
I still want to try one last time to see if we can mend
the past. Come to Lassiter Park with me now, Sophie.
I swear I will not attempt anything, I just want to
spend time with you."

She found herself hesitating.

"Sophie, it's Christmas, and I'm *begging* you. Can
you really keep turning your back on a marriage that
was blissfully happy until I let you down? I was the
wrongdoer, I freely admit it, but I'm more repentant
than you'll ever know. So if those vows mean as much
to you as you say, you *have* to let me try to put things
right! Besides, I will not be able to hound you for long
afterward should you wish to sever the relationship,
because I'll have sailed on the *Piper*. I swear upon
everything I hold dear that I will not resort to any
underhanded or unfair trickery with syllabubs," he
added, attempting to lighten the atmosphere.

At that she closed her eyes, and nodded, "Very

well, I'll come with you to Lassiter Park, but I promise nothing, Owen. You've begged me to spend a little time with you; I agree to that, and only that."

He gave her no opportunity to change her mind, but quickly lowered the window glass and leaned out to shout instructions to the coachman.

But a few minutes later, just as the carriage was about to turn across the road through the urn-topped gates, it had to halt because another carriage drove from the opposite direction. Owen's coachman reined in sharply, and both Sophie and Owen glanced out. They were in time to see the other carriage sweep past, and dismay sank through Sophie like a remembered stone, for a strikingly beautiful redhead was seated inside. It was Serena Hetherington. Of all the people to chance to see, it had to be the woman who'd brought about the crisis that had wrecked everything! Serena gazed out in startlement, perceiving Owen, but not the fact that his estranged wife was with him. There was no mistaking the delight and predatory anticipation that leaped to her almond eyes for the split second before her carriage carried her past, and Owen's coachman flicked the reins to urge his team into action again.

Sophie's lips parted in consternation, and in the space of a heartbeat she'd changed her mind again. Seeing Serena made all the difference in the world. Suddenly Lassiter Park was out of the question; in fact it was the very last place on earth she wished to go to! Bitter memory relit her eyes as they flew toward Owen.

His face was a study of perturbation, for he knew only too well the effect seeing Serena had had upon the situation. "Sophie—" he began.

She broke in. "I—I can't stay. Not now."

He leaned forward urgently. "You said you'd spend time with me, Sophie," he reminded her.

"Yes, I know, but—"

"There can't be any buts, Sophie. Serena meant nothing to me then, and still means nothing."

"The same can hardly be said of her. Joy was written all over her when she saw you!"

"Does it matter what *she* feels?"

Sophie looked away, her hands twisting anxiously in her muff.

Owen still leaned forward. "Please stand by your word, Sophie. Spend this time with me, and don't let Serena Hetherington spoil anything."

Tears shone in her eyes, and after a long moment she nodded. "Very well, I'll still stay," she whispered, but her misgivings were many, and ran very deep. She'd been uncertain enough before the chance glimpse of Serena; now she felt she was making a very grave error of judgment.

She gazed out at the remembered scene, the beautiful park, the red deer that fled at the sound of the carriage, and, above the trees, the first view of the Jacobean chimneys and ornately gabled roof of the seventeenth-century house. The water of the lake was very still and dark at the narrow neck where the drive passed over the stone-balustraded bridge, and now the carriage had drawn so much closer, the prospect tower seemed to reach up into the clouds that were gathering swiftly across the entire sky.

This was how she'd first seen her new home when she'd come here as a bride. Owen had held her hand as they drove up in an open carriage. It had been a beautiful summer's day, her frilled pink parasol had twirled above her head, and her eyes had shone with happiness. There was no sunshine now, just the bleakness of a Christmas Eve morning, and a sky that was heavy with the yellow-gray clouds that so often meant snow. And there was, too, the shadow cast by Serena Hetherington ...

She watched as more and more of the house became visible. It was a small, very beautiful mansion, built of red brick with stone facings, with the Dutch-style gable ends and large mullioned bay windows that were so fashionable at the time of its building. The shutters were closed, and the place would have looked deserted had it not been for the curls of smoke rising from the chimneys because the servants were keeping all the rooms warm and aired. She pondered the consternation their unexpected arrival would cause, and the hurry-scurry to open all the shutters and whisk the dust covers off the furniture. As for the kitchen, there'd be uproar because the larder was bound to be trimmed to cater just for the staff, not for the return of Captain and Mrs. Lassiter! Was Mrs. Barnsley still the cook? And Brewster still the butler, she wondered?

The unexpected arrival of the master's carriage did indeed cause consternation on a grand scale, but it turned to astonished delight when he was seen assisting Sophie down at the door, for there wasn't a servant at Lassiter Park who hadn't been sad when she left. As Owen and Sophie entered, the sound of hastily opening shutters was already echoing through the house, and a footman was snatching dust sheets off the sofas in the dark-paneled hall, where the painted ceiling depicted the myth of Prometheus. Two maids were endeavoring to fan flames from the banked-up fire in the hearth, above which rose a chimneypiece that was a glory of carved birds, leaves, scrolls, and musical instruments.

As Owen helped her with her cloak, Sophie gazed around at the house she'd once loved so very much. She knew this could be her second homecoming if she wished. But did she wish? Was this house and its master what she still *really* wanted, or would she always be too hurt to ever forgive enough?

She and Owen walked by the lake that afternoon. Snowflakes drifted idly in the air, clinging to her hood and cloak, and brushing her face. In spite of all her doubts and fears, she was beginning to relax a little. She felt almost at ease as they strolled companionably together. She watched a horseman ride down the drive to the house, and hand something to Brewster at the door, but then Owen drew her attention to the waterfowl on the lake, and she thought no more of it.

The horseman had ridden away again by the time they reached the stone bridge, where a holly tree was so bright with scarlet berries that she had to stop and gather some. Owen helped her, and soon she had a huge armful. He smiled into her eyes over the shining berries and greenery. "I'm glad you didn't change your mind about coming here today."

"I am too," she replied after a moment's hesitation.

The pause wasn't lost on him. "Sophie, you have no need to fear Serena." He caught her gloved hand so she dropped all the holly, but he took no notice as he drew her fingers to his chest, pressing them against his heart so she could feel its steady beat. "I'm yours, Sophie, not hers, and this heart beats only for you," he said softly.

"Does it?" she whispered, unable to stem the wretched flow of doubt that spilled through her merely at the mention of her rival's name.

"Yes, it does, as you'll soon realize now you're here."

She met his eyes again. "Don't hope for too much, Owen. The fact that I've come here doesn't mean I'm going to stay."

"I know."

"Do you?" She searched his face. "*Do* you?" she asked again, her voice dropping to a doubting whisper.

"I'm not deluding myself, Sophie. I'm well aware that the past cannot be dashed aside in a moment, and that trust cannot be regained simply because I *wish* it. I need you to spend these hours here with me, in the hope that you'll remember the good things we had, not just the bad, but you need not fear that I'll fling myself at your feet in a paroxysm of unmanly tears, or grovel for a crumb of kindness from my lady's plate. I promise not to resort to shabby seductive wiles, nor force more kisses on you, or creep to your room tonight. You're my wife, but you're also your own woman now, and any decision you make will be binding upon me. But just remember this, I love you with all my heart, Sophie." He gazed into her eyes for a moment longer, and then looked up at the snow-laden sky. "Come on, let's go inside in the warmth," he murmured, releasing her hand and then bending to gather the holly.

Moments later they walked back toward the house, but as they entered, Brewster hastened toward Owen with little silver tray upon which lay a sealed note. "This was delivered a few minutes ago, sir," he said.

Owen dropped the holly on to a table, then took the

note, and stared at the writing without breaking the seal. Then he strode across to the fire, and tossed the unread note upon the flames. Brewster glanced at him and then hurried away.

Sophie gazed at the burning note as it curled into ashes. "It was from her, wasn't it?" she said quietly.

"I wouldn't know," he replied unconvincingly.

"Oh, really, Owen, who else even knows you're home again? Don't pretend. It was from her, and we both know it."

"Very well, it was from her."

"And you'd have read it, if I hadn't been here."

He shook his head. "No, Sophie."

"Oh, yes, you would," she whispered, then gathered her skirts to hurry up the staircase.

Owen gazed after her, then turned to look at the glowing embers in the hearth.

As darkness fell and the hour for dinner approached, candles were lit. Firelight leaped over the rich wooden paneling and the green brocade hangings of the bed as Sophie combed and pinned her hair, an art she'd more than perfected over the past year. Outside it was still snowing, but inside it was warm and cozy. She wore the dark-green velvet gown again, and was seated at the dressing table as she teased a little frame of curls around her face. Then she took a little sprig of holly selected from the bunch she and Owen had gathered. It consisted of two leaves and six berries, and she used a hairpin to attach it carefully to the knot of hair on top of her head. It was a simple but very seasonal effect, although the last thing she actually felt was seasonal. Serena's presence seemed to be everywhere, as if she were in the house at this very moment ...

Sophie got up and went to the window. Beyond her reflection she could see the park. The snow had settled, and from time to time flakes glided past the windowpane. She remembered her first Christmas here. She'd been standing at the window waiting to go down to dinner, just as she was now, and Owen's reflection had appeared in the pane behind her. She'd turned, and smiled as he'd come to kiss her. After that it had been some time before they'd eventually gone down to the dining room ... She gazed at the pane for a long moment, half wishing Owen would appear again now, but he didn't, and besides fate seemed to be conspiring to force Serena to the fore.

The dinner gong echoed through the house, so she picked up her shawl, took a lighted candle from the mantel, and left the room. The passages at Lassiter Park had settled unevenly over the centuries, so there were steps here and there to compensate, but the long gallery was still as splendidly level as it always had been. The gleaming floor reflected the candlelight as she walked, and statues gazed after her. The walls were covered with carved paneling, and hung with tapestries and gilt-framed paintings. Heavy plum velvet curtains were draped on either side of the many doorways, and drawn across the impressive line of windows.

The candle flickered as she paused at the top of the grand staircase, with its unicorn newel posts and splendidly carved rail. The servants had hastily put up what greenery they could, and she caught the scent of pine from the branches that had been fixed among the banisters.

Owen was waiting at the bottom. He wore his dress uniform, and the epaulettes and abundance of gold braiding shone as she went down toward him. His gaze swept approvingly over her. "It brings back good memories to see you coming down these stairs again," he said, taking the candlestick from her and blowing out the flame because the hall was lit.

They crossed the hall to the dining room, yet another beautifully paneled room, this time with carving that was said to be the work of the great Grinling Gibbons himself. The quality of the flowers, winged cupids, and laurel wreaths was certainly exquisite enough for the master sculptor, as indeed were the many other examples throughout the house, but there was no record that he had actually been engaged or employed. The candlelight made the carvings seem to come to life, as if the cupids would suddenly fly free around the room.

The long dark-oak table was exquisitely laid with a white cloth. In the center stood an epergne that tumbled with holly and red ribbons, and there were a pair of four-branched silver gilt candelabra that cast a pleasant light over everything.

Sophie's eyes met Owen's as he pulled out a chair for her, and she looked quickly away again.

The meal of roast capon with all the trimmings was very agreeable, and they both found it particularly nice to eat plain English cooking again after the rather formal fare served at the Hôtel d'Angleterre and the rue Ducale. Sophie even found herself beginning to enjoy herself and laugh a little as Owen regaled her with tales of the strange and exciting things he'd seen in the Caribbean. For a while she forgot Serena Hetherington, but then, right at the end, when the dessert was served, everything went wrong and the past swept ferociously back to remind her how much of a fool she would be to return to him.

Mrs. Barnsley herself bore the dessert in, and proudly set two elegant little crystal dishes before them. She was a plump, homely woman in a beige woolen dress and starched apron, with her graying hair tucked up beneath a mobcap. She straightened to look proudly at Sophie. "Syllabub, madam, made to the recipe you brought with you when you first came here."

Sophie's eyes flew to Owen, who avoided her gaze. Somehow she managed a smile for the cook. "Thank you, Mrs. Barnsley, it's most kind of you," she said in a rather tight voice, maintaining the smile as the pleased woman bobbed a curtsy and then bustled out again, causing such a draft that the candles flickered.

As soon as she'd gone, Sophie looked contemptuously at Owen. "So *this* is how you keep your word!"

"Sophie, I swear I had nothing to do with it."

"What was it you said? No underhanded or unfair trickery with syllabubs? And yet what do I see on the table before me? Why, syllabub, I do declare!"

"Would it avail me of anything to say I didn't order them?"

"No? Forgive me if I find that hard to believe. Mrs. Barnsley wouldn't have presumed to serve this, she'd have taken instructions from you!"

He sat back, his eyes a little cool. "You're very quick to accuse me, and to dismiss my protests of innocence."

"Because I think even you will agree that this particular choice of dessert is somewhat suspect!"

"Believe me, you're reading far more into this than actually exists!"

"Am I?" She looked away.

Angrily he tossed his napkin onto the table, then his chair scraped as he rose to his feet. "Forgive me if I decline to finish the meal, but I fear that right now I have a huge desire to be elsewhere! I rather fancy that Serena would welcome my company a little more than you do!" Turning on his heel, he strode out.

Tears streamed down Sophie's cheeks, and she gazed through a blur at the syllabub before her. What a fool she'd nearly been again, for if he hadn't done this, if he'd served apple tart, fruit cream, meringues, *anything* but syllabub, she'd have found it very hard indeed to resist her heart tonight. It had been so good to be with him again, enjoying his company and conversation, that Serena had very nearly faded completely from her thoughts.

There was an anxious tap at the door, and Sophie looked up, hastily dabbing her eyes with her napkin as Mrs. Barnsley came in. "Yes, what is it, Mrs. Barnsley?"

The cook came hesitantly to the table. "Begging your pardon, madam, but there is something you should know."

"Yes?"

"I—I was coming back to the dining room because I'd forgotten the lemon peel on the syllabub, so I couldn't help overhearing what you and the captain said. Captain Lassiter didn't order the syllabub, madam, it was *my* doing. I—I thought you and he were, well, you know, together again, so I was sure the syllabub would be the perfect thing. And that's the God's honest truth, madam. I remembered how much you always liked the syllabub, and I just made it. I'm so sorry if I did something wrong, madam, but I had to let you know it wasn't the captain's fault."

Sophie stared at her in unutterable dismay. Oh, no, and she'd said such dreadful things to him! Slowly she got up. "Where is he now?"

"He went to the stables for his horse, madam." The cook shifted uncomfortably, having heard absolutely everything that had been said in anger.

Sophie looked away wretchedly. He'd gone to Serena, and she, Sophie, had driven him there.

"I'm so very sorry, madam," Mrs. Barnsley said unhappily.

Sophie pulled herself together. "It wasn't your fault, Mrs. Barnsley, you did it for the best, and under any other circumstances it would have been a charming gesture. I leaped to conclusions, and let my unforgiving nature and sharp tongue get the better of me. I really don't have anyone to blame but myself."

The cook looked sadly at her, then went unhappily out again.

Sophie leaned her hands on the table, and bowed her head. Why couldn't she have held her tongue this time? Why couldn't she have accepted the truth about herself, that she still loved Owen Lassiter with all her might, and wanted to return to him? The truth had stared her in the eyes today when she'd been so fearful about the lost snuffbox. She'd feared he might come to harm, and it was more than she could bear. She wouldn't have felt like that if she didn't care deeply. He'd done all he could to win her heart again, but she'd been more concerned with her own bruised pride and obsession with past injuries, determined to see falsehood in everything he said or did! Oh, fool, *fool*, letting all go to ruin because of an innocent dessert.

She gazed at the syllabub in front of her. How light and dainty it looked, prepared with such loving concern by a cook who'd been overjoyed at the reconciliation she believed had taken place. Slowly she dipped her finger in the creamy confection, then tasted it. More tears welled from her eyes as visions of the past skimmed past her tear-drenched eyes. She saw that first Christmas with Owen at her parents' home; then she saw the wedding night, and a dinner that had ended with this same simple dish . . .

Owen's voice suddenly spoke from the doorway. "Tears? Perhaps Mrs. Barnsley has been too generous with the lemon."

She whirled about with a gasp. He was leaning against the jamb, his naval uniform very striking in the candlelight.

She hastily wiped her eyes, and tried unsuccessfully to look composed. "I—I thought you'd gone."

"I didn't even really consider it."

She looked at the floor. "I could not have blamed you if you had," she said quietly.

"Well, you *do* try a man's patience, even a guilty man," he murmured.

"I *wanted* to forgive and forget, truly I did, but . . ."

"Can you forgive and forget now?" he asked softly.

Fresh tears stung her eyes, and she nodded. "Yes," she whispered.

"Do you really mean that?"

"Yes, oh, yes. I love you, Owen, deep in my heart I knew it when the snuffbox fell into the water. I was so afraid for you. I could hardly bear it!"

"Are you sure you don't still fear I will betray you with Serena?"

"I'm quite sure," she replied truthfully, for suddenly that fear *had* gone.

He straightened, and in two strides had reached her. He pulled her close, crushing his lips upon hers, and tasting tears and syllabub in a heady blend that made him feel weak. His mouth moved luxuriously over hers, and he felt how her body softened willingly, molding to his in a remembered way that brought tears to his eyes too.

He drew back, resting his forehead against hers. "Oh, Sophie, my dearest darling, I've dreamed of this moment so many times over the past year that I began to think it would always remain just a dream. I've faced hurricanes, icebergs, pirates, French men-o'-war, and every other hazard the high seas can hold, but the only thing I really feared was not winning you back. It was my love for you that carried me through it all, even though I'd lost you through my own foolishness. I won't fail you again, I swear. Let this Christmas mark a new beginning."

She nodded. "Let it be the best Christmas ever," she breathed.

He kissed her again, holding her to him and savoring the contours of her body. The taste of syllabub was intoxicating, and he drew away once more, smiling into her eyes. "Mrs. Barnsley went to a great deal of trouble on our account, so perhaps we should sample the syllabub after all," he said softly.

"Perhaps we should," she answered, smiling too. Happiness bubbled irrepressibly through her. Suddenly the past year had been swept aside, and all was as it should be again.

He reached across to dip his finger in the little dish, and placed a little dab of dessert on her lips. "Tasting such a wickedly delicious dessert on the lips of one's dearest love is pleasurable beyond belief," he murmured, beginning to bend his head to kiss her again.

She drew back for the briefest moment. "Pleasurable to the point of being seductive," she whispered.

He paused, looking deep into her eyes. "Indeed?"

"Oh, indeed," she murmured, stretching up to give him the sort of kiss that could only lead to the bedchamber.

The Christmas Goose

❄

Patricia Rice

Despair blew across the cliff with the December wind, pummeling Simon LeMaster with the same gale force that tore open his coat and whipped at his cravat. He heard the resounding trumpet call to arms in the high whine through the rocks, heard the clash of artillery in the crash of the waves, and the sound of men dying in the mournful cry of the gulls. The smoke of too many battlefields cluttered the sky in boiling gray clouds.

He blamed the wind for the moisture tearing in his eyes, but he knew his own soul responsible for all else. He glanced down at the rocks below his feet, imagined the height of the waves at high tide, and wondered if he had the courage. Deciding he had no more of that honorable asset now than he had when he led his men into battle, he gathered his weight on his walking stick, and limping, turned his back on the sea.

He supposed a bottle of laudanum more his style if this soul-wrenching melancholy became more than he could bear. In any event, the holidays were no time for such thoughts, although the holidays had brought them on in the first place. For the first time in six years, he had come home for Christmas. No living in a tent in the middle of a mud field, no lounging on a

APPLE DRESSING

2 cups diced crustless bread
½ cup melted butter or
  drippings
1 cup cubed apples
½ cup chopped walnuts

¾ cup chopped cooked
  prunes
1 tablespoon lemon juice
½ teaspoon paprika
1 teaspoon salt

Lightly toss the ingredients together in a large bowl.

---

bug-infested mattress in a bordello where everyone
spoke a foreign language. The voices around him
spoke clear crisp English with a rural accent, the air
smelled fresh and sweet, and childish laughter echoed
up hill and down valley. He couldn't bear it.

He kept seeing the shadowed eyes and hollow
cheeks of children so starved they could barely lift
their feet. He saw their mothers, exhausted from years
of fighting and surviving, often not knowing the father
of their children, victims of rape and necessity. With
enough liquor and distance, he might eventually erase
their faces; they were foreign faces, after all. But he
couldn't erase the faces of those children on the docks,
the hope and despair in their mothers' eyes as they
waited for their menfolk to descend from the boats
returning them home, menfolk missing limbs or other
vital parts making them useless as wage earners for

the rest of their lives. Those faces were English, the wives and children of men he'd led into battle. Those men had fought more fearlessly and bravely than he ever had, but only he had emerged relatively un-scathed to a wealthy home and a family who could support him should he never do another day's work. His men had come home to nothing but a hero's pride, a cold fireplace, and empty bellies.

Simon had tried talking to his superiors. He had gone over their heads and talked to every government official he could find in London at this time of year. He'd met stone walls everywhere he turned. Finally stumbling upon one of his brave men begging on a corner and having only a few coins to help him, he'd let the melancholy overwhelm him to the point that he had to come home. At least in battle he'd felt some sense of accomplishment. He could make a difference occasionally. But back in the security of England, he could do nothing. He had no power, no wealth of his own, no status to change a system so archaic it would treat men as pawns to dispose of at will.

He had to stop thinking like that. The anger and frustration had long since dissipated into this endless despair. He would throw himself off on the rocks of a certainty if he kept up this train of thought. He had to divert his attention, think of the gingerbread cook-ing back home in the kitchen, decide on presents for his niece and nephew, search for the happiness that eluded him when he should finally be at peace. He had everything. Why should he mourn for those who did not?

Simon heard the sharp yip of a dog somewhere far-ther down the cliff path, and he scowled. People ought to keep their dogs at home, not let them run the dangers of these crumbling cliffs. Too often loose dogs ran in packs, endangering the sheep. He debated searching for the culprit or leaving it be. He had difficulty making any decision at all these days. He found sleeping through the days easier than choosing whether or not to get out of bed.

A sharp yipe called him to action much as the call of a trumpet once had. Cursing his aching foot, Simon hobbled over the rough ground, searching for the source of the sound. He found it in a pile of rubble and boulders a little way down the path. A young collie, tail flapping like a flag, worried at a paw caught between two stones. Liquid brown eyes turned trustfully to the stranger approaching.

"Stupid, fool animal," Simon muttered, wincing as he slid on his bad foot. The path could be treacherous to the sure of foot, and he most certainly was not that at the moment.

With malice aforethought, he unwrapped his cravat and tied it to the dog's collar. He intended to find the owner of the mongrel and lecture them thoroughly on the care and upkeep of stupid animals. The dog made no protest but licked his hand gratefully. Maybe the animal wasn't so stupid after all. At least it had the sense to offer gratitude and respect to those who came to its aid.

The stone dislodged easily. The dog presented another difficulty entirely. Leaping and bounding and smearing Simon's doeskin breeches with mud, he nearly jerked his rescuer from his feet when he raced for the top of the cliff.

Still, it gave Simon something to think about besides his melancholy state of mind. The walk back to town was considerably brisker than the one coming out. The dog remained mercifully quiet now that it was free, but it tracked the scent of every rodent to cross its path until the hampering neckcloth brought it back in line. It proceeded at a run so as not to miss a single moment of the romp. Simon had practically lost his breath by the time he reached Lymeshead.

The main street of the village wound lazily along the creek meandering through the town square, around a hill, and over a stone bridge on the far side. Fortunately for Simon, the vicarage stood on this side of town. It made as good a starting point for his search as any.

The fair-haired young vicar wandered into his cottage garden at the same moment as Simon opened the gate. They hailed each other, and the vicar leaned over to pat the tail-wagging collie.

"Leopold! What are you up to now?" the young man asked, scratching behind the dog's ear and glancing up to the stiffly correct man holding him. He'd never seen the younger LeMaster in such disarray, with his cravat off, his shirt open, and his expensive trousers mud-streaked.

"Then you know this wretch, Richard?" Simon demanded. "He nearly got himself killed out on the cliffs today. I mean to give his owner a severe upbraiding. Could you direct me to the culprit?"

Straightening, Richard smiled at the young lordling's outrage. He'd known Simon since childhood. The younger son of a viscount, Simon had all the stiff-necked pride of the aristocracy, but a sense of responsibility wider than the sea lapping at their doorsteps. No man could shoulder the weight of the world. Even Richard had abandoned that hope at an early age. But Simon was too stubborn to admit defeat. Richard pretty much figured Simon would have single-handedly defeated Napoleon if necessary, for he would never have come home otherwise.

"Oh, I don't think there's a culprit involved. Leopold is a stray that landed on the Widow Tarkington's doorstep some months ago. She's done everything within her power to find the dog's owner, while attempting to teach the rascal manners. Unfortunately, animal training is not one of her strong suits. I should imagine Leopold either escaped the barn or chewed off his rope."

"Widow Tarkington? Matthew married?" Thunderstruck, Simon stared at the amiable vicar.

Richard shrugged. "Men do, you know. He came home long enough to meet and court her, then went off to get himself killed. There's times I think he married her because he knew he would die, and he wanted someone to look after his sisters."

"Stupid nodcock," Simon grumbled, staring past the vicar's head to the gray-shrouded sky over the sea. The wind was less here, on the lee side of the hill. "A soldier should never marry. There ought to be laws."

"Yes, well, I suppose if that went into law, we wouldn't have many soldiers. Not a bad thing to consider if all countries enforced it, I suppose, but I can't see it happening in our lives."

Simon ignored this wisdom. Grasping the collie's impromptu leash more firmly, he took his leave. "I should call on the widow, in any case. Matthew would have wanted it. I wish someone had told me sooner."

Richard shrugged. "Someone would have soon enough. You've only been home a few days. I truly don't think Matthew is frowning at you from heaven."

Ignoring that small admonition also, Simon followed

the collie through the garden gate and back to the main street. Although they were much of an age, he'd never been particularly close to the vicar, who had always been sickly and something of a scholar. But Simon and Matthew had got into romps together through most of their lives. They'd gone to war together, but in different units since Matthew couldn't afford colors in the more prestigious guards Simon had joined. It must have cost the better part of his mother's savings to have bought colors at all, but there had been little other chance of Matthew making a living. His acreage was too small and too rocky to produce the kind of income needed to support a country squire in these times.

Wondering which of the village girls Matthew had chosen for his wife, Simon wandered the familiar path through town, past overgrown hedgerows, and down a dirt lane to the old farmhouse where Matthew had grown up. Matthew's father had once been owner of sufficient land to scrape a comfortable living, but bad investments, a bad economy, and an early demise had brought the squire's living to an end. Simon remembered hearing some time back that Matthew's mother had died also, but he had just assumed the girls had gone to live with family. It hadn't occurred to him that Matthew had chosen to raise his sisters by himself. Although, now that he thought about it, Simon couldn't remember ever meeting any of Matthew's relatives other than his parents. Perhaps there hadn't been any.

The collie sensed he came close to home and jerked and strained at his leash. Simon's damaged foot ached with the exertion, and he found his pace dragging in direct proportion to the dog's need to go faster. Wearily, he contemplated unfastening the leash, but he refused to allow the dog to come out ahead. He would see it firmly secured first.

The stone farmhouse looked shabbier than he remembered, but the front door had been freshly painted, the knocker polished, and the steps swept. Simon pounded on the knocker, listening to it echo through the hollow inner hall. He and Matthew had frequently tested its echoing capacity in years past. With no furniture or wall to obstruct it, the knock resounded quite clearly through to the kitchen.

Still, no one came to the door.

Remembering the Tarkingtons had kept few servants, Simon surmised they had none now. He waited a while longer, giving the occupants time to set aside whatever they were doing, but still no one responded to his call. He meant to turn away and loose the mongrel in the barn when a high-pitched squeal sent him racing as fast as the dog toward the rear of the house.

As Simon came around the corner, a fleet-footed creature dashed between his legs, and his weakened foot finally gave out under him, landing him firmly on his rear in the muddy yard. The makeshift leash slid from his hand and the dog ran off, barking, in the direction of the squealing pig, trailing the cravat after him. Before Simon could attempt to right himself, a tall figure in skirts, racing around the corner, screaming in fury, stumbled over his outstretched legs and fell smack into the dirt beside him.

Simon only had a dim impression of angles and bones and creamy skin before the female gave him a surprised look, darted a glance in the direction of the racing animals, and leaped to her feet again. Without a word of apology, she charged after pig and dog.

Shaking his head to clear it of the cobwebs evidently replacing his brain, Simon staggered upward. His fleeting impression was enhanced now by the sight of the tall slender figure outracing the pig to shoo it awkwardly with her long skirts. With the aid of the barking collie and a fence, she managed to trap the animal sufficiently to confuse it, but not necessarily to send it in the appropriate direction. With a sigh, Simon limped to her rescue.

Even the pig had a collar, Simon noted wryly as he swatted a porky rear end with his walking stick, sending the obstreperous animal back toward the barnyard where it belonged. The collie followed at its tail, shepherding it as he ought to shepherd sheep. The sight made Simon's lips twist in a smile he hadn't felt on his face in quite some time.

"I apologize, sir," the woman said breathlessly as she walked at his side, holding her ribs as she gasped for air. "Just look at you! You're all over mud. As soon as I get those dratted animals locked up, we'll go inside and I'll see what I can do to right the mess. Although I daresay that mud will stain," she said doubtfully, giving his trousers a second look.

"I've had worse than mud stains before," he answered, the smile disappearing as he remembered the valiant soldier who had served as his valet these last years. O'Hara had always known how to remove mud and blood and the scars of war. The man had been blown to bits in a retreat that went astray. "You need to find some way to control these animals of yours."

She shrugged, and he noticed the muddy tear in her shawl, apparently another casualty of their fall. She had the shawl tied loosely over her bodice, so he could see little of the figure beneath, but her reed-slimness gave the impression of fraility, although she stood nearly as tall as he.

"The girls insist on making pets of them, and I haven't the heart to tell them all creatures have a purpose. I'm afraid we'll end up feeding that rapacious pig for the rest of our lives instead of turning him into the ham he's supposed to be."

They shooed the pig back into its sty and locked the protesting dog in the barn before turning back toward the house. Only then did she stop and give him a quizzical look. "We haven't met, have we? I'm sorry. My manners are abominable these days."

Simon would say her manners were immensely practical, but he supposed one didn't address an unknown lady with such familiarity. He'd been too long from civilization himself. He made a brief bow, only then realizing his state of undress. The last he'd seen of his cravat, it had trailed through mud and briar in the front hedge.

"I apologize. I'm Simon LeMaster, an old friend of Matthew's. I just heard he'd left a widow, and along with returning your dog, I meant to pay my condolences. I hadn't realized I scarcely look the part of proper caller." He gave his rumpled clothing a wry look. "I think I'm the one whose manners have gone begging."

"LeMaster!" she exclaimed with a little more enthusiasm, her wide lips turning up in a brilliant smile. "Matthew told me all about you and the escapades the two of you indulged in. It's a wonder either of you lived to see maturity. I keep congratulating myself that I have only his sisters to contend with and not any little brothers who might resemble either of you. I'm Rebecca."

She calmly led him through the kitchen door as if he were one of the family instead of a guest. She gestured toward a bench near the fire. "Take off those wet boots while I make some tea. Your feet must be frozen."

She'd no doubt attributed his limp to wet, cold feet. If he didn't remove his stockings, she'd see no less. Simon shrugged and did as told. In truth, it felt good to remove the confining boots from his aching toes. "How old are the girls now? They were always pests we managed to elude. Surely they're nearly grown?"

"Just old enough to cause trouble. Mary is twelve, and Lucille's fifteen. Matthew always said had his sister Johnna lived, he could have left the lot to her, but she died in childbirth some years ago. I don't mind, though. Had it not been for the girls, he would probably have waited until he returned from war to marry me, and then I would never have married at all."

She said it quite matter-of-factly, without a hint of anguish as she went about setting the teapot on the stove and measuring the leaves. Simon noted she measured very carefully, as if the tea leaves had the value of gold. Glancing around, he could see little in the way of edibles. Behind the open pantry door he could see a sack of flour and a tin he thought might contain sugar. No meat cooked over the fire or hung on the drying rack. He remembered a time when this kitchen was redolent of baking pastries, roasting meats, and savory stews. The weak concoction simmering on the old stove now barely carried the odor of turnips.

"Would you like a bit of apple tart with your tea?" she asked, removing her torn shawl and attempting to disguise an expression of dismay as she noticed the tear. Biting her lip, she slipped on a clean apron and washed her hands at the pump.

Not seeing anything resembling a tart anywhere in the kitchen, Simon was about to politely decline when she removed the cold pastry from a shelf above the stove. From his sitting position, he couldn't have seen it up there. He couldn't remember Matthew's mother ever keeping anything on that shelf, but then, old Mrs. Tarkington had barely stood five-foot high. This Widow Tarkington had sufficient height to dust the low kitchen ceiling without standing on a chair.

Stomach rumbling, he could scarcely decline. Simon remembered the apples he and Matthew used to filch from the old trees out back. They'd always tasted sweeter than any others he'd ever eaten. He couldn't remember the last time he'd eaten crunchy apples or even a tart.

The Widow Tarkington moved gracefully for a tall woman. A steaming hot cup of tea appeared before him along with the tart topped by a little cream. With the fire warming his back and hot tea in his stomach, Simon felt transported to a time when he'd thought those niceties constituted heaven. He closed his eyes and savored the warmth and aromas, then found himself noticing the fresh mild scent of the widow's skin as she refilled his cup.

His eyes flew open again, but she hadn't noticed his momentary aberration. She merely took a seat at the table with him and warmed her fingers on her hot cup. Simon wondered about her background, where Matthew might have found her. She certainly didn't come from the village. She had thick whiskey-colored hair pulled back in an unfashionable bun, and eyes he could call neither gray nor green, but she possessed a calm air of assurance none of the village girls would have shown in this situation. Most of them giggled and looked at the floor when he was around.

Before he could open his mouth to ask the question hovering on the tip of his tongue, the front door slammed open and the echo of girlish laughter drifted down the long hall, followed by the loud tramp of feet and the shouts of young voices.

"Rebecca! Rebecca! We talked to the vicar's wife!"

Simon couldn't distinguish one voice from the other, but he could tell both talked at once. Rebecca winced and rolled her eyes at their unladylike exuberance, but she rose with a smile on her face to greet them.

"Lucille, Mary, we have company. Mind your manners," she admonished gently, catching the youngest by the shoulders to gently brush her long hair back out of her face, turning her to face their guest properly.

Both girls bobbed hasty curtsies and made polite murmurs of greeting, but instantly turned back to Rebecca for the topic most on their minds.

"Mrs. Lofton says you might go a'Thomasing. She says it's perfectly proper. Then we might have enough for a goose and to buy those ribbons in the window." As the eldest, Lucille spoke first, keeping her voice just short of pleading.

The color in Rebecca's cheeks faded, but she managed to speak quietly and proudly, not even looking at their guest. "We will not discuss this again, girls. Begging is only for those who have nothing, and we have a great deal. Now run upstairs and wash. We need to begin dinner."

She tried to behave as if the girls hadn't embarrassed her to the bottoms of her feet as they ran, protesting, from the room. She set her cup on the sink, cleaned up an apple spill on the side of the pan, and carefully replaced the remains of the tart back on the shelf. She'd left just enough to split between the two girls. Mr. LeMaster had eaten the piece she had meant for herself. She didn't mind. It had been rather pleasant having an adult conversation in the middle of the day like this. She didn't often have time.

She felt his silence and wished for something with which to fill the void. They both spoke at once.

"I don't suppose you . . ." he started to say.

"I apologize for the . . ." she began and stopped.

She turned, and they smiled hesitantly at each other. He wasn't at all a bad-looking man when he smiled. She'd thought him harsh earlier, with grim lines along the side of his mouth, and cheekbones hollowed to rawness, but when he smiled, she could see the laugh lines beside his eyes, and his face took on a whole new demeanor. She could picture him swirling lovely young ladies around the dance floor, their eyes sparkling up at him as he whispered pretty words in their ears. He was that kind of man. The handsome, wealthy, spoiled kind. The kind who ignored gawky, intelligent, plain women like her.

"Ladies first," he murmured politely. "Although you really don't need to apologize for the girls. They're young and it's Christmas. They want everything they see. I have a young nephew who's convinced I can give him the stars if I so choose. He's demanding a big one."

She laughed. That was the awful thing about handsome, charming men. They could make you laugh and feel good with just their words. They meant nothing by them. The charm just came easily to them, smoothing over rough spots, getting them out of difficult situations without harm to themselves. If they eased someone else's way in passing, fine, but more often than not, they ended up leaving a trail of tears. She was too wise to see more in his words than was there.

"I'm not at all certain those two would be satisfied with a star unless they could wear it in their hair. It's been a rough few years for them, but they still believe Christmas is a magical time, one when miracles come true. I have yet to teach them that we must make our own miracles."

He leaned over and pulled on his boots. "It's a shame we can't all keep that belief. What I started to ask was if you would mind sending your apple tart recipe up to our cook. I would be happy to deliver it myself. I have never tasted anything so delightful in my life."

Rebecca found herself blushing. She knew better. She kicked herself mentally. But Matthew had been dead well over a year and not home for longer than that before his death. She had very little experience in dealing with a man's flattery, in any event. Obviously, she must be starved for masculine attention.

She tried to respond coolly. "The type of apple makes all the difference, and the amount of seasoning. A sweet apple needs less sugar, a tart apple cooks better but requires more cinnamon. And since tastes differ, not all cooks produce the same results."

He gave her a quick glance as he straightened his last boot. "I suppose that goes for a lot of things. If I bring you the other ingredients, do you have enough apples to make one of those tarts for me? I'll be happy to pay you for your labor."

Rebecca narrowed her eyes in suspicion, but he seemed perfectly sincere. "You needn't go to that trouble. I'll send a tart up to the house on the morrow. That's my baking day anyway." She lied through her teeth, but she wouldn't have this man seeing her as a charity case. She had little left but her pride, and she would cling to it for as long as she could.

He stood up, towering over her as few men did. The laugh lines had disappeared. "It is foolish to give away what others will buy. The labor and ingredients for a tart like that come dearly. We pay our cook and the grocer and the kitchen maids for the likes of that. Why should you not be reimbursed as well? Then the girls could have their ribbons."

She wrapped her hands in a towel and tried not to glare at him. "I am not your cook or your kitchen maid or your grocer. I am your neighbor. In case you have not noticed, I am not in trade."

He opened his mouth to argue, thought better of it, and wisely nodded his head before stalking to the door. Rebecca couldn't call it anything else but stalking. Simon LeMaster liked to have his own way. He was the type of man who liked to reorganize the world around him to match his ideals. And she hadn't conformed. Her father had tried for more than twenty years, and she'd never learned the knack. God had given her height instead of docility. Mostly, she didn't mind. But Simon LeMaster wasn't precisely happy with the arrangement.

"I thank you for the tea, Mrs. Tarkington," he said stiffly, opening the door. Then, with a brief nod, he was gone.

She wanted to sigh in relief. She wanted to be glad that the meddlesome man had received his comeuppance. But it had felt so good having a man in the kitchen again, hearing a deep voice praise her cooking, having a helping hand with the wretched animals. She had nearly wept with relief when he'd come to rescue her from the dratted pig. She had instantly given him the part of conquering hero: strong, brave, handsome. But he was made of clay like all the others.

Quashing her easily aroused daydreams, Rebecca returned to the real world with the advent of the girls to help with dinner. Assigning each of them a task, she tried not to let their chatter pierce her easily wounded heart. They thought all adults invincible. They needed to believe that. She wouldn't allow them to learn otherwise.

"Molly said last year she got a fur muff *and* hat," Lucille declared. "And this year she's asked for a fur-lined cape to match."

"Just think of all the bunny rabbits that must have died for her," Rebecca responded absently. She had given up hope of convincing the girls they didn't need everything they saw, but she couldn't give up the practice of teaching them.

"Bunny rabbits?" Mary asked, wide-eyed. "That's bunny rabbit fur? Oh, how awful!"

"Fur has to come from animals," Rebecca answered calmly, hiding her smile. "And I shouldn't think there's much left of it to match this year. Rabbit fur sheds abominably."

"You're making that up," Lucille said suspiciously, chopping at her carrots.

Rebecca raised her eyebrows. "And when have I ever lied to you?" She waited for that to sink in before continuing, "Once I learn the knack of weaving wool into yarn, I can make you warm gloves and hats and coats, and they will all match, and no one will have anything like them. You just have to be patient."

"Molly says only peasants wear wool and make their own yarn," Lucille muttered scornfully. "Her mother buys velvets and the prettiest embroidery thread in London. Papa used to buy us velvet dresses every Christmas. And we used always to have goose with apple dressing for Christmas dinner."

Rebecca tried to keep the tears away. Once upon a time, she'd had a father who bought her velvet and silk dresses, any kind she'd ever asked for. She'd had cooks and maids and a horse of her own. She'd never worn wool, knew nothing of where it came from. The only practical thing she had ever learned was how to cook and bake, and that was because she'd spent so much of her time mooching from the kitchens. She'd lost all that and would never see it again. She'd traded it willingly for the chance to be Matthew's wife, but she knew how Lucille felt. She couldn't fault the child for expressing the same desires and thoughts she had when she donned her scratchy woolen gown each morning, or stared at another meal of turnips.

"Maybe next year the sheep will have a finer wool and will bring a better price," she answered without too much hope. She knew nothing of sheep. Matthew had left a manager in charge of the few they possessed. The sum the man had given her after the shearing hadn't been enough to do more than pay their most pressing debts.

"Do you think we might have a plum pudding this year?" Mary asked timidly. Of the two girls, Mary was the quietest, the easiest to frighten, the one who tried the hardest. Rebecca understood that the three people Mary had counted on most in this world had been ripped from her short life without warning, and the child feared Rebecca, too, would one day disappear.

It was an impossible fear to ease. She could only love the little girl and pray circumstances would improve.

Rebecca had no idea how she would make one of the elaborate plum puddings her family used to serve, but perhaps she could come up with a more modest version. Brushing a kiss over Mary's hair, she gave her a hug. "Let's see what we can do, all right? Tomorrow I must make a tart for the viscount's family, so I will go into town and see what I can find."

Both girls cheered considerably at the prospect, and Rebecca nearly wept at the easiness of pleasing them. At their age, she would have thrown a tantrum had she not received a dozen gifts, had her plum pudding and cooked goose, and a Yule log larger than two men could carry. She had been spoiled horribly. Perhaps that was why she had been so determined to have Matthew after her father had said she could not have him. Still, she refused to regret the few short weeks they had together. She just regretted the result.

As if reading her mind, Lucille asked, "will your papa come to visit this year, do you think, Rebecca? You must miss him."

Rebecca wiped her eyes with the back of her hand, leaving a floury streak across her face. "No, I think not, Lucy. He's old and set in his ways. We'll just send him a cheery note, shall we?"

She didn't expect a reply this year any more than in years past, but she refused to be as cold as he.

"My word, Simon! What have you done to yourself?" Looking alarmed, the Viscountess LeMaster studied her younger son's ruined clothing as he came through the upper hall. "You have not been to the cliffs, have you? You could have fallen!"

He could have taken a bullet or a cannonball any number of times these past years, Simon thought dryly, but his mother hadn't been there to see that. She only worried about those things she could see.

"I did fall, but not on the cliffs. Why didn't you tell me Matthew left a widow? I should have called sooner." He was impatient to change out of his filthy clothing, but he had a restless need to learn more about the woman he'd just left. Where could Matthew have possibly met her? She had too much sophistication for a village girl, but she wore none of the physical attributes of a lady.

"I didn't realize you hadn't met her, dear. Why don't you go change those horrible clothes while I call for tea? You must be starved."

He had a thousand questions he wished to ask, but Simon nodded and wandered off to his own chamber first. He would never get a word out of his mother otherwise.

Once properly bathed and attired, he returned to the parlor, where the entire family had gathered in front of the fire. His father sat scribbling at a small desk, only occasionally sipping at his tea or nibbling at a sandwich. His elder brother, Thomas, had his head together with his wife, Helen, obviously discussing Christmas preparations, while the twins bounced merrily on the sofa, entertaining their grandmother with this unexpected visit in adult company.

Again, Simon felt the pangs of melancholy strike. The family seemed entirely whole without him. He'd not graced their presence at this time of year for six years or more. The twins thought him no more than a visiting stranger. Thomas and Helen had their own lives, revolving around their children and their friends and their social life. His father had made an idle inquiry as to his plans now that the war seemed over, but he'd scarcely acknowledged his younger son's presence since. Only his mother fussed and bothered over him, as if Simon were still a small child. He just couldn't seem to fit his adult self into this picture.

Why did he feel so out of place with the people he loved when he'd felt comfortably at home in the kitchen of a woman he didn't know?

Shaking his head at the perversity of his nature, Simon forced himself into the middle of this family scene. Perhaps he'd become used to crude conditions, and a simple country kitchen had felt more like home than this elegant parlor. He didn't mean to analyze it. He took a seat beside his mother, across from the twins, and accepted the cup handed to him.

"May we have your cherry cake if you don't want it?" four-year old Tobias asked, his face already liberally smeared with the remainder of an earlier cake.

"But I mean to eat them all up," Simon responded soberly, "even the chocolate ones. You may have sandwiches, if you like."

Beside the brash Tobias, dainty Tabitha puckered up. "I wanted a chocolate one," she murmured.

"They're nasty pasty sandwiches," Tobias declared. "You can't have all the cakes."

Amazing how even at an early age the boy learned to stand up and argue while the girl just sobbed to get her way. Simon hadn't had enough experience with children to notice that until now. He thought back to the two young girls in Rebecca's kitchen. Those two hadn't sobbed or protested. They'd merely stated their case and went about their business when told. He wondered how the argument fared after he'd left.

What was "a'Thomasing" and why had Rebecca gone so pale at the thought?

"One more cake for each of you," his mother said, interrupting his thoughts. "Then back to the nursery with you. You're all over crumbs."

While the children carefully chose their favorite cakes, Simon turned to his mother. "I've been from home so long, I've forgotten it all. The vicar mentioned something about a'Thomasing, but I had to pretend to know what he was talking about. Is it related to St. Thomas's day?"

Lady LeMaster gave him a little pat and handed him a plate full of sandwiches. "It's just the day some of the widows in the village come around to visit with gifts of holly or mistletoe. We leave a plate of shillings at the door in exchange. We have a sip of tea and talk a bit, then they help themselves as they go out. It's a polite way of helping out this time of year. It's so hard on some of them, and this year it's particularly bad. The wool brought in nothing at all, corn prices are down, and with many of the miners out of work, there's no extra to be had anywhere. And there are so many widows these days, with the war and all. I'm afraid the poor rates will have to go up to take care of them all. We do what we can."

Stunned, Simon sank back against the cushions. "Does the government not provide pensions for the military widows?"

His mother sent him a shrewd look. "I suppose, of some sort. It doesn't seem enough to live on, though. I'm not certain they all receive it, and of course, they can't afford solicitors to look into the matter. It's a sad business, but there is little we can do about it. Did you say you met the Widow Tarkington today?"

"I returned her collie to her. I hadn't realized Matthew married. She's not from around here, is she?"

"I haven't really inquired, dear. Matthew didn't bring her around and introduce her before he returned to war. I've seen her in church, of course, but we're not in the same circles. I can't imagine how Matthew found her."

Simon gritted his teeth and tried not to condemn his mother for her attitude. She had thought little of Matthew's mother, calling her a "common woman from the village." But the squire's wife had been as educated and well brought up as the viscountess, perhaps more so. He couldn't remember Mrs. Tarkington ever condemning anyone for their lack of breeding.

To Simon's surprise, his father intruded upon the conversation, leaving his desk to help himself to one of the cakes the twins hadn't mangled before departing for their nursery. "Met her in London, he did. He was on leave, she was there for her come-out. Right smitten the moment he laid eyes on her, I believe. Came to my office and asked for my aid in winning her father to his suit. Didn't make much difference. Botherwell always was a hard-headed ass."

"Botherwell? The only Botherwell I remember is the baron who turns coal into cash. She's his daughter?"

The viscount shrugged. "His only child. Spoiled her. Told him so myself. Not that she took well in society in any case. Too tall for most of those lazy young louts. Botherwell should have known something of the sort would happen. Gal had too much sense to fall for the fortune hunters who swarmed around her, so she found herself a pretty face instead."

Simon sifted through his father's laconic explanations for the whole story. The conclusion he reached raised his eyebrows. "She eloped with Matthew?"

His father filled his plate and wandered back toward the desk. "So I heard. Matthew didn't ask me about that part."

By this time, Helen and Thomas had finished their discussion and now returned to the table. Helen set her cup down and asked, "Are you talking about Rebecca? Sad case, that, but she should never have gone against her family's wishes. Matthew Tarkington only wanted a mother for his little sisters."

Simon scowled. "I don't believe that. He wouldn't have eloped with the daughter of a wealthy baron unless they'd made a love match. He was always impetuous, but he wasn't selfish."

Helen smiled daintily. Simon could see where her daughter learned her mannerisms.

"Men always defend each other. He took a wealthy young girl from her loved ones and dumped her in the middle of nowhere to look after two little girls, then he returned to war and left her to fend for herself. If that's not selfish, I don't know what is."

"If I recollect rightly, it takes two to make a marriage. She must have had something to say about the matter. Perhaps she didn't realize her father was so opposed to the match. I suppose he cut her off?"

Helen nodded as she delicately wiped her fingers on a linen napkin. "No dowry, nothing. He'd had grand plans for her. He probably could have bought her an earl, if she'd wanted. He doted on her. I never had a chance to talk with her much, but Rebecca never seemed interested in owning an earl. Growing up without a mother, she lived a little wild at home. She had some strange ideas."

Strange ideas like wanting the same love and affection from a husband as she'd received from her father, Simon supposed. She hadn't grown up wild. She'd grown up naive. No one had explained the facts of life to her. He began to understand a little better why she'd practically thrown him from her kitchen for offering her money. He'd made an ass of himself.

As he left his family to go on to other topics, Simon found himself wandering in the direction of the billiard room. He hadn't practiced in years. He and Matthew had used to enjoy the challenge of a good game of billiards. Thomas never had the eye for it. He wondered who he would play against now. Not having Matthew here left a gap he hadn't expected. Maybe Richard played? Probably not. A vicar wouldn't.

Simon couldn't keep his mind from straying back to Matthew and his widow. Matthew had married a wealthy baron's daughter. It seemed too incredible to be true. Of course, Matthew had always had a way with women. He'd seduced his fair share in the village and even had a few swooning when he and Simon had gone to London to buy their colors. They'd thought it jolly good fun at the time. At the age of twenty-one, fun was the only thing of importance on their minds. Marriage had never occurred to either of them. They'd meant to be war heroes.

Simon shot his cue into the ball so sharply that it bounced back and forth across the table without ever hitting a hole. Cursing, he put the cue back in the rack. War heroes. A lot of good they were, dead and buried in some stinking hole.

"My, how lovely you look today, Mrs. Tarkington!

And Miss Tarkington! Soon enough, you'll have all the lads stumbling over their feet around you."

"That's about all they're good for," Lucille muttered under her breath, making Rebecca smile. Lucille had just had a major tiff with the butcher's boy, until now her favorite suitor, if he could be called that. Mostly, he gave her meat pies and showed her where the frogs swam.

Rebecca smiled at the friendly grocer and produced her shopping list. "You flatter us, I'm sure, Mr. White. It must be the Christmas spirit come upon us." She handed the list over the counter to him.

"Just a few weeks more," he declaimed merrily. "I've got the gander all picked out. How about you? Will you have goose?"

Rebecca clasped her gloved hands tightly but managed to return his good cheer. "If I had my way, we'd have roast pork, but the girls treat that little monster as a pet."

White laughed and turned to find the supplies listed. "Going to have plum pudding, I see. Haven't had a good plum pudding in years. Wife says they're too much trouble without the children there to enjoy it."

"You're welcome to join us, if you'd like, sir. I'm sure we'll have more than we can eat. It's a modest recipe, not as grand as you remember, perhaps, but we'll have the usual surprises, I'm sure." Rebecca shook her head silently at Lucille's frown. The child would have to learn it was more pleasurable to share treats with others than to keep them to themselves.

"That's right kind of you, Mrs. Tarkington, right kind. Might take you up on that. Squire always dressed a good table. Remember sharing his punch many a year. Here you are." He returned to the counter, piling up the supplies that would provide a Christmas baking of tarts and pudding as well as the usual staples for cooking.

"Put that on our bill, if you would, Mr. White. Matthew's pension money should come in after the first of the year." She crossed her fingers as she said this. She hoped the pension money would appear then. She'd written. They'd acknowledged her petition. When the money hadn't been forthcoming, she'd written again, mentioning her father's name. The reply had promised. Surely, they wouldn't hold out any longer than the first of the year.

A frown of concern replaced the grocer's earlier good cheer. He glanced at Lucille, who had gone to look at something in the window. Quietly, he whispered, "I'm sorry, Mrs. Tarkington. The bill's higher than is good for both of us. What if I put a few of these extras back? Then it won't come to so much."

The extras, like the expensive cinnamon for the tarts and the candied fruits for the pudding. Rebecca bit her lip, trying not to let him see it quiver. She had nothing to give the girls this year. She had thought and thought and found no money for anything. She'd hoped the pudding would lift their spirits. Mr. White let her run a generous bill, knowing she paid what she could whenever she had it. Now even he threatened to cut off her credit. Much more of this, and she would be forced to take charity. Or sell tarts to the odious Simon LeMaster.

With a calmness she didn't feel, Rebecca removed her glove and pulled off the simple gold band on her finger. "Will this help pay toward the bill, Mr. White?"

He looked shocked. "I couldn't take that, Mrs. Tarkington. That's your wedding ring."

She smiled bitterly. "But I'm not married anymore, am I? So it's of little use to me. And I promised the girls plum pudding."

She could see the indecision on his face, the goodness of his heart warring with the instincts of a businessman. He had a wife and home and shop to run. She could understand his fear that he would end up supporting the Tarkingtons if they never paid their bill. She lay the ring down on the counter. "I don't wish to take charity, Mr. White. I'll trust your judgment on the fairness of the payment."

"I'll have a jeweler weigh it," he promised, slipping the ring in his pocket. "You'll get the best offer I can find."

She hated to see the pity in his eyes. That was the worst part of poverty. She could learn to deal with recalcitrant pigs and smelly sheep and scrubbing floors and all that. She just couldn't abide the pity. She moved to examine an exotic assortment of spices on the wall while the grocer packaged up their order.

With their supplies neatly tucked into their bags, Lucille and Rebecca returned to the unpromising gray light of the street outside. Heavy clouds still hung over the sky, and a brisk breeze whipped their skirts, cutting right through their flimsy cloaks. For the hundredth time, Rebecca wished she'd had foresight to elope with her winter clothes as well as her summer gowns. Of course, at the time, she hadn't thought her father could be so unforgiving.

"Isn't that Mr. LeMaster coming toward us?" Lucille asked as Rebecca stopped to tie her woolen scarf more securely around her neck. The girls had knit it for her last winter. It had odd lumps and knots in it, and the red, green, and brown made a strange combination of colors, but it accomplished its purpose.

Rebecca looked up in time to see the young soldier advancing on her. She could tell he had been a soldier even though he wore civilian clothes. The military stride and determined expression said it all. She would find herself outflanked if she didn't surrender her position immediately.

"Good morning, Mrs. Tarkington," he said in clipped tones that almost demanded a salute. "You're out early."

"The same could be said of you, sir," she answered politely, ignoring the stirring of interest in her more feminine side when his gaze seemed to soften as it fell on her. "We decided we wished to make plum pudding as well as apple tarts today, and I needed a few ingredients."

His eyes lit with anticipation. "Would you need any help, then? I haven't stirred a good plum pudding in years."

Surely he couldn't be setting up a flirt with her. He'd said he was Matthew's friend. A friend wouldn't try to seduce his friend's widow, would he? Remembering herself, Rebecca laughed inwardly at her misplaced vanity and gave the answer she would have given Matthew. "We'll make the tarts first. How good are you at peeling apples?" A man as handsome as Simon LeMaster would never set up a flirt with a woman as plain and unappealing as herself.

"Quite good, as a matter of fact," he stated, falling into step with them. "Even better if I'm allowed to munch a few while working.'

They didn't make it past the village tavern before

Mrs. Lofton, the vicar's wife, came hurrying forward to greet them.

"Rebecca! There you are. I've just been out to the house looking for you. We needed you at the Ladies' Meeting last night. We've decided to have a holiday festival to help the needy this year. Everyone will bring in odds and ends of things: baked goods, knitted garments, Mrs. Baker will bring some of her fine jams, you know the kind of thing. And we'll auction them off! We'll have refreshments and entertainment for the children, then the proceeds will go toward buying coal and supplies for those who need it. We were hoping you could contribute some of your baked goods, both for the auction and the refreshments."

Rebecca hesitated for only a second. She couldn't lower herself in the eyes of Lucille and Mr. LeMaster and the vicar's wife by saying she couldn't afford the expense. She certainly couldn't admit that they could use the coal and food themselves. She had been raised as a lady, and it was a lady's duty to help those with less. She knew for a fact that many families had a great less than they did. The Tarkingtons had been landed gentry in these parts for centuries. She couldn't sully their name by acting any less. She nodded quiet agreement, discussed the refreshments briefly, then left Mrs. Lofton on her round of errands.

Rebecca felt Mr. LeMaster's questioning gaze on her as they set off down the path, but she refused to meet his eyes. Making more tarts would use what sugar remained in the larder, and most of the flour. If they received the pension in January, they wouldn't have to go without. If they didn't . . .

She couldn't let herself think of that. Instead, she turned her attention to the nonsense Mr. LeMaster and Lucille exchanged while her mind wandered elsewhere.

He had them laughing as they scuffled through damp brown leaves and frozen ruts back toward the house. Rebecca had seen the sternness in his face yesterday, but she had recognized the charm in him from the first. Matthew had possessed that same ingenuous charm, the easy smile, a manner that made her feel wholly feminine and like the only woman in the world for him. She couldn't say Simon LeMaster made her feel like that, but she suspected he could should he turn his mind to it. The thought made her uneasy. She knew her own vulnerability too well.

That was one too many things to worry about.

As they hurried around to the kitchen door so as not to clutter the parlor with their muddy boots and damp cloaks, Mary came running from the back field, shouting with hiccuping sobs, "Ginger's in the pond!" The rest of her cries were mostly incoherent until she came closer, and Rebecca's stomach sank further as she understood the extent of the disaster.

"Leopold was chasing a mouse, and he scared Ginger, and she broke the rest of the stall door, and now she's wandered down to the pond and I can't get her out!"

Rebecca tried to stay calm. She was the adult here. The girls needed her to behave accordingly. But without Ginger the cow, they would have no milk or cream or butter. And the foolish animal would freeze herself in the pond if Mad George didn't come out and shoot her for trespassing as he'd threatened to do the last time she'd muddied up his fishing pond. The cow weighed eight times Rebecca's weight and had the mind of a mule. The animal didn't go anywhere she didn't want to.

Even as she thought that, the squeal of a rambunctious pig warned of impending chaos. Sure enough, Pigmalion came rushing through the gate Mary had left open in her haste, charging directly toward them as if the only escape route she knew involved flying between the legs of humans, tumbling them like bowling pins.

"Not this time, you nuisance," Mr. LeMaster declared, hopping aside and swinging his walking stick toward a piggy snout.

Pigmalion squealed and tried to dart around the swinging stick, but he applied it firmly to her snout again, steering her back toward the open gate.

"I'll get her leash!" Lucille cried, dropping her groceries and rushing toward the barn.

"Ginger! We've got to save Ginger!" Mary cried in dismay as attention seemed diverted from one crisis by another.

"Find me a stout stick and I'll go after her," Rebecca declared, marching off in the direction of the pond.

"You'll hurt her!" Mary protested.

The cow was Mary's particular pet, while Pigmalion belonged to Lucille. At the moment, Rebecca would gladly take both to the butcher's. She ignored Mary's protest and started toward the open field, knowing full well the hopelessness of her quest. She'd never persuaded the wretched cow to do anything it didn't want to do before. She didn't expect it to happen now. But she had to try. If nothing else, she had counted on selling some of the cream and butter to Mr. White in exchange for some of the staples they would need if the money didn't come soon. It smacked of trade, but not charity, at least.

She heard pounding footsteps running up behind her. Turning, she saw Mr. LeMaster coming after her. Behind him, Lucille had her pet safely leashed and was leading the pig back to his pen. Astonished at the swiftness with which they had caught the animal, she remained stationary. Maybe Mr. LeMaster was a miracle worker.

"I'll get the cow," he informed her, not even breathing hard as he limped up beside her. "You'll get your skirts wet, and if Mad George is still as mad as he used to be, I don't want you near him. He's as likely to shoot you as the cow."

"Then he's as likely to shoot you," she answered dryly. "I don't think your family would appreciate that." She started back down the path again.

"I assure you, I can handle George. You needn't waste your time. Your nose is turning blue with cold, and I daresay your fingers are the same. Why aren't you wearing a hat and warmer gloves?" He traipsed beside her, their long strides evenly matched.

Fool question, Rebecca thought sourly, but she didn't say it aloud. She'd admired his leather fur-lined gloves earlier. She wondered if gloves like that could be made for women. She supposed not. But even mittens would do. She understood Lucille's envy of Molly's fur-lined muff. She clenched her shivering fingers into balls and kept on walking.

"Stubborn woman," LeMaster muttered beside her. "Why don't you sell this dump and find a snug little cottage somewhere?"

"Do you always dispense unasked-for advice?" she asked curtly. She shouldn't do that, she knew. He was offering help, and she should act helpless and grateful. Right now she was too cold and frightened to care.

He didn't reply immediately. But as they came in sight of the cow standing in the pond, he said, "You're right. I apologize."

They didn't have time to exchange any further pleasantries since Mad George chose this moment to race out of his house carrying an antiquated musket that might just shoot off of its own accord from the force of his gestures.

"Stay here!" Simon ordered.

She didn't, of course. She hurried in the direction of the mule-headed cow as he intervened with the irate farmer.

Rebecca had to wade into the icy water to grab the cow's halter. Her teeth instantly began to chatter as she tried to persuade the recalcitrant animal to turn around and walk out of the bone-chilling cold. Big liquid brown eyes looked at her, and she could swear she saw the devil in them as the cow let out a long moo-o-o and refused to budge.

On the bank, Mad George ranted and raved and swung his musket, while Mr. LeMaster talk soothingly, easing closer to the dangerous firearm. Rebecca couldn't think about the consequences of that. Her mind had grown as numb as her toes and fingers. She tugged at Ginger's halter, alternately cursing and pleading.

"... out of my pond now!" The words floated over the water, accompanied by the loud boom of gunpowder.

Ginger jerked free of Rebecca's numb fingers to run in panic to the far bank. Losing her balance, Rebecca tumbled seat first into the water, her frantic gaze going to the far shore for certain signs of bloodshed. Instead, she saw Mr. LeMaster heaving the old gun into the pond and running toward her. Mad George, apparently intent on capturing the cow, now stormed around the far bank.

Had her teeth not chattered so fiercely, she would laugh at the scene. Maybe in the future this would make a hilarious dinner story. As the bone-chilling water soaked through her skirts, and Mr. LeMaster raced to Rebecca's rescue, the obstinate cow calmly climbed from the pond, heading for home. On the far bank, George jumped up and down in fury, unleashing curses to hurry her along. With more resignation than amusement, Rebecca watched Mr. LeMaster wade into the water, heedless of his impeccably polished boots. At this point, she really had no idea if she could stand on her own.

"You'll catch your death of cold out here!" he scolded, sounding more annoyed with her than with the cow. "I told you to wait. Look at you—you're soaked!"

Teeth chattering, Rebecca couldn't make a suitable reply. As he helped her up, she tried to pull away from him so he wouldn't end up as wet as she, with little success. He wrapped her in his arms and kept her from falling as she stumbled back to dry land.

He cursed and fussed all the way back to the house. They heard Mary's shouts of delight as Ginger plodded back to the barn in search of fodder after her little escapade. Rebecca again tried to escape her protector's hold as they approached the house, but Simon threatened to pick her up and carry her if she tried again. Feeling as if her feet were blocks of ice, Rebecca had to acknowledge his better judgment.

"Run, build up the fire," Simon shouted at Lucille when she came racing toward them.

She took one look at his face and ran to do as told without question. Rebecca wearily thought that nothing short of a miracle in itself. Lucille never did anything without question these days. Shivering violently, she allowed herself to be led into the kitchen.

"Hot tea," Simon demanded, and Mary scurried to pour two cups.

When he kneeled on the floor to remove Rebecca's ruined shoes, she finally managed to squeak a protest. He gave her a look from his position on the floor, took notice of her chattering teeth and blue fingers, and ignored her protest. Peeling off his gloves, he removed both her shoes and stockings and began to hastily massage her toes between his warm hands.

She wanted to die of utter embarrassment, but she was too cold. She wrapped her frozen fingers around the hot cup Mary handed her, but she still shivered too much to bring it to her lips. Simon looked up and noticed it.

"Get the tea down," he ordered. "You'll stop shivering with something warm inside. Spill it, if you must, but get it in you or I'll pour it down you myself."

She thought him an extremely presumptuous man. She would have told him so, but she couldn't get any words out. He had no reason to come in here and order her around like that. He didn't even know her. She could freeze to death if she wanted. It wasn't any of his business.

But she managed to bring the cup to her lips and sip cautiously. She would have to stop shivering if she meant to yell at him.

"Go get a fire started in the bedroom," he was ordering now, talking to Lucille. "You'll have to get her into bed. Mary, find a warming pan and heat the sheets."

That was absolutely the outside of enough. Kicking her feet from his hands, Rebecca did her best to stand, though he kneeled too close for comfort. The tea had warmed her thickened tongue enough to scold. "I have work to do. I have no intention of lounging about in bed all day. Now let me up, Mr. LeMaster. You'll need to go home and find something warm for yourself. You're almost as soaked as I am."

He got to his feet only to tower over her, trapping her in the chair. "I see the tea has finally warmed your tongue, Mrs. Tarkington. You will have lung fever if you don't warm yourself. Do you wish to spend the holidays in bed with a vinegar poultice on your chest?"

She blushed heatedly at the reference to her chest but refused to acknowledge her embarrassment that he should notice she had such a thing as a chest. "The kitchen is the warmest place in the house. There is no sense in wasting good coal in heating the bedroom during the day. Now either get yourself home to change, Mr. LeMaster, or take off those wet boots. Lucille can find a pair of Matthew's stockings for you to wear until yours dry."

She had him there. He could not in all good conscience demand that they use coal that cost so dearly, nor could he offer to supply them with more. He understood that now. Frowning, he stepped away from the chair and the now blazing fire. "I'll accept the offer of Matthew's stockings and go into the parlor to change, if you'll have sense enough to stay before the fire here while the girls fetch you some dry clothes."

They practically stood toe-to-toe, eye-to-eye. Simon found this new angle of looking at a woman more fascinating than he cared to admit. She had lovely gray-green eyes with golden specks surrounding the dark centers. Her lips were just inches from his. One small move and he could capture her mouth, feel its warmth and sweetness against his. Gad! Had it been that long since he'd felt a woman's mouth beneath his? He remembered distinctly every line and curve of this woman's body beneath his fingers as he'd helped her back to the house. She was too slender. He could nearly feel her ribs. But she was round in all the right places. The desire for her burned hot and quickly through the length of him. He had to turn around and leave the room to conceal the extent of his need.

Shivering in the unheated front room, Simon stripped off his boots and stockings and accepted the warm woolen ones Lucille threw in to him. He waited while the girls hurried up and down stairs, bringing Rebecca dry clothing. She had been wet to the skin. He'd seen every curve, every bit of lace and ribbon beneath her soaking clothes. He had no difficulty at all imagining how she would look before the fire, her skin glowing as she toweled herself off. All the cold in the world couldn't suppress the heated blood flowing through his veins at the moment.

It startled Simon to realize he hadn't felt like this in a long time. He hadn't sought out any of London's numerous courtesans when he was there. It hadn't even occurred to him. His thoughts had stayed entirely with the cause he fought—and lost. But now, when he felt as if he'd fallen to the very depths of the Slough of Despond, his body awakened, and his best friend's widow had caused it.

He didn't know how to act. He'd never found himself in such a predicament before. He couldn't take advantage of Rebecca. She'd suffered enough. He would have to take this momentary aberration and find another direction for it. But the hours that followed did nothing to relieve his growing desires.

Once the warmth of the kitchen seeped through them, Rebecca and the girls turned their tasks into laughter and song. They giggled and gossiped and poked fun at each other and everything around them. Shriveled apples became talking doll's heads with the addition of currant eyes and carved mouths and Rebecca's mincing voice speaking for them. Simon watched jealously as she kissed Mary's brow and hugged her when the younger girl spilled her bowl of cream and almost cried. He listened raptly to their crystal-clear voices blending in an old Christmas carol as they rolled out pastry dough. He didn't attempt to join in, knowing his own voice poor and rusty from disuse. He merely peeled his apples, soaking up the merriment, and remembering happier times when he and Matthew had used to sneak into the kitchen to filch whatever crumbs they could find, only to find themselves caught and put to work. There had been laughter and warmth and the rich scents of baking cakes and roasting geese then.

Still, nothing could replace the six years hollowed from his soul by war and death and destruction. The ghosts of dead men haunted this room, Matthew's among them. Simon could see them now, shivering over meager fires on distant shores, teeth chattering as they sipped boiled water to keep warm, uniforms torn and ragged from months of fighting. Hunger, thirst, filth, and disease had killed as many of them as bullets and cannonballs. And while they died, people back home had sat in their warm houses, drinking hot punch and wishing each other good cheer.

He couldn't mix the two scenes together. They wouldn't settle into one whole. He felt as if he still lived back there by those distant fires, and he merely looked through some window to this happy interior now. He wanted to join in. When Rebecca teased him into a fa-la-la-la, Simon did his best to enter the spirit of the song, but his spirit had long since departed. He merely wanted to warm his body next to hers.

By the time they reached the stirring of the plum pudding, the girls were feeling reckless enough to tease him as much as they did Rebecca. They insisted on blindfolding him as he stirred the pudding and made his wish, while Rebecca added whatever charms she'd bought for surprises. Then they did the same for themselves so they couldn't see what else she added.

"What did you wish for?" Mary asked excitedly as Simon handed over the wooden spoon to her.

He hadn't wished for anything. He already had everything, and it seemed pointless to ask for more than he needed. But he merely smiled and chucked her under the chin. "Wouldn't you like to know? Maybe I wished for a big hairy dog to chase Ginger when she gets out."

"We already have Leopold," she pointed out reasonably. "He just doesn't understand he's supposed to chase her back to the barn and not play with her."

"If Ginger had claws like Miss Kitty, he'd learn soon enough," Rebecca responded dryly, tying the blindfold around Mary's eyes. "No wishing for the moon," she reminded the girl as she took the spoon. "There's no sense in wasting a wish."

"Oh, I'll not waste it. I know just exactly what I want." Eagerly, the small girl took the spoon and pushed it through the thick batter.

Simon wondered what a twelve-year-old could want so passionately as he watched her purse her mouth in intense concentration. He would have liked to provide it for her. He could have bought anything their hearts desired, but he knew their guardian wouldn't allow it. He had to find some way of providing what they needed, without making them accept charity. A flicker of a thought played at the back of his mind as they made the final stirs to the pudding.

"Now, we put it in the pot and bring it to a boil," Rebecca was saying. He admired the way she taught the girls without seeming to preach. Matthew had chosen well. Simon wished he'd been half so wise.

All too soon the day came to its end. As Rebecca proudly handed him the apple tart to take home, Simon wished more than ever to give her something in return. He wasn't much good at gift giving, but he had to try. Perhaps he couldn't help the men in his company or their families, but he ought to be able to help Matthew's widow. If he could just do this one small thing, perhaps some of this despair and frustration would dwindle a little.

He had the tart for dinner that night, and the next morning, for the first time since he returned to England, Simon woke early, refreshed and ready to meet the tasks ahead.

"Mother, do you still send Christmas baskets to the neighbors?" Simon asked over breakfast, causing his mother to glance up at him with surprise. He'd not come down for breakfast since he'd returned home, preferring sleep to meeting the day, but he'd never been inclined to conversation in the morning even before he'd left home.

"Yes, of course, dear. It's tradition. They expect it of us."

"Could we send a goose this year instead of the basket?"

"A goose?" She glanced at him speculatively, as if wondering if he'd taken leave of his senses. "I don't see the purpose, dear. Everyone is expecting the baskets."

"That's just it, Mother. Everyone must be bored silly with baskets by now. Christmas should be full of surprises. Can't you imagine how thrilled they will be to receive a goose instead?"

She inclined her head in thought. "It would certainly be easier. I could just send for the poultry and have them delivered to each family, all in one swoop. I wouldn't have to buy the baskets and apples and oranges and spend days putting them all together and hoping they don't get bruised. Are you certain they wouldn't mind?"

"Quite certain. And just in case, I'll tell the vicar that the oranges were bad this year, and we looked for something a little more satisfying. He'll pass the word around the village fast enough. They'll be expecting something different. Are the Tarkingtons still on your gift list?"

Amusement flickered briefly in his mother's eyes, but Simon chose to ignore it. "I debated it after Matthew's death, of course, but I couldn't see any reason I shouldn't send a basket to the girls if I sent one for

Matthew. The widow usually sends up an apple tart in return. Very well bred girl, apparently."

Simon nodded in satisfaction. "Shall I make the arrangements for you, then? I know a poultry dealer who might handle the order."

Letting the look she gave him speak for her, his mother merely replied, "I'll fetch my gift list, shall I?"

Sneezing violently, Rebecca watched with dismay as the farmer deposited the goose from his cart onto the front lawn. Giving a cheery wave, the man called, "Greetings from the LeMasters!" and merrily drove his cart down the drive, the caged contents squawking and squealing as the wheels jostled through the ruts.

The gray gander on the lawn chased wildly after its departing companions.

Rebecca cynically contemplated letting the wretched bird go, but the goose was too valuable to let run free. Besides, the girls would be hideously disappointed if they knew their Christmas dinner had escaped. The basket of fruit that usually arrived at this time of year had become expected, as pleasant and unsurprising as the first snow. But a goose! They would be beside themselves.

Rebecca groaned at the thought of all the ramifications of cooking a Christmas goose, but she didn't have time to contemplate them. She had to catch the escaping bird.

Hearing her shouts, Lucille and Mary came running from the house, lending their efforts to trap the terrified bird. The goose squawked in outrage. The girls squealed and darted from vicious pecks. The yard erupted in a chaos of shouts and flying feathers. Un-

able to allow everyone else to have the fun, Leopold
found his favorite bolt-hole and joined the fray.

Had Rebecca any experience whatsoever at killing
poultry, she would have wrung the gander's neck right
there and then. As it was, they could only herd the
protesting bird into the barn to join the other animals.
Wondering vaguely how one went about keeping a
goose until one was ready to eat it, Rebecca allowed
the girls to feed it corn, and sneezing, made her way
back to the kitchen. The drenching in the pond had
apparently had its effect. She thought she might have
a bit of a fever. Looking on the bright side, she would
need less coal to keep her warm at night.

By the next day, she didn't feel quite so optimistic.
Her hands shook as she prepared the chamomile tea
her mother used to prescribe for head colds. She
wrapped herself in blankets and lingered by the
kitchen fire to drink it. Heaven would be lying in bed
in front of a roaring fire, buried in blankets, with tea
in one hand and a good book in the other, as she had
once used to do when feeling under the weather. But
she had the pastries to bake for the church auction,
the hems to sew into the gowns she'd made the girls
for Christmas, and the house hadn't been dusted and
swept in days. And now she had to come up with the
recipe for the apple dressing the girls insisted upon.
She couldn't afford the luxury of pampering herself.

She should have known Simon LeMaster would pick
that day to pay a visit.

She had pulled on one of Mrs. Tarkington's frilled
caps as much to keep her head warm as to keep her
hair neat. She wore a wool gown she'd made for her-
self that first winter of her marriage, the warmest
gown she owned but far from the fashionable confec-

tions she had once worn. Flour dusted her sleeves, and the hem was stained where she had gone out into the mud with it once too many times. On top of that, her nose was red from holding a handkerchief to it all day, and her eyes felt strained and teary. She almost didn't answer the door when she heard the knock.

Her heart plummeted when she opened the door and saw Simon standing there, glorious in his bottle-green fitted morning coat and pristine cravat, his boots polished to a shine she could probably see herself in were she inclined to look at his feet. That first day when he'd appeared sans cravat and muddy from head to foot, she'd accepted his presence much as she had Matthew's familiar countenance. Today, he stood before her as a stranger, a wealthy, aristocratic stranger who must see her as little more than a housemaid. She had the urge to slam the door in his face.

His expression of alarm certainly didn't enhance Rebecca's feeling of well-being. She swayed slightly and caught the door, but she sneezed before she could think of an appropriate greeting.

"Why in hell aren't you in bed?" he exclaimed, grabbing her arm to hold her steady, then practically shoving her into the hall to close the door on the chilly air outside.

Rebecca wanted to chide him for his inappropriate language, if only to remind him that she was a lady and not a housemaid, but another fit of sneezing kept her from anything resembling a coherent reply. When he led her toward the cold and drafty front parlor, she managed a struggle of protest, but even limping, the ex-soldier had greater strength than she.

"Where are the girls? They ought to be here taking care of you. I'm certain Matthew didn't intend for you

to act as slave to their whims. Sit down here while I
build up the fire."

She started to protest the wicked waste of fuel, but
he turned and glared at her. "One word more and I'll
set fire to this barn. I've seen enough wasted lives,
thank you very much. Throwing yours away to save a
few pennies isn't in the least sensible. Now where are
the girls?"

Reluctant to admit to the relief she felt that some-
one else had come in to take charge, Rebecca sank
into the ancient overstuffed sofa and applied the hand-
kerchief to her nose again. "The dratted goose chased
the cow through the barn doors. They're trying to herd
the cow back, but I fear the goose is lost." She didn't
mention that she feared the barn doors were a loss,
also. She had no experience in carpentry. "I'm really
quite fine. It's just a head cold."

"And tomorrow it will be a chest cold, and the day
after that, pneumonia, if you don't keep warm and get
some rest. I'll fetch Mrs. Lofton. She can look after
you for a bit while I help the girls find Ginger."

Rebecca shook her head. She tried not to look at
the man crouched at the fireplace lighting the fire as
if he belonged there. He had swept into their lives
like a summer breeze, and he would sweep out again
just as swiftly. She would not come to rely on him like
some helpless invalid, or widow. She'd seen the elderly
women in the village relying on others to provide their
fuel and look after them, as if being female made
them helpless to do it themselves. She refused to be-
come like that.

"I cannot ask you to go out of your way. The goose
was a lovely gift. Send your family our gratitude, and

I will pen an appropriate note just as soon as I can. We needn't take up more of your time."

The glare he gave her now should have formed ice crystals in the air. Apparently satisfied the fire had caught, he rose to his full height and towered over her. "Oh, yes, the goose was a truly lovely gift. It gave you one more animal to look after and feed. Just exactly what you needed. Have the girls named it yet?"

She heard his sarcasm but wasn't certain of its direction. Did he complain of his mother's choice of gift? Her inability to tend livestock? The girls' tendency to turn food supplies into pets? Her head ached too much to puzzle it out. With a wry tone, she admitted, "They called it Betsy. I didn't think it wise to explain it was most likely a Bill."

A flicker of a grin bent his harsh lips for just a moment. Grabbing a neatly embroidered pillow from one of the side chairs, Simon handed it to her along with an aging afghan thrown over the loveseat. "Wrap yourself up and don't move. I'll have Mrs. Lofton here shortly."

Rebecca shook her head. "She has her hands full with the charity auction and Felicity Smythe's new baby. She can't be in three places at once. I'm quite fine. There's no need for this concern. Perhaps if you have a moment to spare, you could help the girls fetch Ginger. She's rather contrary and doesn't always respond to orders."

"Just like another female I know," he muttered, shaking his head. "However did you and Matthew get along? He always swore he meant to marry a docile female who would bow to his every wish. I cannot imagine the two of you together."

Simon didn't wish to imagine the two of them together, that would be to acknowledge that this bristly woman on the sofa had shared a bed with his best friend, putting her beyond the bounds of propriety for him. Even with her nose red and runny, he found her immensely attractive. Or perhaps it wasn't her physical appearance causing this unprecedented display of concern so much as the combination of fraility, helplessness, and damned stubborn hardheadedness. In his world, widows were fair game for seduction, and he had to admit he'd come here this day with something of the sort in the back of his mind. But though his body still responded to just her proximity, he wasn't listening to his body at the moment. His head screamed "off limits," and his heart shivered with fear.

"I am a docile female," she muttered from behind her handkerchief. "But sometimes it is impossible to take orders from every male who swaggers into my sphere. One has to draw the line somewhere."

Amusement finally drew a smile from him. "Point taken. All right, I shall find the girls and send them back here to pamper you. Then I'll take the wretched goose to the butcher shop where he belongs."

"It's too early to keep it for Christmas dinner," she pointed out sensibly.

"You want me to put it back in the barn with the damned cow?" he asked, raising an eyebrow. He almost regretted his harsh tone when a look of resignation briefly crossed her face. Only then did he remember she mentioned something about the cow breaking down the barn door. "You can't run this place by yourself," he bit out angrily, stalking toward the door rather than face that look of resignation. He preferred it when she argued. "I'll have someone come take a look at the barn." He slammed the parlor door before he could hear her protests.

He found the girls tugging on the cow's halter, the dog barking on its heels, half a mile down the lane. The goose, of course, was nowhere in sight. Taking the cow's lead and smacking it sharply on the rump, Simon got it started in the right direction. Within minutes, Mary had her mittened hand tucked firmly around his arm while she skipped beside him, chattering merrily. Matthew had undoubtedly spoiled his sisters dreadfully for them to accept him with such ease.

"I'll put Ginger back in the barn, but you two must go in and persuade Rebecca into bed. She'll be of no use to you at all if she comes down ill. I'll try to send Mrs. Lofton up here to tell you what to do, but she must have rest and lots of hot tea and warmth. Can you do that?" He directed this mostly at Lucille, the eldest, who nodded her head solemnly and tried to fight back tears. He wondered if he'd spoken too harshly. He was more accustomed to ordering soldiers about than dealing with little girls.

It was blithe Mary who put their predicament into words. "We were to write to her papa today. We write every Christmas, telling him everything we have accomplished this year and wishing him a merry holiday, even though the grouchy old bear never answers Rebecca's letters. She cries a lot when Christmas comes, although she tries not to let us know. I know she hopes he will come and visit, but now we won't even be able to write if Rebecca is ill. It wouldn't be seemly for us to write to a man we don't know, would it? And if it is not written today, Mr. White cannot take it with him when he leaves for London tomorrow.

Rebecca says we must not waste our coins on postage."

My word! Simon had never considered the details of poverty before. His father had always franked his missives, and he'd never given thought to how his pen scratchings got from one place to another. He remembered now how his men had carefully crosshatched their letters on a single page. He'd assumed they conserved the costly paper, but no doubt they meant to keep the cost of mailing down also. And more than one sheet of paper would involve an excess of sealing wax, another luxury he took for granted. Shaking his head at his obtuseness, Simon tried to come up with a solution to the problem that didn't involve charity.

"If you take good care of Rebecca, I'm certain she will feel like writing in a day or two, and then I can take the letter to town with me when I go," he said, surprised by his own decision. He hadn't meant to make the long journey to London in this wretched December weather, but if that's where he could find Rebecca's father, that's where he meant to go. The idea hadn't been so clear to him the other day, but the fiasco with the goose had made the decision urgent.

The girls accepted his announcement with aplomb, as if they knew of people traveling to London every day of their lives. Once they reached the house, Lucille even managed to pull him aside to ask, "Will you be seeing Baron Botherwell?"

Trying to hide his surprise, Simon nodded. "I shall deliver your letter personally."

Cautiously, digging her toe into the dirt and watching it rather than him, she asked, "Do you think you might mention how much an answer would mean to Rebecca?" She looked up at him with sudden defiance, although tears still rimmed her eyes. "It is Christmas, after all. He could be just a little generous with his heart. Could you do that for us, please? We have not been able to make anything really special for her this year, and this would be like a gift, wouldn't it?"

Something once solid in Simon's heart cracked a little as he looked down into that tearstained, windblown face. She asked the impossible of him, just as he'd asked the impossible of himself—and failed. He knew he could never persuade the baron to do anything he didn't wish to do, but he couldn't ruin this child's Christmas by telling her so. Perhaps he could think of some solution between now and Christmas, pull some strings, bargain with the devil. He didn't know what he could do, but he knew he couldn't disappoint Matthew's sisters.

The girls darted into the house as Simon towed the cow back to its stall. The barn door had, indeed, come down under Ginger's assault, although looking at it, he could see it hadn't taken much pressure. It was a pure miracle the whole structure didn't fall down about their heads in a strong wind.

Cursing Matthew for not providing better for his responsibilities, cursing himself for not understanding how strapped for funds his friend must have been, Simon shoved the barn door upright and made a makeshift bolt to hold it in place. One more of Ginger's batterings ought to shatter it into sawdust.

He checked on Rebecca before he left. He really ought to think of her as the Widow Tarkington, but she was too young to be a widow, and the girls had him thinking of her in their terms. He found the trio ensconced before the roaring fire, sipping hot chocolate and engaged in some game of cards that involved wagering with hairpins. Half Rebecca's hair was already down about her shoulders. The disheveled locks made her look as young as her youthful charges.

He didn't have the heart to scold them for not allowing Rebecca to rest. Simon suspected the rosiness of her cheeks had more to do with fever than the fire, but he wasn't in a position to play the part of nurse. He would see that Mrs. Lofton visited, despite Rebecca's protests. He took his leave, vowing to himself to see that they had ample fuel to keep the drafty old house warm.

Upon a sudden intuition, Simon took the path across the fields instead of the road and found the gander chasing minnows in Mad George's pond. He had little experience with geese, but he knew the secret to dealing with animals was firmness. He was wetter than when he started by the time he had the goose firmly tucked under his arm, his other hand holding its vicious bill closed. He'd intended to feed the Tarkingtons with Christmas goose, not the crotchety farmer, whether the blamed bird accepted its fate or not. Satisfied he could still control members of the animal kingdom even if he could control nothing else of the world around him, Simon deposited the goose in the Tarkington's rickety chicken house, threw in some corn, and bolted the door shut, leaving the bird squawking its protests.

A light flurry of snow dusted Simon's caped greatcoat as he stepped down from the carriage at the door of Baron Botherwell's London town house. Impressive walls of limestone block towered against the smoke-choked London sky, with only an occasional glimmer of lamplight from behind heavily draped windows to brighten the facade. No festive evergreens adorned this grim structure to welcome a shivering visitor. Simon expected a similar welcome from the human inhabitants.

He felt no particular surprise when the butler placed him in the front drawing room when he sent his card up. The LeMaster name carried significant weight in both social and financial circles, even when carried by a younger son. But a name could get him only so far. His failure at swaying government officials to their duties proved that. Simon held out little hope for the success of this meeting.

The baron appeared in velvet dressing gown and neatly tied cravat, obviously intending a quiet evening at home. He regarded Simon with some degree of suspicion and closed the door behind him.

"Viscount LeMaster's younger son, if I remember correctly?" he said without inflection, coming to stand before a crystal decanter. "Brandy?"

Simon nodded and accepted the glass offered. "I appreciate your seeing me, sir. I have a missive I promised to place in your hands directly."

The shorter, rotund man stiffened and turned his back on him. "From my daughter, no doubt. You may heave it on the fire. She's chosen her life. I'll not heed her pleas."

Simon gritted his teeth and removed the carefully preserved letter from his inner coat pocket. "I doubt that the lady would beg. She has too much pride for that. She and her stepdaughters merely send Christmas greetings, as would any dutiful daughter. The most they hope for is a reply assuring them of your continued good health, I believe."

The baron snorted. "No doubt in order to determine the date of my death and when she can expect to come into her inheritance. I'm a far cry from death's door, be sure to tell her. Although what interest you have in a common soldier's wife, I hate to imagine."

Simon thought he might explode from rage. His grip nearly cracked the fragile crystal stem of his brandy snifter before he had sense enough to return it to the table. Seeing no point in continuing an argument with a man determined to wear blinders, he kept his voice low, but fury colored his words. "A common soldier's *widow,* sir, who is doing amazingly well supporting two young girls and running an estate without any help from anyone, certainly not from you. For a spoiled young rich girl, she's adapted very well and needs nothing from you but assurance that her father doesn't hate her. I'll be happy to tell her that she wastes any efforts to form a reconciliation with you, and the girls may go on thinking they have no one who cares about their welfare except herself."

His angry strides to the door were interrupted by the baron's scathing reply.

"If you think to form a reconciliation between me and my daughter so that you may marry her and gain the dowry her first husband did not, you may disabuse yourself of that notion now."

Simon's hand gripped the door handle and twisted hard before he turned and glared at the bitter old man. "I doubt that you will ever understand that all your daughter needs is love, but I give you her best. Merry Christmas, Baron."

He stormed out, leaving the old man to stare into his warm fire alone.

Only some minutes later, shivering inside the cold carriage, did Simon realize what he'd done, again. He'd failed.

It took Simon a week to admit his failure to Rebecca. He made certain that the physician visited her when Mrs. Lofton reported the widow's illness lingered. He supplied the medicines required and allowed Mrs. Lofton to take the credit. The vicar's wife looked at Simon oddly when he assumed the expense, but she wisely held her tongue. Only when she informed him that Rebecca was back on her feet again did he force himself to admit that he couldn't hide from her forever.

He had spent two nights in London with every intention of finding himself a willing woman to ease his needs, but for some reason he had never felt the urge and hadn't stirred himself to look for what he needed. But this week back in Lymeshead had made him miserable with longing. He saw Rebecca's rosy cheeks and laughing smile every time he walked through the main street. He heard her voice lifted in song whenever he smelled cooking apples. He remembered her soft curves in his arms every time he lay down to sleep at night. The thoughts drove him to madness.

He knew it was madness. He barely knew the woman. She was his best friend's widow. He had no right to think of an impoverished widow with two children in the way he was thinking of her. If he just thought of her in his bed, he might dismiss the matter entirely as lust, but he longed for the warmth and joy of her kitchen, the smile on her face, the loving touches he'd seen bestowed on the girls. He wanted something from her he had no right to ask for, and now he came to her door, hat in hand, announcing his failure. She had every right to never speak to him again.

When Rebecca opened the door, Simon could see the roses hadn't returned to her cheeks yet. She looked pale and drawn, and she coughed when she tried to smile in greeting. She might as well have ripped the heart out of him right then and there. He wanted to grab her in his arms and carry her up to bed and scream for a physician. He wanted to rail against the fates that required her to work when she should rest, when she should rightfully have servants at her beck and call. He could do nothing but take off his hat and find words to lighten the blow.

"Mr. LeMaster! Come in. We haven't seen you in ever so long. I just finished the gingerbread for the church auction. Won't you come in and test it for us?"

She ushered him into the drafty hall, taking his scarf and hat and hanging them on hooks, coughing as she chattered. Without embarrassment, she led him back toward the kitchen and the only warmth the house offered.

He ought to tell her she didn't look well enough to be out of bed, but he couldn't insult her like that. He thought her lovely even in her illness. Her eyes sparkled with delight at his appearance. Her fingers brushed his coat with the same loving attention as she gave the girls, and Simon could see a spot of color return to her cheeks when she looked at him. That look stirred his longings even more strongly than before.

Gratefully, he accepted the chair she offered, but then realizing she meant to wait on him, Simon leaped to his feet again. His injured foot no longer pained him as it once had, but the sight of her coughing from her efforts felt like a stab wound to his heart.

"Sit, and let me wait on you for a change. I suppose you have spent the morning on your feet, baking gingerbread for others instead of caring for yourself," he scolded, catching her shoulders and pushing her down on the cushioned bench beside the fire. "Where are the girls today?"

"Lucille is delivering the first batch of gingerbread and"—she blushed slightly and turned her face away—"I shouldn't tell you this. I'm sorry. I wasn't thinking. But . . ." She shrugged and met his gaze anyway. "I offered the goose to the church for the auction, also. We couldn't feed it, and the girls would never allow me to kill it. We talked about it, and they agreed it was best to give it to charity. Mary's taking it down to the vicarage now."

Simon ran his hand through his hair in perplexity. He'd meant to feed the Tarkingtons on Christmas goose. He'd meant to give them a merry Christmas for a change. He'd meant to do many things, but he didn't seem to have the knack for doing anything right in this civilian life. He stared down into her flushed face and could only think of one thing to say.

"Do you have any idea how lovely you are when you blush like that?"

She blushed even more, and quickly turned her eyes away, brushing at a wayward strand of hair as she did so. "You needn't tease to get even. I know I shouldn't give away presents from others. I debated it long and hard. But . . ."

Giving a sigh of exasperation, Simon caught her chin with his fingers and turned her face up to his. She looked so startled, he couldn't find any words to ease her plight. Giving up the fight, he bent and kissed her.

The startling sweetness of her lips warmed his blood like ripe strawberries on a summer's day. He couldn't indulge in just one. He couldn't keep bending over her like this either. Without any more thought than that, Simon pulled her to her feet and into his embrace.

She struggled briefly, protesting with a push of her hands against his chest, but she never attempted to remove her lips from his. Their mouths had somehow sealed together, nourishing, encouraging, taking and giving with equal parts hunger and need. The black void in Simon's soul disappeared, filling with the bliss of this brief moment.

And brief it had to be. The sound of the girls' chatter as they flung open the front door shattered the intimacy.

They both moved away in embarrassment, afraid to look at each other as the girls ran into the kitchen, laughing and shedding coats and scarves across the furniture.

"Betsy squawked and chased the butcher's dog all the way through the village!" Mary laughed as she reached for the teakettle simmering on the stove. "I don't think she'll end up anyone's Christmas dinner. I think she ought to be a guard dog."

Rebecca tried not to look at the tall man beside her as she carefully spooned tea leaves into the pot. He seemed as rooted to the spot as she felt. She didn't know what had come over them. An excess of Christmas cheer, perhaps. She certainly felt as overheated and excited as if she'd drunk too much Yuletide punch. She had to force herself not to glance over her shoulder to see his expression.

Mary might be oblivious to the tension between the two adults, but Lucille gave them quizzical looks as she set out the plate of gingerbread. More boldly than she ought, she confronted Mr. LeMaster with the questions Rebecca had refused to put into words.

"Did you see Rebecca's father? Did he read our letter?"

Rebecca could feel the way he stiffened, felt the tension as surely as if it were her own. Perhaps it was. She was having difficulty separating herself from that kiss. She felt as if she'd entered Simon's soul when he'd taken her into his arms. It had felt so right. She'd never thought anything could ever feel so right again. But she knew enough now to know Simon LeMaster would never dally with the widow of a friend. He'd meant no insult by that kiss. She didn't know precisely what he had meant, and maybe he didn't either. But she knew the despair she'd seen in his eyes had found its outlet now.

"I saw the baron."

Rebecca wanted to keep her face turned from him, didn't want to see the torment behind his words, but she couldn't resist looking. Perhaps she heard wrong. Perhaps she could see something in his expression that would tell her more than his words. She trusted the unhappy lines of Simon's face. At least they were honest. Unlike other handsome men, he didn't use his charms to hide the truth, not about something that mattered as much as this did. She wanted to make it easier for him somehow, but she couldn't.

Simon looked directly at her as he spoke. She could

feel the distance between them widening as the words came out.

"I delivered the letter into his hands. He knows you're alive and well and doing fine. He appears quite hearty and healthy. He sends you his warm wishes."

She couldn't quite believe she was hearing this. He'd seen her father? He couldn't have. He must be lying about that as well as about everything else. Did that mean her father had refused to see him or was too ill to see him? Panic rose, unbidden, into her eyes, before she could even say the words.

He must have seen the panic, must have recognized her disbelief. His expression shuttered, Simon set down the cup Lucille had handed him. "He's doing fine, Rebecca. You needn't concern yourself about him at all. I think it's time I left. Thank you for the tea."

She let him go. The girls escorted him through the hall, asking excited questions about London and the man they thought of more in terms of step-grandfather than as no relation at all. In their innocence, they saw the baron as an old man, rocking by the fire, reading their letters with loving repetition. Rebecca had never had the courage to correct them. They wouldn't understand how a man could be so cold as to live without love. She couldn't understand it herself.

Unable to fight the tears running down her cheeks, Rebecca turned the bread dough into the flour and blamed her sniffing on her cold when the girls returned.

Simon bought the stupid goose at the auction for a sum so large that everyone attending rose to their feet and applauded his largesse. He had the bird caged and sent back to the manor to guard the stables. What else could one do with a gander wearing a red ribbon around its neck?

After sampling the gingerbread refreshments, the viscountess offered an equally immense sum for the gingerbread auctioned, but Rebecca wasn't there to appreciate the compliment. Only Simon understood the real reason the Tarkingtons didn't join the festivities, and Rebecca's illness had very little to do with it. She would never let a minor thing like a chest cold stop her from going where she wanted. But lack of coin to purchase anything for charity would embarrass her into hiding instantly.

Simon had caught Mr. White having Rebecca's wedding ring weighed at the jeweler's. He still cringed inside when he thought of it. He'd come in to figure out what little trinkets might please his family, but the sight of that wedding ring had decimated any Christmas spirit he may have possessed. The gold had worn to a thin fragment of itself on the fingers of untold Tarkington wives. It was all but worthless in any light. Simon had paid the balance of the widow's bill in exchange for it.

He carried the ring in his pocket now as he climbed the rocks of the cliff. He had the urge to heave the wretched piece of gold into the waves crashing below. In return for that miserable piece of jewelry, a lovely strong woman like Rebecca had turned herself into a drab, worn farmwife when she could have danced in luxurious ballrooms wearing silks and satins. He didn't understand it.

He didn't understand life. How could he be given everything when others had nothing? And having everything, why did he feel so miserable, when the Tarkingtons, with nothing to their names but a drafty old farmhouse, managed to laugh and fill their lives with warmth and joy? Why did he, a hero with dozens of military medals to his name, feel a failure while Rebecca, with nothing more than this plain gold band, see herself as successful because she'd managed a few short weeks of marriage?

A sharp wind blew through him as he stood on the cliff, contemplating these questions and finding no easy answers. Even the weather failed to cooperate. Instead of the gloom and clouds his mood required, a bright winter sun sparkled across the waters, laughing back at him in twinkles on the waves. Simon couldn't even find his melancholy of earlier. Something else had taken its place.

And he knew exactly when it had happened. It had happened the moment his lips touched Rebecca's. Something had opened in him then, something strange and unexplored, perhaps, but something so powerful that he couldn't ignore it as he wished. He wanted to go back and try it again, to explore the feeling a little further, to talk to Rebecca about it, to see if she felt any glimmer of the same thing. He wanted to know if she'd felt that way with Matthew, if she could ever feel that way again. He wanted to know so many things, but instead, he stood on the cliff's edge, a failure, again.

How could he ever face her and tell her the truth about his visit with her father? That he had angered the old man so much that the baron had no doubt flung the letter on the fire, unread, after he'd left? How could he explain her father's bitterness, a bitterness that would continue should Simon attempt to court her?

He didn't possess great title or riches to please the old man. He had the inheritance from his grandmother. His father had offered a small farm with a manor house, but the income from it barely paid the upkeep of the house. He supposed everyone assumed he would marry well, so no one had given the matter of his support much thought. He'd never considered it himself. But if he meant to take a poor wife, he'd have to do more than idly think about it.

Simon blinked and stared out over the ocean as the direction of his thoughts became clear. A poor wife? Had he considered taking any wife at all? Not more than a month ago he'd stood on these rocks and considered throwing himself off. How had he made such a turn around to stand here now considering taking on the responsibility of a wife and children? Children? Where had that thought come from?

In something akin to shock, Simon turned around and faced the rolling land behind him. The wind pummeled his back, driving him farther from the cliff's edge, closer to the village and the road leading to a certain quiet farmhouse nestled in a valley. He couldn't do this. He couldn't go to her a failure. He had no right to think she would accept him. No right to think she would even look twice at him.

But even as he told himself these things, he saw a tall figure appear on the crest of the hill, her bonnet whipped back from her loosened hair, her skirts and pelisse billowing wildly around her as she scanned the horizon. Catching sight of him, she waved with all the joy and excitement and life that was the Rebecca he had come to know and love. The ill woman of the past weeks was just a momentary aberration. His Rebecca possessed a spirit akin to the wind blowing off the water, too strong to ever give in.

Simon found himself running to her, ignoring the ache in his healing foot, ignoring the idiot he made of himself as he raced to capture what was never his in the first place. If he stopped to think, he would throw himself off the cliff. Instead, he let himself hope. He held out his arms, and much to his happiness and relief, she raced into them.

Their lips met and clung, and the icy cold of their flesh warmed quickly to a blazing fire. Simon gasped and came up for air, catching her more firmly against his chest so she couldn't escape in this fleeting moment when he couldn't hold her with his kiss. Joy danced in her eyes, but whether it had anything to do with himself, he couldn't discern. He merely basked in the wonder of it.

"He's come! You did it! You brought my father here! Oh, Simon, I can't believe it. I didn't believe it. I thought you lied. I'm so ashamed. But he's here. It's Christmas and he's here! It's the best gift I've ever had. Oh, Simon, thank you. I can't tell you how much I thank you."

Disbelief widened his eyes as he stared down at her. Simon wanted to protest, wanted to disclaim any responsibility in the matter, but Rebecca tugged on his arm, pulling him back toward town.

"He's being grumpy and obnoxious, but the girls are stuffing him with gingerbread and apple tarts, and I'm basting him with honey, and he's coming 'round, Simon. He's asked about you." She gave him an embarrassed grin. "I think he's checking on your prospects. You made a strong impression, it seems."

A strong impression. He'd yelled at the old goat

and slammed a door in his face. That ought to be strong enough. Still incredulous, Simon followed Rebecca reluctantly. "Stuffed with apples and basted with honey? Are you turning him into the Christmas goose in replacement for the one you gave away?"

Her laugh chimed on the December wind. "Yes, I am. He's a goose and deserves basting, but I've invited him for dinner and not as dinner. He brought us a goose already dressed. I've made apple dressing. Will you have some with us?"

Would he have some with her? He had a family at home no doubt sitting down to a groaning board of a dozen removes from soup to pudding, but Simon wanted more than anything else in this world to share a goose in the warmth and laughter of Rebecca's kitchen. He followed her gladly, willing even to face the baron's outrage in exchange for a few more minutes of her company.

He was insane. He knew himself as a raving lunatic. He'd never done anything so impulsive in his entire life. Even as he walked into the utter anarchy of a farmhouse filled with the screams and laughter of two young girls as they chased Leopold up and down stairs while a crotchety old gentleman yelled at them to sit like proper young ladies, Simon still wrapped a proprietary arm around Rebecca's shoulders as he walked through the door. He knew it was a possessive gesture, and a defiant one.

Rebecca knew it too. She glanced up at him with a trace of uncertainty that disappeared the moment he gave her his best commanding stare. Laughter immediately danced in her eyes. She meant to lead him a merry chase, he could see that now. She would never make a docile wife, but Simon had discovered he didn't want docility. He wanted someone to challenge him, to keep him on his toes, if only to chase her blamed pigs across creation. He gave her a wicked grin before turning to greet the old man who'd suddenly stopped waving his walking stick at the girls to glare in their direction.

"I knew it!" the baron huffed. "I knew you had designs on her! Well, let me tell you this right now, you young puppy—"

Simon helped remove Rebecca's pelisse, hanging it on a hook as if the old man didn't bluster worse than the wind outside. Interrupting the tirade, he held out his hand to the old gentleman. 'Glad to see you again, sir. You couldn't have given your daughter a better Christmas gift. I bet you didn't realize she's the best cook this side of Paris, France. A man could easily breathe his last breath in exchange for one of her tarts."

The baron stared at the proffered hand, glared at his daughter who stood breathlessly at Simon's side, glanced up the stairs at the two girls leaning over the banister in sudden silence, and growling, shook Simon's hand grudgingly.

"I'm taking her back to London with me." He threw out the challenge blatantly.

Simon smiled in return. "It's Rebecca's decision if she wants to go. I've business up there myself." Escalating the attack, he caught Rebecca's cold fingers between his own warm ones, and smiling down at her, asked, "Have you any of that hot cider you made for me last time? I'll have to follow you to London just in hopes you'll occasionally feed me. I'll miss your cooking otherwise."

The wide smile crossing her face made him feel more courageous than any battlefield triumph.

The baron threw in all his field artillery. "I'm bringing her out in society again. She can do better than the penniless son of a viscount. She'll not cook in my kitchens."

This time, Simon squeezed Rebecca's hand and let her reply. No trace of uncertainty lingered in her eyes as she sent him a warming glance and turned to her father. "I like to cook, Father. I'm not any good at dancing and flirting, but I'm a very good wife. And I'm very good at choosing my own husband. I'd like to be a good daughter, if you'll let me, but I won't let you tell me what to do anymore. I'm a grown woman now. I know what's best for me better than you do."

"Good at choosing your own husband! Just look at this hovel! How can you say—" The baron halted his speech when Rebecca leaned over and kissed him on the cheek. Before he could continue, she tugged Simon toward the kitchen and gestured for the girls to come down where they belonged.

"It isn't money that makes me happy, Papa. I thrive on love. Come along before the goose is burned. I'm certain Simon must be starved by now. Lucille, fill the gravy boat and set it out, dear. Mary, it's your turn to light the candles. I think we ought to let Simon say grace today. We have much to give thanks for."

With a grin, Simon pulled Rebecca back long enough to brush a kiss across her forehead. Then he released her to take charge of her particular field of battle. He stayed behind to deal with his.

The baron chewed furiously on the tip of his mustache. A drafty wind blew down the unheated hall, and Simon led the way into the simple country kitchen where the fireplace filled every cranny with glowing warmth. The carefully pressed linen tablecloth gleamed with old china and crystal, handed down from generation to generation. A mismatched plate or two and an occasional crack disappeared easily beneath the beauty of candlelight and fragrant evergreens arranged in the center of the table. The scent of roasting goose and apple tarts erased any disapproval from the hardest of hearts.

"I love your daughter," Simon stated matter-of-factly, watching as Rebecca darted from stove to table to cabinet. She turned and gave him a wide-eyed stare at his statement. He knew he wasn't doing this properly. He had no experience on this particular battlefield. But as a raw recruit, he would learn. His look of confidence received a blinding smile in return. "I'm of good family with many prospects. I'm thinking of taking a seat for one of my father's boroughs. There're things in our country's policies that need changing."

Simon couldn't believe he heard himself saying these words, but he realized he meant them. He hadn't failed yet. He'd just given up too soon. He wouldn't make that mistake again. Watching Rebecca, he knew he would never give up.

Disgruntled, the baron wrapped his hands around the back of the best chair in the house. Glancing from his daughter to Simon, he growled, "Your father's boroughs don't have enough power to change table linen. I've got one in Gloucester that has enough money behind it to make those prigs in parliament sit up and pay attention."

Simon finally allowed himself to relax and admire the slender sway of Rebecca's back as she carefully ladled soup into a tureen. He hadn't won her yet. He had a victory or two under his belt, but he hadn't cleared the battlefield or claimed his territory. But he would. He'd found a prize worth fighting for, a prize who made him want to fight again. He didn't intend to give up this time.

With the scattered remains of dinner still surrounding them and the girls entertaining the gruff old man in the front room, Simon moved a little closer to his goal. Taking the towel from her hands, he turned her into his arms, and watched the pink flush her cheeks becomingly.

"I know it's too soon, Rebecca. I don't want to rush you. Just tell me if I have a chance. I need to hear the words. I haven't misunderstood, have I? I do have a chance?"

Shyly, she brushed a disheveled strand of hair from his face. She made no effort to move from his embrace. "I've only had the opportunity for wishful thinking until now, Simon. But I've seen enough of London and met enough men to know my own mind. You're so much like Matthew in many ways, and in others"—she shrugged and smiled apologetically—"in other ways, you're so much stronger. I loved him as a girl, Simon. I'll love you as a woman loves. Can you accept that?"

The kiss he bestowed upon her then gave his reply and more.

And in the parlor, Mary whispered into her sister's ear, "I got my pudding wish, Lucy. We have our goose and the baron and Simon, too. Isn't Christmas wonderful?"

The Proof
Is in the Pudding

❄

Barbara Metzger

1.

"Faugh," declared Sir Otis Ogden from his place at the head of the long table. " 'Tis a waste of good spirits, I say."

Since Sir Otis considered any spirits not flowing directly down his shriveled gullet a waste, his wife Johna did not bother raising her voice to be heard across the mahogany expanse. Lady Ogden's younger sister, Phillipa, though, seated somewhere in the middle of the table behind an arrangement of pine boughs, holly leaves, and red apples, clapped her hands when the butler and two footmen carried in the flaming pudding on its silver platter. Drenched in brandy, the traditional holiday dessert flared blue and gold and scarlet in the dimmed dining parlor.

"It's beautiful," Phillipa whispered. "It's ... it's Christmas."

"It's poppycock," Sir Otis spit, spewing wine down his shirtfront. The claret stains added a festive touch to the remnants of turbot in oyster sauce, roast goose, and asparagus already decorating the aged knight's neckcloth. If his young wife had thought to sweeten Sir Otis's disposition by serving a fine meal, festooning

CHRISTMAS PUDDING
(makes 4)

2 cups raisins, halved and stoned

2 cups sultanas, halved and stoned, or figs

1½ cups currants, washed and dried

1½ cups candied fruit peel and candied cherries

1 cup almonds, blanched and shredded, or mixed nuts

1 green apple, peeled, cored, and chopped.

1 carrot, grated

1 tablespoon lemon rind, grated, plus ¼ cup juice

1 tablespoon orange peel, grated, plus ⅓ cup juice

rum for soaking (optional)

½ pound beef suet, finely chopped

4 cups bread crumbs

2 cups flour

1 cup brown sugar

1 teaspoon allspice, grated

1 teaspoon salt

½ of one nutmeg, grated

6 eggs, well beaten

1 cup brandy

More rum for soaking (optional)

½ cup brandy for flaming (optional)

Soak the fruits in rum, at least one month in advance. This makes them plump, as in plum pudding.

Mix the fruits and dry ingredients well. Separately, mix the eggs, juice, and brandy, and add to the mixture, stirring thoroughly. Everyone in the household can take a turn stirring and making their pudding wishes. Let the whole thing stand, covered and cool, overnight.

Divide the mix into four greased pudding basins, molds, or bowls, covered with foil, or tie into boiling bags. Place the puddings into large pots of water and bring to a boil. Cover the pot, reduce the heat, and steam the puddings for 8 hours. (Make sure the water doesn't boil away.)

Remove and cool, then cover and store in a cool, dry place, for a month.

One week before serving, soak the puddings in rum if you wish. Just before serving, steam the puddings again, 1–2 hours, before unmolding. This is when coins, tokens, and such can be pressed into the pudding.

To set on fire, warm the brandy and light it, then pour over the puddings.

his dreary house with ribbon and holly, entertaining him with carols in Phillipa's pretty voice and her own pianoforte accompaniment, she was wrong. Again. All the sugar in the gingerbread men, in the marzipan angels, in the candied fruits—all the sugar that got baked, boiled, and blended for a hundred holiday feasts—was not going to improve the curmudgeon's nature. As for peace, goodwill, and Christmas feeling, Sir Otis was feeling bilious.

"Next thing you'll be doing is setting the blasted house on fire," he muttered. "Just my luck to marry a damned arsonist. Fires in every hearth, a fortune in candles gone up in smoke, now you're setting torches to my food. Hell and tarnation, if you had any fire in your blood mayhaps I'd have me an heir."

The servants pretended deafness, a not infrequent malady in this household, while Johna supervised the cutting of the pudding. Her face might be as red as the maroon velvet gown she wore and her lips might be pinched into a thin line, but Johna would not let the old glump ruin Phillipa's Christmas. He'd already ruined Johna's hopes for a happy life with a man who could love her. That was enough.

Obviously, this was not a marriage made in heaven. It was, in fact, a business transaction conducted in a smoke-filled gambling hall, over a table of unpaid and unpayable gaming debts.

Slavery being illegal, Johna's father, Baron Hutchison, sold his elder daughter into matrimony. Johna was eighteen at the time, a raven-haired beauty with her dead mother's blue eyes and levelheadedness. She might have made a splash in the Marriage Market if Hutchison could have dowered her, dressed her, and dropped her into the *ton* under some dragon's watchful eye. But the dissolute baron could barely feed his daughters, much less get them entrée into the *belle monde*. Gambling, drinking, and poor management of his properties, all had combined to keep Hutchison one short step away from debtor's prison.

Sir Otis Ogden was his only hope—and the holder of most of his notes. If Lord Hutchison was barely skirting the fringes of society, Sir Otis was beyond the pale. He'd been able to purchase a knighthood but not respectability. A cardsharper, a moneylender, a fleecer of green lambs fresh from the country, his reputation did not bear scrutiny. His lusting after a young girl did.

So Lord Hutchison got his debts paid and a handsome settlement besides. If his conscience needed more soothing than the sound of rustling bank notes, he convinced himself that Johna would be a widow sooner rather than later, considering Ogden was ten years older than himself, to say nothing of the rough company the man kept. Odds were she'd still be young enough to attract another husband, and wealthy enough to provide for her dear papa in his dotage. He promptly gambled away his windfall, got tossed out of some foul dive into the snow, caught an inflammation of the lungs, and died—before seeing another shilling of his senescent son-in-law's blunt. Which only went to prove that Hutchison never had been lucky at playing the odds.

Sir Otis got his bride, but not quite what he expected of the marriage either. No female of such tarnished pedigree could advance his social standing, no matter how beautiful she was. And no female could put the wind back in his sail, no matter how young she was. After a few sweat-covered attempts at conjugal consummation, Sir Otis gave it up, along with hopes for an heir. No society belle, no son, just a damned expensive piece of goods, that's what his money had bought him. So he fired his housekeeper and two maids.

Of them all, Johna was perhaps the least disappointed in her marriage, especially once the grunting and groping were over. She hadn't expected much, after all, just a better life for her sister and herself. She could have refused the match, could have hired herself out as a governess or companion, but she wouldn't leave fifteen-year-old Phillipa alone in Berkshire. Hutchison Manor's roof was falling in, the staff had left for positions that actually paid a salary, and who knew what misguided notion Papa would get into his muddled head next?

Sir Otis agreed to take in the spotty schoolgirl sister, though, so the marriage contract was finalized. Now, three years later, the sisters weren't hungry and they weren't in the poorhouse. They were, however, bonded servants. The bonds might be those of holy matrimony, but the results were the same. Johna kept house in London for Sir Otis and did half the cooking, mending, and cleaning. Phillipa worked alongside the maids, dusting and washing. She wasn't spotty anymore, and she wasn't a schoolgirl. She was eighteen, the very age at which Johna had been wed. Prejudiced or not, Johna thought her sister was lovely with her brown ringlets and softly rounded form, in contrast to her own straight black hair and tall, willowy frame which Sir Otis, for one, found boyish. Too, Phillipa was an unspoiled, uncomplaining treasure of a girl. She'd make some man a fine wife since, perforce, she knew all about managing a gentleman's household. The problem was, there were no gentlemen.

Sir Otis didn't entertain at home and never invited the two young women to accompany him on his evenings out. In fact, he barely allowed them to leave his house, determined not to share what he couldn't enjoy. Be damned, he thought, if he'd have any dandified nodcocks strutting around his chicken coop. If they could get out of the Albemarle Street residence, Sir Otis and duties permitting, the girls knew no one in London and had barely the fee for the lending library between them. Their few treats depended on what Johna could squeeze out of the nipcheese household budget. The generous allowance her father had negotiated for Johna was going, according to Sir Otis, to pay for the maintenance of Hutchison Manor, to settle the baron's last debts, and to keep the girls in modest home-sewn gowns so they didn't shame him.

'Twould take the devil in lace drawers to shame the old reprobate, thought Johna. And 'twould take the heavenly host to please him. For sure her lovely Christmas dinner hadn't. Johna had hoped to get Sir Otis in a mellow mood, to beg permission to take Phillipa to Bath for the winter. Social standards were less rigorous there, she'd heard, and the place was reportedly full of young army officers, widowers, and second sons. Well, she still had her Christmas wish. While stirring the pudding last month, she'd wished that Sir Otis would relent enough to provide dear Phillipa with a dowry and a future. Meanwhile, Johna was not going to permit the miserable old muckworm to ruin her sister's joy in the holiday season. She'd been working on this Christmas pudding since early fall, just for Phillipa.

First she'd let everyone from the scullery maid to the stableboy help stir the pudding and make their wishes—while the master was out, of course. Then she'd divided the mixture into four boiling bags to steam for hours, then hung them out to set and age, just as in her grandmother's old recipe. According to the faded household book, one was for family, one for company, one for the servants, and one for charity. Since there was no company, Johna had traded the extra pudding for the special tokens she'd hidden that morning in the family's dessert, the one that had been soaking in rum for the past week.

As she carefully cut the pudding in precise sections, Johna asked, "Do you remember Mama's little charms, Phillippa? The ones she used to hide in the Christmas pudding?"

Phillipa clapped her hands again, beaming around the centerpiece. "Never say you found them, Jo. I can't wait to see. Oh, hurry, do."

"What's that you two are nattering on about now?" Sir Otis demanded. "Mealymouthed chits talk barely loud enough to be heard."

The footmen passed the plates while Johna tried to soothe her husband. "It's just an old tradition, like making wishes when you stir the batter."

"Balderdash. Tommyrot. More nonsense to fill a gudgeon's empty head." He stuck his spoon into the dish before him.

"Look, Jo, I got the ring! That means I'm going to be married within the year!"

Johna smiled. Of course Phillipa had found the ring, right where Johna'd planted it. She dug around in her own portion and came up with a coin.

"What's this blasted jibber-jabber?" Sir Otis shouted around a mouthful of pudding. "Is this food or some tomfool parlor game?"

"It's just for fun—" Johna started to explain, and Phillipa chimed in with, "It's part of the Christmas magic. I got the ring, and Jo got the coin. That means she's going to come into great wealth this year."

Sir Otis took another heaping spoonful into his mouth, then banged his fist on the table and thundered, "You mean you stuck a coi—A ch—"

Phillipa answered: "Not a real coin, sir, a special token. Besides the ring and the coin, there's the shoe that means a long journey, and the key that portends a wonderful opportunity. What else, Jo?"

But Johna was watching her husband down the length of the table. She was frozen in her seat, horrified, as Sir Otis went "Ch—ch—" a few more times, his face turning purplish, before he fell over, right into his dish of pudding.

Sir Otis had gotten the shoe.

Six months of mourning was all the respect Johna was willing to accord her departed husband, and that was five months more than the dastard deserved. No improvements had been made at Hutchison Manor, no outstanding debts had been marked paid. And Sir Otis's own private papers showed exorbitant interest rates on loans, dealings in smuggled goods, a strongbox full of nefarious and underhanded dealings. Johna relocked the box and hid it deep in her clothespress, wondering if a man could be more despicable dead than alive.

Not when he'd left her a fortune to rival Golden

Ball's, he couldn't. Not when he'd *left,* by heaven's grace. Johna was twenty-one, rich, and free. There was no one to issue orders, no one to criticize her looks or behavior, no one to tell her what to do. Sir Otis's solicitor threatened to challenge her in court: a young woman needed a guardian, a trustee. Johna threatened to find another man of affairs to handle her finances. Mr. Bigelow withdrew his complaints.

For six months the Widow Ogden could not go to the theater or the opera or even the assemblies in Bath, not without permanently destroying her reputation. But she could spend her husband's ill-gotten wealth, smiling with every bank draft she wrote. Johna refurbished the London residence top to bottom, with enough servants that she had a maid just to tidy the other maids' rooms. She hired a manager for the Berkshire property, and made sure he had ample funds to restore the manor house to a glory never seen in her lifetime. She set up a bank fund for Phillipa's dowry that made Mr. Bigelow's hand shake. And then she called in the dressmakers.

By the end of June they were ready. Johna wore pale grays, silvers, the smoky lavenders of half-mourning that became her better than any colors she might have chosen, while the fashionable high waists emphasized her slender elegance. Phillipa's gowns were pretty pastel muslins, trailing ribbons and rosettes. The fabrics were the finest to be had, the styles absolutely à la mode.

The Prince Regent went to Brighton for the summer and the cream of society followed. So did the Hutchison sisters. They rented a lovely house on the Steyne, frolicked in the sea, rode the little donkeys, and partook of every public concert, every promenade, every open-air pastry shop. To no avail.

Johna made no secret of her widowhood or her wealth, and made sure to mention Phillipa's dowry in the hired staff's hearing. To no avail.

They were noticed, of course, as two beautiful young women would be noticed anywhere, but not by the right people. The only persons who approached them, who tried to scrape up an acquaintance, were half-pay officers, basket-scrambling fortune-hunters, or outright rakes. The Regent's set seemed to consist of an inordinate amount of all three, plus a contingent of bored, blasé snobs. Acknowledging any of their suggestive smiles, accepting a rum-touch as escort, being at home to a here-and-thereian, would have put paid to Johna's hopes of seeing her sister creditably established. She knew what they all had in mind for a wealthy widow and she wasn't having any of it. Not yet.

By the end of summer, back in London, they were no closer to Johna's goal of seeing her sister dance at Almack's. Johna had overestimated the value of her father's title and underestimated the stench of Sir Otis's. She thought of hiring one of those well-connected ladies of the *ton* who, for a fee, acted as chaperone, social mentor, matchmaker. If they were so well-connected, though, Johna couldn't help wondering, why did they need to hire out their services? Besides, she couldn't bear putting herself under the thumb of some prune-faced dragon. Not yet.

Johna wasn't giving up her reputation, her independence, or her dreams for her sister's future. Not yet. Instead she called in her markers.

2.

Duty and dignity. Those were words a man could live by. A dainty morsel like the Black Widow was a delight a man would cheerfully die for. Merle Spenser, Viscount Selcrest, tapped Johna's thick vellum note against his booted leg as he sat in his library, thinking. And smiling.

Oh, the viscount had noticed the stunning widow in Brighton, all right. A man would have to be deader than that dirty dish Ogden not to notice her. Like every other man in Brighton, Selcrest had even tried to strike up a conversation with the dasher, at the library one day, at the jeweler's on another occasion. Both times she'd turned her fine-boned shoulder and ignored him with a faint tilt to her rose-petal lips. His grandmother the duchess couldn't have depressed his pretensions more elegantly or with more finality. The chit had style.

She also had a younger sister in tow, a pretty bit of fluff and frill. The reluctant consensus among the sporting gentlemen in Prinny's circle was that the widow wouldn't be entertaining any proposals—honest or otherwise—while chaperoning the girl. Even before Selcrest entered the lists, enough money to pay half the Regent's debts had been wagered and lost on which lucky swell would capture this so-ripe plum. Odds changed when the well-breeched, well-favored viscount took the field, only to go down in ignoble defeat.

And now, that same speedily dispatched challenger to the widow's supposed virtue wondered, what had changed her mind? Had she sent the sister back to school or off to the country? Or had she finally realized she'd never reach respectability, not with the baggage she carried? Marrying a disreputable old man for his money and then, rumor had it, killing him to get it sooner was not a high recommendation. There were at least four loose screws in Brighton who needed her blunt badly enough to marry Johna, Lady Ogden, despite the *on-dits*. She hadn't given them the time of day either. And she hadn't sent for them in London.

Viscount Selcrest had a broad chest. It swelled a tad broader as he called for another tub and shave—his second of the day. His only problem, as he sat in his sandalwood-scented bath, was the wording of her message: Could he please call at his earliest convenience, on a family matter. A female like Lady Otis Ogden had nothing to do with his family. Not ever.

Duty and dignity meant everything to the viscount. Granted he hadn't gotten around to marrying and filling his nursery but, 'struth, he was only twenty-eight and did have his brother Denton to ensure the succession. Other than that minor detail, he tried to lead an exemplary life, guarding the family honor as zealously as he protected his property and dependents. Perhaps because of his own unfortunate beginnings, Merle firmly believed that his sons had as much right to inherit a good name as a good income. The viscount was a conscientious landlord, a dedicated member of Parliament, and a devoted son to his widowed mother. He wasn't a gambler, a drunkard, or a womanizer—not by the measure of the day, at least. That's where discretion mattered.

And that was why the viscount stepped down from his curricle two blocks from the address on Albemarle Street and handed the reins to his tiger. "Keep walking them around the square. I'll find you when I have concluded my business."

Contrary to his preconceptions, Merle was impressed with the widow's home. The entry was light and airy, furnished in the best of taste with priceless Chinese vases filled with flowers and a Turner scene he'd love to own. The liveried footmen were properly deferential as they accepted his hat and gloves, and the bewigged butler's backbone was as starched as his shirtpoints as he announced that, yes, milady was receiving.

Here was another surprise: she wasn't receiving him alone. The sister sat on the sofa beside the widow, sharing the latest issue of *La Belle Assemblee*. A pretty little filly, Merle noticed in passing. Too bad she came from such a dicey stable. While the widow asked his preference for refreshment and gave directions to the butler, Selcrest made a mental list of suitable chaps to match the gel to, one of his local squire's sons out in Suffolk, or a distant cousin in the Horse Guards who needed a rich bride-price to further his career. The chit's future settled to his satisfaction— and his convenience—Merle turned his attention to the widow. "Yes, the weather is cool for this season," he agreed, thinking that she was even more lovely than he remembered. She wore a gray-striped cambric gown with a black shawl draped casually over her shoulders. With her black hair and magnolia skin, she looked good enough to undress.

The poker-backed butler returned with a tea cart and two maids. While they were busy positioning the plates of poppy seed cake, macaroons, and raspberry tarts, Johna took time to observe her guest. She congratulated herself on picking just the right name from

Sir Otis's strongbox. Lord Selcrest was as polished as a fine diamond, hard-planed yet vibrant with an inner glow. He had the self-assurance of a born nobleman and more than a tinge of the haughtiness she'd noted in Brighton. And yes, he still had that raffish smile, as if his brown eyes could see beneath her clothes. Johna tugged her shawl closer. "Do you take lemon in your tea? Sugar?"

"Just sugar, please. One lump."

Johna busied herself pouring and stirring and passing plates until all three of them were served and the butler and maids were dismissed. "Phillipa, dearest, perhaps his lordship would enjoy some music while we chat," she suggested, indicating the pianoforte at the far end of the well-appointed room.

Phillipa obediently took her cup and a third raspberry tart and sweetly asked if he had any favorite pieces.

Other than raspberry tarts, Selcrest wanted to say, he favored elegant widows, so she should play anything long and loud. "I'm sure whatever you select will be charming, Miss Hutchison." When she moved off, with still another tart, the viscount resumed his seat on the cane-back chair, nudging it slightly nearer the sofa, the widow, and the platter of pastries. "A lovely girl, ma'am. And you have a fine cook."

Johna smiled. "And you're likely wishing them both to perdition right now."

"What, am I that transparent, my lady? I had hoped to make your acquaintance in Brighton, so naturally I was delighted at your invitation to call. I was hoping we could come to some agreement."

Merle was hoping he hadn't rushed his fences despite her candor, so he was relieved when the widow said, "Good. I am hopeful of that myself." Then, before he could inch his chair a bit nearer, she surprised him yet again with, "Did you know my husband, Lord Selcrest?"

"Why, no, I never had the, ah, pleasure." He'd sooner eat nails than go near a Captain Sharp like Ogden.

"But you knew of him, surely?"

"Yes, but—"

"I was going through some of his papers and came upon this note." She pulled a paper from the journal at her side and handed it to him. "I believe it to be your brother's. Am I correct?"

There it was, as big as life, *Denton Spenser*. The amount scrawled under the unmistakable IOU was bigger than life. Bigger than Den's yearly income, for sure. The viscount was staggered by the sum. He knew his scapegrace brother was running with a rackety crowd, but to fall into the clutches of a makebate like Otis Ogden? And not consult Merle, or ask his help? That was a crushing disappointment when he'd striven so hard to be head of the family. Then his lordship realized an even larger disappointment. "So you didn't invite me here to . . ."

"To throw myself at your feet, to ask you to make a scarlet woman out of me, to beg your protection against the cold, cruel world? To—"

"Enough! I beg your pardon if I have offended you with unwarranted assumptions." Thunderation, Merle could feel his cheeks growing warm, the first time a woman had confounded him in years.

"But you don't think they are unwarranted, do you? Everyone believes Sir Otis's wealthy young widow must be a trollop, so naturally you supposed I'd be amenable to your suggestions."

The bitterness in her voice was unanswerable, and the sadness. He reached for another raspberry tart rather than look her in the eyes with a lie. When the silence became uncomfortable, even with the Bach in the background, the viscount smoothed Denton's note on his thigh. If the widow was too virtuous to join the muslin company, what was she doing taking over her husband's loan-sharking? Merle's compassion for her plight died aborning. He'd redeem the vowel, of course. Devil take him if he'd let some harpy get her talons into his little brother.

As if reading his mind, or his sneer, Johna quietly explained, "When I found the voucher I did not write to Mr. Spenser. I had heard that he is always pockets to let and I did not want to send such a young man to the moneylenders."

Selcrest acknowledged her meager benevolence with a curt nod. "I don't carry that much of the ready. Will a check do?"

"I do not want the money, my lord." She waved one delicate hand at the room, the house, and all its splendor. "I have more than enough wealth for my needs. I do, however, require something that only you can provide."

Now this was more the thing, Merle thought. She wasn't calling in the chit, she was begging a favor. After which minor feat of dragon-slaying, the damsel would likely fall into his arms in gratitude. "I am at your service," he said with that lopsided smile that left no doubt as to what service he'd like to render.

"What I'd like"—she paused while the viscount

helped himself to the last raspberry tart—"is an introduction to your mother."

"My mo—" The notion so startled the viscount that he swallowed wrong. He coughed, or choked, or perhaps laughed.

In any other household, a gentleman might be gently slapped on the back or politely offered a drink of water. Not in this household, not now. Johna leaped to her feet, upsetting her teacup. "Oh no, not again! Pippy, come quickly!"

And then, before Lord Selcrest could swallow the rest of the tart so he could speak up, young Miss Hutchison had rushed over and grabbed his arms over his head, shouting at her sister to remember what Dr. Browne had advised, too late. Her sister did remember, the whole nightmare of her husband's sudden departure. So she drew back her fist and with all her might belted the viscount in the stomach, right below the ribs.

In the ordinary course of events, her fist would have bounced off his lordship's rigid muscles. He worked out with Gentleman Jackson and fenced with Monsieur Lamartine. But he wasn't sparring or parrying; he was sitting in an attractive female's parlor, eating raspberry tarts. The impact of Johna's fist sent the air straight out of him. It also sent the cane-back chair toppling over, with Merle in it, so his head struck the floor right where the thick carpet ended.

"My stars, Jo, you've killed him!"

Johna was on the floor beside the viscount, loosening his neckcloth, shaking his shoulders, and drenching him with tears. "You can't die! Oh, please wake up, my lord. Please please please." And she took to slapping his face.

Merle was seeing a dozen Lady Ogdens and feeling
a million slaps on his aching head. So he made a grab
for her hands, which pulled her off balance and onto
his chest. So he kissed her, which seemed like the right
thing to do at the time. It certainly made his head
feel better.

Johna pulled out of his arms with a gasp. Whether
from relief that he was alive, humiliation at her ac-
tions, or indignation at his, Johna was incensed. She
hauled back that same deadly right and punched the
viscount in the jaw. It seemed like the right thing to
do at the time, and made her feel a great deal better.
Of course it bounced Merle's head on the hardwood
floor again.

This time when he awoke Lady Johna was sending
her sister to fetch the brandy decanter, thank God.
Merle slowly managed to drag himself to a sitting posi-
tion while Phillipa poured a wavery stream into the
tilting glass Johna held, their hands were shaking so
badly. The viscount reached out to take the glass be-
fore they spilled the whole bottle, only to see the ele-
gant widow down the shot in one swallow.

He had to laugh. "Mama's going to love you."

"Then you'll do it? You'll help?"

Phillipa handed him another glass. "He has to help;
we saved his life."

"Saved my life? Bloody hell, you damn near killed
me."

"You took liberties," was all Johna said as she
helped him to his feet and onto the sofa.

"It was a dying man's last wish."

"Fustian "

He smiled. "Have you never heard of the kiss of
life? It worked."

"Rubbish."

"But lovely rubbish, if I remember correctly. Of course I wasn't in any position to truly appreciate your efforts at reviving me. Perhaps you'd care to—"

"I was *not* trying to revive you. That is, I was, but not then." To hide her blushes Johna crossed to the bellpull.

Within minutes her efficient staff had the mess cleaned up and the brandy decanter refilled. The viscount had a full glass in his hand, a slab of raw meat on his jaw, and a sack of ice on his head. He also had his brother's note of hand, rescued from the debris. "I owe you for this, if not my life."

Johna reached for the marker and ripped it up. "No, I was wrong to hold that over you. I know what my husband was. He likely cheated your brother, the same way he cheated Papa. I was desperate, my lord."

"For my mother's approval?"

Johna gazed toward the pianoforte where Phillipa had resumed her playing. "I want my sister to have the chance I never did. She cannot help being Sir Otis Ogden's sister-in-law, any more than I could help being Papa's daughter. She deserves a decent husband, a true gentleman the likes of which we are not liable to come upon on our own, nor back in Berkshire. I found your brother's voucher, but he is too young to lend any kind of countenance. And your escort . . ."

Merle finished for her: "Would have been damning."

Johna shrugged. "If you showed interest in Phillipa, no other gentleman would pay her attention, and if you paid me particular notice, they'd all assume I was your mistress. Either way, Phillipa would not get to meet any decent, worthy candidates for her hand and dowry. We have no female relations, no connections for all the three years we've spent in London. Your mother is known to be ... eccentric. I've heard that she keeps rabbits in the drawing room and plays cards with her butler, but she is still good *ton*. She could lend us that veneer of respectability we so dreadfully need."

"Higbee has been with us forever," was Selcrest's only comment. He leaned back to think, sipping his brandy. To call his mother an eccentric was like calling the Thames wet. It didn't half describe the thing. Mama was downright attics-to-let. The reason Merle clung so firmly to his dignity was because he found so little of it at home. He'd had to fight his way through boarding school because it was public knowledge that he'd been born a scant six months after his parents' wedding. A premature birth, hell; to this day he didn't know if he was the rightful heir or the butler's son! Mama would only answer that she was always faithful to the love of her life.

The rabbits were the least of his embarrassments, just another passing fancy like the seances in the munitions room and the mud baths in the backyard. Merle would not let it happen again, his name becoming a fixture in the *on-dits* columns. He spent his days keeping his mother from her wilder extravagances, like flying her own hot air balloon. When the viscount wasn't scrambling to keep his mother from the brink of social and physical disaster, he was pulling his brother out of scrapes. He was not about to sacrifice years of holding them to the straight and narrow for the sake of these two outcasts.

Selcrest no longer believed that Lady Ogden had killed her husband. That was something, at least. If she weren't quite the innocent her sister was, neither did she seem quite the mercenary baggage he'd assumed. Testing the waters, he asked, "Were there other outstanding loans among your husband's papers?"

She nodded. "I'll burn them tonight. I never intended to ask anyone for money."

Were favors just as bad? Merle's head was aching too much to decide and, deuce take it, the widow was too alluring to let slip away into rural obscurity. "I'll put it to Mama. I'll ask her to help sponsor you and your sister into polite society. But on one condition: if you cause one poor reflection on my mother's good name, one misstep or least hint of impropriety, the deal is off. I'd rather pay my brother's debt in cash, with interest, than let you stir the scandalbroth. Are we agreed?"

"Agreed," she said, holding out her hand.

Merle was about to turn the slender wrist over and kiss her palm, or her fingers, or perhaps the pulse beating through the blue veins. But she wasn't finished: "My sister and I are entirely capable of behaving like ladies." Her eyes narrowed and her chin rose an inch. "Are you agreeing to act like a gentleman?"

Merle looked at that fragile hand and rubbed his aching jaw. He decided a firm handshake was the safer course. "Agreed."

3.

"Coo-ee, gov, wot 'appened to you?" The viscount's tiger looked back down Albemarle Street for the gang of thugs that had attacked his master, perhaps a runaway carriage. But the midday sun was still shining on the quiet street. "I thought you was makin' a mornin' call, not goin' to a mill."

"Stubble it." Lord Selcrest took up the reins and flicked his whip over the horses' heads, forcing the tiger to scramble onto the back of the curricle, lest he be left behind. Merle drove around to the stable mews rather than getting down at the front door of Selcrest House as usual. He thought he could go in the back door, through the service entrance near the kitchens, without disturbing the household.

Unfortunately, one of the maids saw him and swooned dead away. Another started screaming, which brought his high-strung Welsh housekeeper, with the kitchen's largest meat cleaver. What next? Merle thought as he tried to wrest the blade away before Mrs. Reese injured herself. The cooks and scullery maids were shrieking by now, knocking over buckets, barrels, and bowls of ingredients in their hysteria.

Of course Merle's mother came to see what all the commotion was about. She loved a good riot, so joined Higbee the butler under the heavy pantry table. Once they'd placed their wagers, the dowager chirped into the mayhem: "Did you have a nice day, Merry dear?"

Once the viscount was cleaned up, and after Higbee had reassured Lady Selcrest that the stains on her son's neckcloth were raspberry preserves, not blood, she wanted to know all the details. So did Higbee. Merle didn't waste his time telling the old man to go polish the silver or something. Higbee wouldn't do it anyway. Selcrest thought with envy of Lady Ogden's so-correct butler. Then he tried to decide just which of the morning's details he ought to relate to his fond parent. He didn't think his mother would be impressed to hear what a handy set of fives the widow possessed. So instead of explaining how he got the purple bruise on his chin, or what the sticking plaster was doing on his head, the viscount asked: "Do you know the Hutchison family, Mother?"

Lady Selcrest knew everyone. If she didn't, Higbee could find them in Debrett's *Peerage*. "The Devon or the Berkshire Hutchisons?"

"Berkshire. The mother was a Whittaker, I believe."

"Ah, *those* Hutchisons." Lady Selcrest was intrigued. Her dry-as-dust eldest son came home looking like he'd been in a dockside tavern brawl, and mentioned two young females of questionable virtue. Maybe there was hope for the boy after all.

"I know there's been a deal of conjecture about them, but they're not as unacceptable as painted. The younger is a sweet little charmer, all round and rosy, the usual accomplishments. Handsome dowry, I understand."

"And the elder? She's the poor girl who was forced to marry that awful Ogden person, isn't she? It wouldn't have happened had her mother lived, of course. I understand Hutchison fell apart after that. It's no excuse. The varlet should be boiled in oil for what he did to his own daughter."

Higbee was standing by the door. "Lord Hutchison is dead, my lady."

Lady Selcrest smiled over at him. "That's right, he is. Thank you, Higbee."

Merle gnashed his teeth. "Do you think you might give the sisters the occasional invite?"

"Do you mean for tea, dear? Of course, if they are friends of yours."

"Well, I was thinking more in the order of dinner, an evening at the theater, a ride with you in the park." Selcrest brushed at a gray rabbit hair on his burgundy coat sleeve. "We're not friends, precisely. I, that is, we, stand somewhat in their debt. I thought to repay the obligation by helping them find their feet in the social waters."

A debt? This was getting better and better. If there was one thing Lady Selcrest liked more than aggravating her son by creating a stir, it was matchmaking. So far, she'd had lamentably few successes. "Let me think. Whittaker's eldest gel married a Babcock, and so did my brother's wife's sister. Not the same Babcock, of course, but yes, I think we can claim a connection that might explain your chicks under my wing."

"They're not my—"

Higbee cleared his throat. "Ahem. Lady Margaret Spenser was godmother to Clementine Whittaker, Baroness Hutchison."

"Great-aunt Margaret?"

"The same. I am sure Lady Margaret would expect you to look after her loved ones."

"If she hadn't died two decades before they were born," the viscount muttered, but his mother was delighted.

"Higbee, you are a genius. Merle, raise his salary."

The man already earned more than the Prime Minister, but Merle nodded, to get back to the issue at hand. "So you think we can do it? Bring Lady Ogden and her sister into fashion?"

"It's quite a challenge, but not beyond my powers, of course. Don't you agree, Higbee?"

"If anyone can reclaim two fallen sparrows, my lady, it is your gracious self."

The viscountess was almost purring. The viscount was almost puking. He got up to leave, but his mother called him back. "I cannot perform miracles, Merle. If your protégées are hopeless rustics or of dubious character, the venture is doomed to failure. I doubt that even I could foist milkmaids, fortune-hunters, or Haymarket ware on the *ton*."

"That's what most of the young misses at Almack's are, Mother, which is why your efforts at matchmaking always fail. Great-aunt Margaret's grand-goddaughters will fit right in."

"Ahem. May I suggest that my lady invite the two young females to tea before undertaking a public appearance? That way we might be certain of their suitability before committing the Selcrest name to their advancement."

"Excellent, Higbee! What would I do without you?"

Most likely find a lonely old duke or an eligible earl to marry, but Merle wasn't that lucky.

"What do you mean, Mama says we have to show a united front of family approval?" Denton was proving more difficult to convince than Lady Selcrest, after the viscount managed to track down his errant brother in the billiards room. "Do the pretty with two harum-scarum females I've never met? Not for the price of that new hunter I saw at Tattersall's."

Merle reset the balls and waited for his brother to take aim. "How about for the price of your gaming debt to Otis Ogden?"

The balls scattered wildly, two landing on the floor. "My, ah, debt?"

"What, did you think a sum like that would never come to light?"

"But the man is dead!"

"So you thought you didn't have to pay?" Merle had retrieved the balls and his own cue stick. He was calmly, methodically, sending his shots into the appropriate pockets. "I wonder, if I should die, would you feel you didn't have to pay the coal-hauler or the vintner? Perhaps I had better be thinking harder about my successor." Merle set his stick aside, leaving Denton an almost impossible shot.

Denton threw his stick down and faced his brother. "Dash it, this was different. I think the wine was tampered with."

"Most likely it was. If you were fool enough to enter a snakepit like the Black Parrot, you should have expected to be stung in some fashion. Marked decks, uphill dice, or footpads in the alley when you left, should you have been unfortunate enough to win."

"Exactly. But the fellows were going, so I went along."

"And gambled away your patrimony and part of mine. It's a debt of honor, you cloth-head. Play and pay. If you thought you were cheated, you should have called the blackguards out."

"They would have killed me."

"And I still might if you won't help launch those two females. We owe them."

"But, Merle, come-out balls and afternoon teas?" Denton shuddered. "I'd rather face Bonaparte's cannons." His face brightened. "In fact, you can reconsider and purchase my commission. That way you won't have to keep bailing me out of these scrapes. I might even bring some glory to the family name, as you're always lecturing about."

"I don't lecture and I'm not going to send you off to get blown apart in some act of bacon-brained bravado. You are still my heir."

"I know the solution then. Why don't you marry Miss Hutchison and beget your own heir? You said her mother was of decent lineage. That way her place in society would be guaranteed and I could go off to the Peninsula, instead of to perdition at Almack's."

The viscount was tossing a billiard ball from hand to hand. He stopped. "What, marry a chit from the infantry? I don't recall Nurse dropping you on your head, but someone must have. She's a sweet child, but I'd be bored within a week."

"Then marry the widow."

Merle placed the ball in the exact center of the table. "What, take Otis Ogden's leavings? Pigs will fly first."

The tea went well, Selcrest thought. He was relieved to note that the sisters were dressed in modish modesty, curtsied to the proper depths, and didn't sit mumchance like so many fledglings he'd seen, intimidated by their betters. He carefully suppressed the notion that Lady Ogden did not consider the Selcrests her betters. Restored to her cool elegance, she was remarkably unfazed by his mother's current penchant for Gypsy attire, the peasant blouse, tiered skirts with billowy red petticoats, and chains of coins and hoops. Merle even thought she sounded sincere when she commented, "How gay you look, my lady," as she took her seat. One would think the female used her fan daily to sweep rabbit pellets off damask chairs. No, he did not think the Hutchison sisters would embarrass his mother.

The alternative was more likely, however. Merle refused to consider the possibility that Selcrest House and its inhabitants mightn't pass muster, nor why the idea so distressed him. He ought to be feeling relieved that Lady Ogden might show them her heels. He wasn't. Deuce take it, she was exquisite. If his mother could get the sister fired off in this fall's Little Season, the widow just might be more amenable to dalliance before the *ton* left town for the holidays. Merle daydreamed of how he'd like his Christmas present unwrapped, while the ladies furthered their acquaintance.

Lady Selcrest was charmed. She declared that, had she known young women could be so enchanting, she'd have had daughters instead of sons. The younger girl read the viscountess's favorite Gothic romance novels and the older one played cards. What could be more accommodating? Lady Selcrest delightedly announced that she couldn't wait to introduce the girls to her circle of friends, to arrange parties in their honor, to take them shopping with her. Her stiff-rumped son may have cringed at this last item, Lady Selcrest observed, but Johna didn't. Excellent female. She'd do, especially if Selcrest continued to watch the beautiful widow like a fox eyeing a particularly plump partridge. He was practically drooling, the gudgeon. Lady Selcrest had only to make sure that the bird stayed just out of reach until the clunch was well and truly caught. She'd have a grandchild before the cat could lick its ear, and before Higbee won their wager.

After showing the Hutchison sisters to the door, Higbee pronounced them prettily behaved misses. "Not at all above themselves like some of the gentry." He shot a meaningful glance at his employer. "And most of the nobility." Higbee's money was still on Selcrest's bedding the lass, not wedding her.

Happily unaware of the machinations at Selcrest House, Johna was happy with the tea, with the meeting, with the arrangement. Their new benefactress was definitely an Original, which could only work in their favor. And, to Johna's relief, Lady Selcrest's son minded his manners in his mama's presence. Johna still remembered the tingle of Selcrest's arms enfolding her, the thrill of his warm lips on hers, the cad. He'd promised to keep his distance, and seemed to be keeping his vow, the cad. No matter, Phillipa was going to have her Season.

Any fool could have predicted a success. Money, looks, and the Selcrest cachet could easily whitewash a checkered past when the females were also personable and eager to please. Besides, the dowager and her butler weren't the only ones to notice the sparks flying between Selcrest and the Black Widow. White's betting book required a new page. Every hostess wanted to provide this latest spectator sport at her do. Invitations started trickling into Albemarle Street, then turned into a veritable deluge of requests for the ladies' presence at routs and ridottos and rides in the park, balls and breakfasts, and balloon ascensions. They even received vouchers to Almack's, that pinnacle of social aspiration. Handsome, intelligent, and wealthy gentlemen left cards from daybreak to dinner, and the floral deliveries left scant room for them to sit down in the few scattered moments when the sisters were home to receive callers. The gentlemen were short and tall, dark and fair. They were peacocks and poets, soldiers and sportsmen, students and statesmen. Surely among them Phillipa could find one man to make her happy.

Everything was perfect, just as Johna had planned, except for one minor detail: Phillipa had already fallen in love.

4.

"I won't have it, Selcrest, do you hear me?"

"Everyone in the cursed ballroom can hear you, dash it. You're creating a scene. Do you want to ruin your sister's chances after we've all worked so hard?"

Johna and the viscount were one of the few couples waltzing at Almack's. The patronesses did not approve of younger girls indulging in the wicked dance. Married ladies and widows, however, were considered experienced enough not to be led into indiscretion by a man's hand on their waist. Hah! Selcrest had been waiting all night in hopes of just such an opportunity. Instead of melting in his arms, though, his partner was boiling mad. Instead of the gossamer butterfly he'd hoped to whirl around the dance floor till her senses were disordered, he held a buzzing, stinging wasp. Deuce take it, she looked like she wanted to box his ears. "Smile, confound it, everyone is watching."

"Not everyone," she replied through clenched teeth, her mouth fixed in a grin that would have done Grimaldi proud. "Half of them have run off to change their bets. What do you mean, not dancing all night and then singling me out for a waltz?"

"I meant to honor my mother's guest with a dance, that's all. It would have been discourteous, else."

"Fustian, you were hiding in the card room all night because you were afraid to face me earlier. Now you've set the cat among the pigeons, and after you were the one preaching discretion and decorum. You have to know what the gabble-grinders will make of this."

"They'll make note that I had one dance with the most beautiful woman in the room." Or they would, he thought, if she weren't as rigid as the carved figurehead on a ship.

Specifically intending to avoid bringing attention, to avoid giving credence to any rumors, Selcrest had left for the card room after escorting his party through the receiving line of curious doyennes, dowagers, and dragons that made up Almack's patronesses. What harm could one dance do though, he'd thought, especially if he also stood up for a *contra danse* or such with Phillipa? The more he thought, the more that one dance with Lady Ogden took on the aspect of a drink of water to a man parched by the desert sun. He lost three hands in a row to Lord Carville, thinking of holding her in his arms. Then he'd heard the strains of a waltz. They would have had to tie him to the mast, like Odysseus, to keep him away from the widow in silver tissue with its black border and scattered sequins.

Johna almost relented to savor the compliment and the feel of Selcrest's firm touch on her skin through the thin layers of her gown's fabric. Almost. But the viscount twirled her about so that she was facing the gilt chairs set along the edge of the dance floor. Phillipa was quite properly sitting out the waltz at Lady

Selcrest's side, surrounded by her usual coterie of beaux, with the Hon. Denton Spenser standing behind her chair—with his hand on her shoulder!

"Two dances they've had. Two. And now this ... this blatant public display! If your gallows-bait of a brother thinks to force me into countenancing such a connection, he's even more of a fool than I thought, and that's saying a lot." She'd stopped dancing in the middle of her diatribe, so other couples were bumping into them.

"That's saying too much about my brother, madam, and too much for this company, dash it." He dragged her off the floor so fast her slippers almost left skid marks on the highly polished surface.

By the time he found a secluded alcove in the fish-bowl of Almack's, Johna was panting and smoke was almost pouring out of her ears. She stamped her foot, only accidentally stomping on Selcrest's instep. "I didn't go to all this effort just to see my sister wasted on a half-breeched basket-scrambler."

"Smile, damn it."

"Smile? When my only relation in this entire world is about to ruin her life after I married that awful old man just to provide her the chance for something better?"

Merle stepped in front of her, his back partially shielding them from the avid watchers. "Do you think I want this any more than you do? My brother aligned with a—"

Johna crossed her arms over her chest. "Go ahead and say it, sirrah."

"With a female too young to know her own mind, is what I was going to say."

"Oh, but Phillipa assures me she does. We've met every sprig and noble spawn on the town, bucks and beaux and all manner of gentlemen. She won't look at any of them, and it's almost November."

"And Denton's never been serious about a female before. He's actually stopped complaining about having to attend those tedious picnics and afternoon dancing-lesson parties. I thought he was sick."

"Lovesick, more like, the moonling. You have to do something!"

"Me? You're the one who let the chit read those romance novels. Just what do you expect me to do about your sister's infatuation?"

"End it! Let Denton join the army. He's been wanting to this age and more. In fact, if you didn't keep him on such a tight rein, he wouldn't have tried slipping his lead in the first place. The nodcock even confessed to me that he believed you would buy his commission if he caused enough aggravation."

"He *is* a fool."

Johna unthinkingly took Merle's hand in earnest entreaty. "Let him go, sir. Let him grow up, make something of himself besides the Viscount Selcrest's brother. Separated, they'll get over this silly calf-love. My sister will find a young gentleman who won't gamble away her dowry or break his neck on some untried hunter."

"Confound it, my brother is not the villain you make him out to be. He is merely full of the usual high spirits, sowing his wild oats."

"Let him sow them in Spain where they might do some good ending this stupid war!"

Merle suddenly realized he'd been staring at the skimpy bodice of the widow's gown as her chest heaved with her passionate plea. Worse, he'd been holding Johna's hand for the last few minutes, in front of half the *ton*. He couldn't decide whether to drop it like a hot coal, or bring it to his lips. Gads, his wits went begging every time he was near the impossible creature! For sure his backbone turned to porridge in her blue-eyed gaze because he heard himself say, "Very well, I'll ask around about commissions in a decent regiment."

"Good." Johna patted his hand. "See that you do, or I will purchase the ninnyhammer's colors myself."

The more she thought about it, the more Johna liked the idea. Perhaps the Selcrest coffers weren't as deep as rumored. Perhaps the viscount saw Phillipa's dowry as good riddance to his expensive brother. Perhaps he would have kissed her hand if they'd been less in the public eye. Great heaven, she had to get disentangled from the entire family! Denton was not a bad sort, at heart. He was just young and unsettled— and his handsome brother was unsettling.

Why couldn't Phillipa have thrown her bonnet at any other man in London? Johna would have seen her wed and gone home to Berkshire in two shakes, with no temptations, no lingering regrets. If her sister married Denton, Johna would be thrown into the viscount's company for the rest of her life, and thrown into a bumblebroth every time he gave her that seductive smile. By heaven, she would *not* be seduced! Johna didn't even want to be married again, not after the first time. Marriage wasn't the remotest possibility, of course, for Selcrest would never lower himself to marry her, the arrant egotist, so his uppity lordship could just go to the devil—and take his brother with him.

Johna couldn't make arrangements with the devil, but she could with the War Office, if that was how one went about starting a young man on an army career. Her solicitor would know the procedure and the expense. It was time she paid a call on Mr. Bigelow anyway, concerning her own expenses. The Season had been more costly than she'd figured, what with both sisters needing new gowns for every occasion and changing ensembles four times a day. Johna had also purchased a fashionable barouche for drives in the park, which meant she then needed the most elegant and thus extravagantly priced pair of matched bays at Tattersall's. The horses required an additional driver, more grooms, and higher stable fees. There was also the lavish ball in Phillipa's honor that Johna and Lady Selcrest were planning for late in the Season, just before everyone left town for Christmas at their country estates. With even the highest sticklers sending their acceptances, Johna's respectability and Phillipa's eligibility were finally being recognized. Johna meant to give them a party they wouldn't forget.

Between her outlays here in London and the staggering sums her manager at Hutchison Manor deemed crucial for the estate's recovery, Johna was noticing her bank accounts dwindle. They seemed to be shrinking at an ever faster rate.

"That's because you are earning less income, my lady," Bigelow explained, as if Johna couldn't figure that out for herself by comparing one month's statement with the next. She didn't care for the patronizing little man, but supposed one solicitor was as prosy and prejudiced against her gender as the next. Johna only wished he'd get on with it, instead of dragging out ledgers and bank slips.

She had left Phillipa behind, not wishing to discuss army business in her sister's hearing, nor financial matters. Lady Selcrest had agreed to chaperone a group of young people on a visit to the British Museum this morning if Johna didn't get back in time. The dowager was a delightful companion, their social savior, and a fond chaperone. Fond of whom, though, was Johna's concern. The widow didn't want Denton and her sister disappearing behind any marble statue. Everyone knew what those old Greek and Roman gods were up to, by Zeus. So Johna was in a hurry.

"Please, Mr. Bigelow, just get to the heart of the matter. I know how much I am spending, and it should be well within my income without disturbing the capital. Suddenly it is not. I wish to know why."

"You do? Ah, of course you do." Bigelow closed the ledger and picked up a quill and a penknife. He concentrated on his new task until Johna cleared her throat. "Actually, my lady, it's quite simple. Without your husband's touch, some of his investments have not been earning the same profit."

"Which investments might that be, sir? The consols pay a fixed rate, the shipping ventures were for speculation, and we sold the foundry at great profit to those steam-engine people."

A tremor in Bigelow's hand caused the penknife to gouge a furrow in his desktop. "It's the gaming parlor that's losing money."

"Excuse me, I thought you just said gaming parlor." The solicitor coughed. "Why yes, and very profitable it used to be, with Sir Otis at the helm. Made his fortune that way, he did."

Johna sat forward on her seat. "A gambling den? I own a gambling den?" All she could think of was Selcrest's hearing this news. He'd have her tossed out of the *belle monde* so fast her new horses couldn't keep up. No scandals, he'd said. No improprieties. The only thing more improper than owning a gaming hell was owning a bordello. Johna might as well tie her garters on Bond Street as let it be known that she was financing her sister's debut with the profits of such a place. Lud, how did she get into this coil?

"Mr. Bigelow, how is it that you let me be ignorant of this fact, when I specifically mentioned that I wished everything aboveboard?"

"Ahem. I, ah, didn't want to bother your head with too many details. New widow and all. It was an emotional time, and I was trying to spare you more agonizing decisions. And you mentioned costly renovations and repairs. I was right: you did need the additional income."

"I wonder how much additional income *you* were earning from this arrangement that you let it continue." Johna was seething by now, that this greedy little man with his thinning hair and trembling fingers, this toad, might lose her everything.

Bigelow could hardly pick up the pen. "But, but that was my percentage, for handling the bookkeeping for the Black Parrot."

"The Black Parrot? That's known to be one of the worst hellholes in London, where young men are regularly cheated out of their fortunes and estates."

"Not always. They were often permitted to mortgage them back, on loans. That was how your husband made such a profit."

"That was how he destroyed my father, charging blood money! I will shut down that cesspool before one more life is ruined."

"Oh, but you can't. The proprietor holds a lease."

"I don't care if he holds a gun to your head, I shall not own a havey-cavey establishment."

Bigelow was starting to develop a twitch in his right eye. "Perhaps Marcel will be able to purchase the building from you. He used to cook for Sir Otis, you know, excellent French cuisine. I had the pleasure of dining with Sir Otis on a number of occasions. Marcel wanted to go into business for himself, so Sir Otis helped finance a gentlemen's club, with supper and a card room. Then it seemed that the gambling became more profitable than the cooking. And the money-lending was most profitable of all. Unfortunately Marcel doesn't seem to have the touch for that. Blancmange, yes. Interest rates, no. I do not know how much Marcel will be able to pay you for the building and for your share of the business."

"I will not sell it. I will shut it down. Today. Get your coat."

He had to wear it open. Buttons were beyond his shaking grasp.

5.

The lawyer was shivering, and not just from the cold. He didn't dare reach into his pocket for the silver flask of comfort, not with those blue eyes fixed so accusingly on him. The widow was worse than the old codger, Bigelow thought. Ogden had been greedy; this female was righteous. One was predictable; the other made no sense whatsoever to the self-serving solicitor. Well, if the lady couldn't see where her best interests lay, Bigelow could. That was his job, after all, protecting his clients from risky ventures. Charging into the Black Parrot like Joan of Arc, intent on displacing a corrupt cook, wasn't just risky. It was suicidal.

As he scurried out of his office, therefore, Bigelow managed to whisper an urgent message into his clerk's ear: "Find Viscount Selcrest. Tell him his lady is at the Black Parrot." Bigelow had heard the rumors and believed them to be true. No man could *not* be interested in this black-haired beauty who was an heiress besides. And passionate, to judge from her outrage. A downy cove like the viscount would know how to take the female in hand, out of a gent's business.

Who knew when Selcrest would get there, though? Marcel had a true Gallic temper—and a criminal past. Trust a makebate like Ogden to latch onto a convict no one else would hire. They said he'd stabbed his former employer because the man complained his roast was too well done. Then again, perhaps Marcel and the widow could compare recipes, like what was in that pudding she served Ogden. The devil take it, Bigelow would rather stand between a wolf and its next meal than get between these two. His father was right: he should have chosen the military instead of the law. He'd have lived longer. Bigelow kept shaking.

So did Johna. Was she out of her mind, she asked herself, going into the bowels of London with no more protection than her spastic solicitor? She'd been concerned about gossip when she sent her coach home, along with the driver, the footman, and the maid who would have noted her destination. Johna insisted Bigelow hire a hackney, to protect her reputation. Lud, she should have worried about her life. This section of town was dark and dirty, filled with the reek of poverty. No one would know where she was going so no one would know if she ever got there.

Johna wished she had a pistol. She wished she knew how to use a pistol. She vowed to learn tomorrow, if she lived that long. No, she'd look on the bright side: it was still morning. Surely villains waited for dark to go about their evil business. After luncheon, for certain. Johna could get this imminent catastrophe averted and still be home in time for the jaunt to the museum, or a fit of apoplexy, whichever came first.

The hired coach pulled to a stop at the entrance to a shadowed alley. "Oi'll bide 'ere an 'arf an 'our, then ye're on yer own," the jarvey told them, shaking his head at their foolhardy errand. He spit over the side of the carriage to punctuate his disdain for cork-brained Cits like Bigelow, bringing his gentry mort to a dive like this.

Bigelow gestured toward the painted board on the corner building. "Are you sure you want to do this, my lady?"

The black parrot on the sign looked more like a vulture to Johna. "What happens to this place if I die?"

Bigelow had his hand on the carriage door, rattling it. "Then it becomes your heir's property, of course. According to the will you drew up, your sister's."

Nothing could have put courage into Johna's steps faster than being reminded of the threat to Phillipa's well-being. "Never!" She got down, holding her skirts away from the foulness in the street. She let Bigelow take her arm up the four grimy steps to the black wood door that had a parrot's head for a knocker.

"Should we knock?" Johna was sure her knees were already knocking. "Is there a footman?" Was there a certain etiquette involved in evicting an unknown, unwanted tenant?

Mr. Bigelow just pushed the door open and led her inside. It took a few moments for Johna's eyes to adjust from the dismal gray of the street to the more dismal gray of the interior. She almost gagged on the stench of rancid smoke, unwashed bodies, and cheap perfume. "I own this horrible place?"

The Black Parrot had its head tucked under its flea-bitten wing this early in the day. There were very few patrons, a handful of huddled men Johna didn't recognize, thankfully, looking as if they hadn't gone home for the night, for many nights. Two or three women sat or sprawled in the corners. One snored. Johna decided she wouldn't examine the women too closely.

"Dealers," Mr. Bigelow whispered, mopping his brow, hoping she wouldn't ask what they dealt in. "I'll go find Marcel."

What, and leave her here? "I'll go with you."

"You cannot go upstairs!" Bigelow squeaked. "That is, perhaps the man is in his office. We'll look there first." He led her down an even darker corridor where damp-stained paintings of nude females hung unevenly on the paneled walls. Thank goodness for mildew, Johna thought for the first time in her tidy life.

The office was better lighted, so Marcel could count the piles of coins in front of him. He looked up with a snarl, a hyena defending its carrion booty. *"Qu'est-ce que c'est?"* He stood when he recognized the lawyer, unfolding to spindly height.

The man was so emaciated, his cooking must be dreadful, Johna thought. And he was so dirty, filth under his nails, oil pasting his hair to his scalp, that she wouldn't have let him in her kitchen to clean the stove.

Bigelow made the introductions.

Marcel turned to Johna with an unctuously ingratiating smile, blackened teeth and all. "Ah, but you find me unprepared. If I had known of your visit, I would have made my *specialité,* mousse a la Marcel." He kissed his dirty fingertips, then waved them around the nearly empty room. "Instead I do not have even the chore to offer you."

"He means 'chair,'" Bigelow interpreted. At Johna's nod of encouragement, he went on: "And this isn't a social call. Lady Ogden wants to close down the Black Parrot and sell the building." Having explained their mission, the solicitor spotted an unfinished glass of wine on Marcel's desk. If the Frenchman was drinking it, the stuff couldn't be dangerous. Bigelow gulped it down, almost wishing it were drugged.

Marcel was still being polite, although he did not offer her any of the wine. "Then I am sorry you made this visit for nothing, Madame Ogden. But you cannot close the Black Parrot, *n'est-ce-pas?* Your husband and I, we have the partnership."

"My husband is dead. The partnership is dissolved. Besides, I thought it was a lease."

Marcel shrugged. "Lease, partnership, my *Anglais* is not so good. *Tant pis.* Either way, you cannot be throwing me up. Out? *Oui,* throwing me out. You tell her, Monsieur Bigelow. It is a matter of law, no?"

Bigelow was feeling better. He'd feel better still if Marcel weren't towering over him, so he backed toward a dark corner of the office, pretending to read the titles on the bookcase shelf. "I tried to explain."

Johna had faced the Almack's patronesses. One filthy French felon was not going to faze her. She did take a step backward, though, so she wasn't having to crane her neck upward, and so she did not have to inhale Marcel's foul breath. "What Mr. Bigelow tried to explain was that the usual money was not being paid to my account. That sounds very much as if the terms of the agreement are invalidated."

"Ah, the money. Now I see. Marcel has a bad month, and madame grows impatient to buy another trumpet."

"Trinket? No, you don't see. I would not keep this ... this insult to decency open for any amount of money, and there is nothing you can do about it. Are you going to take me to court? Do you think your operations will stand the light of day?"

"Bah, you will not make me try. You would not want your connection here to be made pubic."

Bigelow choked. For once Johna didn't care, she was so angry. Let the man suffocate on his own guilt. "Are you threatening to expose me? I'd rather it be known that I was trying to rid myself of this hellhole than that I condoned it! The club is closed as of immediately. You and your slime will be gone by the end of the week. The building is now for sale. *Le Parrot Noir c'est fini.*"

"Your accent, feh! And your demands, they are like cockroaches in the kitchen. You sweep them away or step on them"—he made a damp, sucking sound—"or you add them to the stew."

Johna's stomach turned at the thought. "No wonder you couldn't make a go of this place as a supper club."

"*Tiens,* now you insult Marcel's cooking?"

Bigelow groaned.

"I don't care if you cook bat blood for Beelzebub! You will *not* do it here!"

With a guttural roar, Marcel lunged. Before Johna could step back, his hands were at her throat, squeezing. "What, do you think Marcel takes orders from some murdering English whore? I'll teach you to stick your nose in my business, *chérie*. I cut it off, eh, so you don't have to smell Marcel's bad breast. Close my rooms? I close your mouth—for good."

Johna was struggling mightily, kicking out at his legs, trying to connect her flailing fists with the Frenchman's head. The dastard's arms were so wretchedly long, though, that she wasn't reaching. A red haze was beginning to cloud her eyes, and she could barely hear Mr. Bigelow's hysterical shouting. She started clawing at Marcel's hands at her throat, digging her nails into his fingers.

"*Chien!* I'll see you in hell. When you get there, say *bonjour* to your murdered—"

Marcel's next words were abbreviated, stoppered by the fist in his mouth.

Merle didn't know why Johna was here. He couldn't begin to imagine, but he'd shake that out of her later, after he took apart this ape who dared to lay his foul hands on her.

Marcel shoved Johna away from him, into a wall, so he could face this new challenger. "*Mon Dieu,* the Black Widow has a new *chevalier.* You chose better this time, *chérie,* but this one won't stick his fork in the wall so easily. Marcel will help, no?"

"No!" Johna croaked. "He's not my—"

The men were trading punches. Selcrest had the strength and the science, but Marcel had the reach.

One of the viscount's eyes was swelling shut, but Marcel kept spitting blood and teeth out of his mouth. When Selcrest's next punch connected with the Frenchman's nose and flattened it against his face, Marcel had enough.

The cook was cadaverously thin but he was strong, and he was a dirty fighter. A knife appeared in his hand. Johna screamed. Selcrest backed out of range. Hadn't he played this role before, the day he met the impossible female? He shook his head to clear it.

"*Que mal* you didn't get a ring from this one," Marcel mumbled through battered lips. "You'd be a richer widow tomorrow."

Mr. Bigelow peeked over the desk he was hiding behind to see what was happening. He saw Marcel's back and he saw Marcel's knife shifting from the Frenchman's right hand to his left. So he picked up the desk chair—the only chair in the room—and brought it down on Marcel's head. The fight was over.

Johna snatched up the knife and waved it under Marcel's streaming nose where he lay on the stained carpet. "If you're not gone by tomorrow morning, or if you ever bother us again, his lordship will ... will have your guts for garters."

Selcrest raised his eyebrows but he nodded, taking the knife from her hand. "Count on it, you miserable scum." He turned toward Bigelow. "I don't know your name, sir, but I am in your debt." They shook hands, then the viscount softly inquired, "Are you quite finished here, my lady?"

Johna ignored the dripping sarcasm. "I do believe that I have made my position clear to Monsieur Marcel. Mr. Bigelow, I shall be leaving with his lordship. You shall find a buyer for this hellish place tomorrow or you shall find a new client. I do not care what pittance you accept, just get rid of it."

"Is your throat very sore, Jo?" Somewhere between the Black Parrot and her place by his side on the curricle's seat she'd become Jo to him.

"N-not terribly, Merle."

"That's good. And it's also good that my hands are busy with the reins."

"It is?"

"Oh, yes, or I'd strangle you too."

6.

"How could you be so blasted stupid?" Selcrest yelled as soon as they were alone in Johna's drawing room. He'd held as tight a rein on his temper as on the horses during the drive back to Albemarle Street. Then came the interminable wait for the servants to bring tea—with honey for her bruised throat—and brandy for his bruised nerves. Selcrest's mood wasn't improved by the sideways glances he received from the footmen and maidservants. Nor by the niffy-naffy butler's inquiry: "Another steak, milord, for your eye?"

He couldn't see out of it, so the thing must be deuced ugly. He'd worry later how the devil he was going to get past his mother and Higbee this time. Right now his swollen phiz couldn't be half as ugly as the red welts he could see on Johna's slender neck. Ugly? Those marks turned his stomach inside out. Hell and damnation, he should have butchered the bastard who did this to her.

Merle kept pacing, trying to keep his blood from boiling. "Dash it all, woman, what were you thinking, going to a place like that? And going alone?"

"I thought I was doing the right thing," Johna managed to whisper through trembling lips. Turning her head to watch him walk from her sofa to the mantel to the window and back was making her neck ache even more. "And Mr. Bigelow was with me."

"The pinchbeck pettifogger who got you into the mess in the first place? The man's a tosspot if I ever saw one." Merle took another sip, frowning into his glass of spirits as he remembered the solicitor's quaking hand. He slammed the glass down onto the mantel and resumed his circuit. "And a scurvy lot of help he was, hiding under the desk. I didn't even know he was there until he crowned that maniac. And you tell me what's right about a lady traipsing through London's worst stews. Nothing, that's what! If you had a problem, why the hell didn't you come to me, Johna? My mother is looking out for you. That makes you my responsibility!"

"No, your mother has done a world of good for my sister and myself. That's enough. You are not obliged to do anything more, certainly not act as guardian to us, or trustee. And I suppose I didn't think my actions through," she conceded. "I was so disgusted, I just wanted to get the deed done." Johna was close to tears from the pain, from the shock, from the anger she read in his one-eyed scowl and relentless pacing.

"I know you are furious with me for landing you in such a hobble. And I know I broke our agreement that there would be no scandalous behavior. So what now? Will you wash your hands of us or denounce me to your mother's friends? I've blotted my copy-book, but poor Phillipa doesn't deserve to be ostracized. That's what will happen, you know, if you ... if you turn your back on us."

Merle strode over to the sofa and bent down so he could look her in the eye. Hers were damp; one of his was swollen shut. "Are you that big a peagoose, or do you think me that much a snob? Can't you see that I don't give a rap about the scandal, Jo? My God, you could have been killed."

"Oh, and you too, coming to save me. I'd never have forgiven myself. And your poor eye." She was crying in earnest now, so it was only natural for Merle to take her in his arms for comforting. She fit so perfectly, it was only natural for him to kiss away her tears. And then her fears. "It's all right, sweetheart. Everyone is safe now. Nothing is going to happen to you or your sister. I won't let it."

Amazing how a kiss could cure a sore throat and a stiff neck and shattered composure. Johna sighed.

"What, did I hurt you?" He jumped back. "I never meant—Lud, only a ham-handed cad would paw at you at a time like this. I beg your pardon, my lady."

Johna sighed again, in contentment. "You do care."

"Care? I ..." It was obviously a new and troubling concept for the viscount. He tried to fix Johna's disarranged hair, tucking a black lock behind her ear. It felt like silk running through his fingers. Care? Oh, Lud. "I care that my mother would be devastated if anything befell her protégée."

Johna touched his cheek and smiled. "You care. I know you do."

Merle turned his head and kissed her palm. "I care enough that if you ever give me such a fright again, I'll thrash you within an inch of your life."

So she sent for him that night, when Marcel tried to burn down the Black Parrot.

If Marcel was going to lose his investment, so was Ogden's widow. He waited till early evening, before the club was officially open for business, then tossed some Blue Ruin at the heavy, faded draperies that kept the gaming parlor shielded from the street. But the pervading dampness and years of leaks made the fabric hard to burn. That and Marcel has used the watered gin. So he went back to the kitchen.

There was so much grease on every surface, so many dirty rags, he had no trouble getting a good fire going, before he got going. Marcel left a message on the front door, right under the parrot's beak: "Ogden's widow owns these asses."

So the constables knew right where to come, to report the fire. "He must have meant ashes, ma'am."

Johna sent a note to Bigelow, another to the viscount. Merle was easily found at Selcrest House, at home like Johna was, hiding his bruises. She could cover the marks with a high-necked gown or scarf, not unreasonable with the November chill. There wasn't much Selcrest could do with a swollen, empurpled orb, except lie. He'd already told his mother and Higbee that a sparring partner at Jackson's had landed a flush hit, but he couldn't tell that to the chaps who'd been at the boxing parlor that morning. A riding accident? Footpads? Neither reflected well on Lord Selcrest, so he stayed in, waiting for the morrow when the swelling would go down and cosmetics should cover most of the violent colors. Perhaps by then he'd come to his senses, too.

He arrived within minutes of receiving Johna's message. "You are not going, period."

"It's my business. I have to go."

"You called on me for help, dash it, now let me help."

"I asked for your help, as you demanded this afternoon. Help, not supervision. The constables said some of the occupants in the building were injured, although there were no fatalities, thank goodness. I couldn't have borne that, someone dying because Marcel hated me so much. But I own the building, therefore it is my duty to see that the people in it get care. I can make sure they are taken to the hospital if they need it, or found a place to spend the night."

"What, you are worried about the dregs of humanity who live and work at a place like the Black Parrot? I admire your sense of duty, but that rabble can find their own way around the back alleys and gin mills. It's too dangerous for you to go. Didn't you learn anything this afternoon?"

"The constables said Marcel was likely halfway to France by now. His note was practically a confession of guilt, so he wouldn't chance being caught and hung."

"One cockle-headed cook isn't half as dangerous as the rest of the neighborhood. You saw it at its best, by daylight. By night every kind of slime crawls out from under their rocks to prey on unwary strays. You're not going, and that's final."

The fire wasn't even smoldering when they arrived. Most of the crowds dispersed when the constables from the sheriff's office joined the Watch, the fire inspector, and two runners from Bow Street. A small knot of women surrounding Mr. Bigelow were passing a bottle of rum, for their tiny coal-filled brazier wasn't putting out nearly enough heat in the raw night.

Bigelow separated himself from the group when he recognized the viscount's curricle. He carried a lantern over to the open carriage, where Selcrest's tiger had gone to the horses' heads to keep them calm amid the threatening cloud of smoke. Bigelow waited for the viscount to help Lady Johna down. "According to the fire inspector, the structure appears sound. He won't know for sure until daylight, of course, but the interior is pretty well demolished." He shook his head. "No one will buy the place now. Costs too much to renovate these old buildings."

Johna was staring at the handful of women who were inching closer. The shape of one in particular caught her eye. "That's fine, I'm not selling. I'll turn it into a home for unwed mothers instead. It will be a memorial to my husband."

"But ... but Sir Otis would have hated the idea!"

"Yes, I know. That must mean it's a worthy cause. The Otis Ogden Hospital and Foundling Home."

Selcrest patted her hand, which he was holding firmly by his side. "And I'll help finance the renovations."

One of the women, the one who had put the idea in Johna's head in the first place, called out, "That's the ticket, lovey, then I'll have somewheres to go."

"That's all right for Mimi, for later," the oldest of the drooping females said, "but what about the rest of us, lady, for tonight?"

All of the women came forward now. They ranged from younger than Phillipa to tired middle age. The card-dealers had soot-darkened faces, some with tear streaks running down their cheeks.

"Is anyone hurt?" Johna asked.

"Lorraine found some salve in the pantry," Mimi told her. "It works fine."

Lorraine was also the spokesperson for the others. "Marcel took everything with him, without leaving our fair share. All our clothes and such is burned and ruined. We ain't got nothing, and nowhere to go."

Johna started to say, "I have roo—" when the viscount's arm clamped down on hers.

"No!"

"Then perhaps you could give them shelter until other arrangements can be made. Surely there's more than enough space to spare at—"

"No," Merle hissed in Johna's ear. "Think of your sister!"

"I am. I wouldn't want her left out in the cold."

Selcrest dragged her a few steps away from the others. "Deuce take it, Jo, they're prostitutes!"

"Not dealers?"

"They might cut the deck for an occasional hand, but that's not their purpose for being here, or for all those little rooms upstairs."

"They still need help." Obviously, Johna was going to have to do it herself; his lordship couldn't lower himself to expend his pity on these unfortunate females who had to put up with the likes of Sir Otis on a nightly basis. She shook his arm off.

While she was thinking what was best to do, another one of the women peered in the viscount's direction, clutching a thin blanket around her shoulders. "Silky, is that you?"

"Silky?"

Everyone turned to stare at Lord Selcrest: Johna and the lightskirts, Bigelow and the minions of the law, two would-be customers at the Black Parrot, three passersby, and his own tiger. The only ones not gawking at him were the horses.

Lorraine pinched the speaker's arm. "Hush up, Kitty."

But Kitty waved the bottle of rum in the air and giggled. "At least I didn't call him Shorty." She giggled again. "Or Speedy."

Two of the other tarts and one of the Runners thought this was hysterical. So did Johna. The great and noble, high-and-mighty, stuffed-shirt lordship had feet of clay after all! And he'd just fallen off his pedestal. She joined the others' laughter.

At least no one could see Merle's scarlet blush. He grabbed Johna's arm and none too gently turned her toward his curricle. "You wait in the carriage. I'll make arrangements for your new friends."

When Selcrest came back to take the reins from his tiger, he told the grinning servant, "If one word of this night's work gets out, I'll make a rug out of you." After he settled next to Johna on the narrow seat and gave the horses the signal to start, Merle stared straight ahead. "Don't ask. You don't know those females, you never saw them. And if you don't stop giggling, I'll leave you here with them."

Merle wanted his family—and Johna's—to leave for his country estate on the instant. They'd avoid any gossip, have an extra week or two to prepare for the holidays, and put Johna out of harm's way in case that thatchgallows Frenchman tried more mischief. The paperwork was completed for Denton's commission, so there was nothing holding them in London.

"Nothing? What, did you forget that I am throwing a ball in two weeks? The acceptances are in, the food is ordered, the orchestra—"

"Confound it, Jo, it isn't safe! The man is a Bedlamite, setting fire to places where people live."

"Then I'll hire some extra watchmen. And thank you for the invitation"—it was actually more of a summons—"but Phillipa and I intend to spend Christmas in Berkshire."

"I think your sister will have something to say about that. If Denton is shipping out in the New Year, don't you think you should let them spend Christmas together with Mother at Seacrest?"

"Perhaps Phillipa could go by herself. Your mother is adequate chaperone, of course. It's time I saw how the renovations are going to Hutchison Manor."

"What, go off by yourself to have Christmas alone in a moldering old pile under construction? Are you dicked in the nob?"

No, she was just afraid to spend any more time in the viscount's presence.

7.

Johna opened the ball with Selcrest as her partner. Let the tongues wag, Johna had decided, she was going to enjoy her last night among the *ton*. In three days, Selcrest was escorting all of them to Suffolk. Johna had agreed, in return for Phillipa and Denton agreeing not to become engaged before they left London. An understanding between them was obvious,

Phillipa, glowing like a sunbeam in her primrose gown, danced with the handsome young officer, so proud in his scarlet regimentals. Johna couldn't deny them their last few weeks together.

She was adamant, though, about not having a formal announcement. That way, for one thing, Phillipa could change her mind, or Denton could. The looks they shared, the adoring gazes, the thread that seemed to connect them even when others were present, didn't make such an occurrence likely, no matter how long he was off fighting. But, too, Phillipa would not be plunged back into mourning if, heaven forbid, Denton did not return from the war. Johna prayed nothing would happen to break her sister's heart.

It was too late for her own. Going to Merle's home in Suffolk was what she wanted to do, of course, but what she positively knew she shouldn't do. The more she saw of Selcrest now, the more she'd hurt later. There was no later for them.

Johna saw the way Merle resigned himself to his mother's foibles, the way he fretted over his brother's welfare. He'd even hired a squad of Bow Street Runners to watch over her and her household. His own mother might call Selcrest a twiddlepoop for his fastidious decorum, but Johna knew better. The man was genuinely kind. He wouldn't mean to break Johna's heart, but he would. He wasn't going off to die for his country; he just wasn't going to offer for her. When she and Phillipa went home to Berkshire after Christmas, Phillipa would wait for Denton to come back. Johna would wait for Merle to come to his senses. One sister had hope; the other, none.

Johna was sure he liked her and cared for her, beyond feeling responsible for her well-being. Even Sir

Otis had a favorite pointer in his kennel. Selcrest might just be coming to love her. Lud knew he was attracted to her, and had been right from last summer in Brighton. He would never be happy with all her fits and starts, however, the legacy from her husband and father. It would be torturing him with another Original like his mother. Johna wouldn't have a spouse like her own parent, so she couldn't blame him, but no matter what she did, scandal was always a hairsbreadth away, it seemed.

But, oh, it felt good to be in his arms for this dance! Later she'd remember the dreams she'd had, dreams that had all fallen short. Her sister'd had her pick of all the eligibles—and had chosen a hot-spurred second son. Johna'd fought for her legitimate place in society—and found it was not worth holding when she couldn't hold this man. Where she thought she'd never marry again, now she felt she'd never be whole again.

She was glad that the ball was a success, at least. There'd been thirty to dinner earlier, and that too had been superb, with compliments to her on the menu, the service, the urns of flowers everywhere. The company enjoyed the extra remove or two that she hadn't recalled ordering, so she did not fret over the meal. She'd been too nervous to do more than nibble at anything herself. Perhaps Cook had trouble with the preparations or ingredients and had to make substitutions. Johna well knew that good cooking had to be a flexible art form.

That dinner was about as flexible as cooking could be: eel in aspic—and arsenic; carrots with caramel sauce and castor oil; ipecac in the poached perch; mouse poison in the mousse.

Mousse? Johna assumed Gunther's had made an error. She'd never have ordered such a dessert, not after— No, she wouldn't think about it!

Unfortunately Lord and Lady Throckmorton couldn't stay after dinner for the ball; his gout was acting up. Princess Lieven and the dyspeptic Russian ambassador left early too. Everyone else stayed to greet the rest of Johna's nearly two hundred guests. Her ball was not quite a squeeze, there still being room to sit or stand, but it was definitely a success. Long after the receiving line had been dispersed so that Johna could open the dancing, the butler was still announcing names. Every title, every prominent honorific, was a sonorous declaration of Johna's social standing. The only one missing was the Prince Regent himself. That would have put the seal on Johna's triumph, but she couldn't have everything, she allowed.

Everyone was eating and drinking, laughing and gossiping. The talk was mostly about Johna and Selcrest, not Johna and the Black Parrot. Speculation reached a new high when he stood by her side after the opening set, greeting latecomers instead of fleeing to the card room. He had to know they were feeding the rumor mills, so she didn't bother to mention the lapse, not when it seemed the most natural thing in the world to have him next to her.

Then one of Phillipa's friends got sick. Johna had to escort the girl to the ladies' retiring room where her own maid could tend the chit until her mother could be found.

"Too much excitement, don't you know," that lady declared. "Silly twits starve themselves, then sneak off to the punch bowl. They'll learn," she added as another green-tinged female entered the room.

Johna went back down to find Selcrest waiting at the foot of the stairs, with his mother accepting farewells in Johna's stead as another couple left. "Lady Cheyne's not feeling at all the thing," she told Johna. "An interesting condition, I'd guess."

It might be interesting, but she wasn't alone in the condition. More gentlemen were visiting the necessary out back, more ladies were needing to lie down. More guests were leaving, with regrets.

"Won't you stay for supper, Lord Alvanley?"

"Sorry, another function to attend. Press of invitations, don't you know." That and the pressing pain in his midsection.

"Did you happen to have the truffled grouse at dinner, Jo?" Selcrest asked as they bade another guest good-bye at the door to the ballroom.

"No, I was too tense to eat anything. Why? Did you?"

"No, I never cared much for it. It's always been one of Denton's favorites, though."

"Yes, that's what Phillipa said, so I put it on the menu." She was looking around, searching through the thinning crowds. "Oh dear, I don't see either one of them. And they promised not to go off alone."

"Don't worry, Denton is out in your garden, wishing he were already in Spain eating army food. And I believe one of the footmen carried Phillipa up to her room."

"And you think the grouse was tainted? Good heavens, how could such a thing happen?"

"It happens all the time, cream gone rancid, oysters out of season." Selcrest was patting her hand for reassurance, but he was frowning, scanning the row of gilded chairs where the chaperones and companions sat. They were almost all nodding off to sleep or fallen over in their seats. "But not all of these people were at dinner. I don't understand what's going on."

Neither did Johna, when they returned to the hall-way and she saw her head footman, not the butler, handing guests their hats and canes and cloaks. "Where is Jenkins, William? It's not like him to be away from the door."

"Mr. Jenkins took ill, milady. Just sort of keeled over, he did, right into a potted fern. But I can manage things here, and the new cook says he's got the late supper in hand, so there's nothing to worry about, ma'am."

"Nothing to worry about when my guests are falling like— What new cook?"

The footman looked at her as if she'd sprouted an-other nose. "The cook who arrived this morning, say-ing you sent for him when his cousin Alphonse came down with the influenza."

"That explains the changes in the menu, but I never sent for anyone—and Alphonse doesn't have a cousin!"

Johna and the viscount looked at each other and simultaneously shouted, "Marcel!"

"Damn, I had all those Runners and guards trying to protect you from someone who was already here!" Merle turned to leave her. "I'll gather them up and go find that hell-spawn. This time he's not getting away."

"Wait! We have to tell everyone not to eat any more of the food!"

"I don't think you have to tell them."

Guests were filing past Johna and the viscount with barely courteous farewells. It was not quite a panic, more a hurried exodus. Then Johna heard some mut-terings about the Black Widow. "Oh, my Lord, they think I've poisoned them!"

Someone heard the word "poison." There was a stampede for the door.

Marcel was having a grand time. He meant to destroy Lady Otis, not necessarily kill her guests, but if they died, *c'est la vie*. Or *la morte*. Revenge was sweet, and so was the syrup of poppies he'd been pouring into the champagne bottles as fast as that so-proper butler ordered them opened. Marcel had seen how Jenkins tasted each bottle before letting the footmen serve it. Jenkins didn't have his nose in the ear now.

Marcel should have left, but he was having too much fun watching all the servants scurry around for basins and bowls and clean towels. When he heard Selcrest shout, "To me, men, secure the kitchen," he didn't bother trying to flee. He'd seen all the guards outside. Instead he pulled a pistol from under his apron.

As soon as Selcrest came through the door, Marcel fired. The distance was too great and Marcel's aim too uncertain for the ball to find its intended target, but it did hit a stack of dirty dishes, sending food scraps and china fragments in every direction.

"Stop," Marcel ordered, "or I shoot again. This time I don't muss."

This time Selcrest was so close that Marcel couldn't miss, if he had another shot. He fired. Nothing happened. The Frenchman stared at the gun. "I told that oaf I wanted a reporter!"

A slim, bespectacled fellow with a pad and pencil stood up. "That's what you wanted, a repeater? You, monsieur, are a jackass. But I thank you. What a story I got. 'Bellyache at the Ball'? 'Misery on Albemarle Street'?"

Now Selcrest had two maggots to dispose of. The reporter was in his way, so he tossed him aside first.

Johna was right behind him, wielding a heavy skillet from the cookstove. "You ruined my ball! You poisoned half the haut monde, and you shot at us! I'll see you in—"

Marcel made a grab for her. Perhaps he intended to take Johna hostage, or just to finish the job he'd started earlier. But he forgot about the broken crockery and splattered foodstuffs all over the floor. So he slipped and skidded, right to her feet—so Johna bashed him over the head with the iron skillet. Runners and hired guards and footmen and grooms from the stable, armed with pitchforks, rushed into the kitchen. In short order they had Marcel trussed like the Christmas goose, ready to be dragged off to Newgate. In all the commotion, the reporter made his escape.

"It will be in all the papers." Johna whimpered into her lemonade—made with her own hands from fresh ingredients.

Merle was beside her, dusting cobwebs from his once-elegant evening attire. He'd been down in the wine cellars unearthing unopened, unadulterated, vintages to serve the few remaining guests. "Yes, but such a juicy tidbit would have made the *on-dits* columns anyway, with so many prominent people involved. It likely would have been mentioned with the criminal proceedings, too. Now, at least, if that reporter does his job, everyone will know that you had nothing to do with the whole mingle-mangle."

"They'll also know I had something to do with Marcel. It will all come out now, the entire sorry mess. My reputation will be destroyed. They'll hold me responsible, anyway, those old tabbies. You know they will."

"So what? You're still the same person, so your friends will understand. And remember, no one was seriously injured. Bow Street found all sorts of bottles and packets, but just small amounts of various poisons. You'll have to throw away anything that dirty dish might have touched, but other than that, you are quite lucky, my dear."

"Lucky?" That wasn't the word Johna would have used.

"Indeed, with a great deal to be thankful for."

"You should be thankful I don't still have the skillet in my hands."

Merle laughed. "Truly, Jo, you can be thankful the Prince didn't come. Poisoning him would be treason."

8.

They'd all recover, the diners, the drinkers, and the denizens of Albemarle Street. Cook was found tied and gagged behind the tavern he frequented, and Jenkins submitted his resignation, for such a lapse in good butling.

Lady Selcrest chose to be amused. "The polite world can use a good purge now and again. They'll get over it by the spring Season. You wait and see, you'll be welcomed back to London with open arms."

Open or shut, Johna wasn't coming back. She'd stay on in Berkshire and raise roses and rabbits, like Lady Selcrest. No, she'd get herself a little dog and name it Sunshine, so she'd have a ray of brightness in her long, empty days.

For now, she couldn't wait to be gone. The knocker was already off the door; they were just waiting for Phillipa to regain her energy before leaving for Selcrest's Suffolk estate. A month in his company, though, might prove more torturous than staying to face the censure of society.

He hated her, that's all she could think. Why else would be leave for the country without them? Selcrest had left her alone to write the hundred notes of apology, to face the hundred curious columnists wanting to see the scene of the crime. At least Jenkins agreed to stay on to keep the onlookers at bay.

Selcrest said he had to go get things ready, as if the man didn't have an army of servants to see to his every comfort and that of whatever guests he might invite. Selcrest said Denton would be escort enough, as if the silly mooncalf had eyes for anyone else but Phillipa. Selcrest said he was looking forward to having Johna at his family home—Hah! John didn't believe a word the two-faced peer said. He'd been bumped and bruised, almost stabbed, almost shot, and almost poisoned—all on account of her. Now his name was on everyone's tongue again, connected to a lurid, ludicrous, hideous hobble. He hated her, and she couldn't blame him.

Everything had to be perfect for his brave girl, Merle decided. No gossip, no danger, no worries over people liking her. If he had his way, she'd never have another worry in this world. Then again, if Selcrest had his way, she'd be in his room, in his bed, in his arms this very minute, so he had to leave London. He'd leave her some shred of reputation while he still had some self-control. A week wasn't long—just two lifetimes.

Everything *was* perfect, Johna thought. Perhaps his lordship had needed the time in Suffolk after all, for she'd never seen a lovelier place. Seacrest was constructed of mellow brick, comfortably nestled among sprawling gardens and stands of wood, evergreens and holly instead of crouching like a fortress on a bare hill, as so many other great houses did. The house itself was immense, but all one style, having been totally rebuilt in the last century, after a fire. Somehow Johna didn't find the place overwhelming, although Hutchison Manor would have fit in the front hall.

Maybe she felt so welcome because he was there, or because Christmas was there. Every sight and smell of the season was present except for the snow, and Selcrest apologized for that, but thought they might have some soon. If anyone could organize the weather, Johna thought, he could.

There were pine boughs and holly and red velvet ribbons, clove-studded apples and scented candles and hanging balls of mistletoe that Phillipa and Denton just happened to find, no matter how often Johna moved them. There were minced meat pies and gingerbread, mulled cider and lamb's wool punch. Every tradition, every special festive delicacy, was done just right, for her.

"Oh, we never bother doing up the whole pile," Lady Selcrest told Johna before disappearing after Higbee to see about releasing her pets from their traveling boxes. "Just the occasional ribbon or wreath if the maids remember to fix them."

Even more telling—and more touching—to Johna

was how Merle didn't appear to be ashamed of her. He invited all of his neighbors in, both high and low, although most of them would have heard of the London debacle. The viscount proudly introduced her to all of them, even taking her with him on his rounds of the estate to meet his tenants, where he knew the name of every child and half the watchdogs. Mounted on a pretty mare from his excellent stables, Johna felt welcome. He let her feel useful, too, helping fill Christmas baskets for his dependents, helping to wrap dolls and toy soldiers for all those children. Her only complaint was that he wouldn't let her near the kitchens. It was her holiday, he argued, but she had to wonder.

Phillipa and Denton, meanwhile, were gone for hours on long walks, sightseeing rides, paying calls on the young people in the vicinity. Rules were more relaxed in the country, Lady Selcrest assured Johna, who was so used to worrying about her sister's reputation. In the evenings when there were no guests they all sang the old carols. Then Phillipa and Denton whispered in the corner of the drawing room while the others—and Higbee—played cards.

Lady Selcrest took to retiring early and taking naps in the afternoon. "Too much gadding about," she declared. "You won't mind organizing the Christmas dinner, will you, Johna dear? We usually have twenty or thirty guests, sometimes dancing after. Do whatever you wish. Talk to Frye. He's the underbutler who stays here when Higbee goes with us to London. The man needs a bit more experience, and I need Higbee with me. There's a new breed of rabbit I want to research. Wouldn't think of bothering Selcrest to escort me."

Frye was well up to the task of planning a small

function, but deferred all decisions to Johna. Then the housekeeper took to consulting her, with Lady Selcrest generally unavailable or uninterested. The gardeners needed to know which plants to bring up from the conservatory, and Mrs. Tibbetts, the wondrously English cook, sought her preferences for the menu. And the rest of the menus, not just the Christmas dinner? Johna agreed to look them over too.

Johna adored the house and its people, the tenants, and the neighbors, and she was pleased to be of service to Lady Selcrest for all that woman had done for them. She just couldn't understand, however, how it came about that everyone considered her, a disreputable widow, as chatelaine of Seacrest. Embarrassed, afraid she was causing him more aggravation still, Johna went to the viscount. She didn't want him thinking her encroaching or a managing type of female.

"But you are, managing the place, that is, and everyone knows it. Capably too, I might add."

They were in his curricle, driving to the next town so Johna could complete her Christmas shopping, now that she had so many new friends among the staff and neighbors. "Silly goose, you've already given us so much just by coming," Merle told her, warming Johna to the tips of her boot-clad toes, despite the freezing temperature. "I cannot tell you how much I appreciate all the help you've been to my mother."

"It's my pleasure to relieve her of any chores, you know that. Lady Selcrest seems less careworn these past days, don't you think?"

"Yes, with your help. I thought she was upset about Denton's leaving. I suppose she's resigned herself now."

"And Phillipa, too. She doesn't have that grim look anymore. You were right about not separating them. She's had this time to learn to be brave."

Johna admired her sister's fortitude. She didn't know if she could face losing the man she loved without falling to pieces. She was having enough trouble facing the man she loved, period, knowing their time was limited. If Johna weren't so busy, she told herself, she just might go into a decline.

Phillipa was being noble, her loving sister thought, hiding her distress for Denton's sake. She smiled as they all drove home from church services on Christmas Eve, and laughed as they exchanged gifts over the wassail cups. Phillipa was delighted with the ermine-lined cape from Johna, and the pearl earbobs from Lady Selcrest to go with the pearl ring Denton gave her. In return she gave Denton a fob watch with her portrait on the inside of the case, and gave Johna the new paint set she wanted. Selcrest gave Johna a gold pin—in the shape of a parrot.

They all laughed then, that Merle thought Johna needed a reminder. He liked his book and the handkerchiefs painstakingly monogrammed by both sisters with his family insignia; Lady Selcrest was pleased with the Oriental jade hare. Everyone agreed, however, that the dowager's gifts were their favorites: scarves and mittens knitted from her rabbits' fur.

Then they sang carols, led by Phillipa's lovely soprano voice as Johna played the pianoforte. They all watched Lord Selcrest light the Yule log from last year's sliver, and joined in when Higbee led the traditional servants' toast to their master's health and the prosperity of the family in the coming year.

More carols, more toasts, hugs all around, then it was time to go to bed before a busy Christmas Day. After a final embrace of her sister, with calls of "Peace and joy to you," still echoing in her head, Johna left Phillipa and Denton to make their good nights. It was Christmas, after all.

While Johna brushed her hair, waiting to hear her sister's footsteps in the room next door, she thought again how cheerful Phillipa was being, how brave.

She kept on thinking that right up to Christmas Day, at lunchtime, to be exact.

Johna was up early on Christmas morning, with many last-minute details to oversee. Then she and all the servants attended service in the family chapel. Merle read the nativity, as heads of households did this morning throughout the land. Johna thought Phillipa and Denton must have decided to attend the village church, after all. Lady Selcrest would still be abed, resting for the evening's festivities.

Then it was lunchtime, and Phillipa still had not returned. That's when Johna discovered that the pea-goose had been brave enough to elope on Christmas Eve.

There was a note. Denton had been offered a better position as aide-de-camp, it seemed, but in the American campaign. It was much farther away than the Peninsula, but Denton liked the idea of seeing the New World, perhaps carving a niche for them there once the conflict was resolved. Phillipa couldn't bear to be parted from him for so long, she wrote, and so had to go along. They'd be married by special license, by the captain of their sailing ship.

Folded inside the note was the little ring from last

year's pudding. "Now my wish can come true," Phillipa wrote. "I pray that yours can too."

"I can't even go after them to try to dissuade her," Johna cried into Selcrest's neckcloth. "They've been gone so long, and they were alone last night. Her reputation is already ruined. And I thought she was being so good, putting on a cheerful face for us."

"She was. It couldn't have been easy for her to leave you." He handed her one of his new handkerchiefs.

"I only wanted the best for her."

"And Denton will see that she gets it, I swear. But now you have to be the courageous one, my dear, for there is more bad news."

She stepped back and blew her nose. "More? My only sister has gone off to some barbaric place with your madcap brother. He'll go away to war and she'll be all alone."

"She won't be alone." He took a note out of his own pocket. "My mother is with them."

"Oh, I'm glad! That is, I'm sorry, Merle. But whyever would your mother decide to go to America in the middle of winter? I mean, even for your mother . . ."

"Higbee went too."

"Ah." There was a world of understanding in that "Ah," understanding how upset Selcrest must be, and how happy his mother and her longtime beau would be in the Colonies with no titles, no prejudices to keep them apart.

"Yes, they've also got a special license, thank goodness. In fact, Mother enclosed a third one, for us."

"Us?" There was no understanding in that syllable whatsoever.

"Well, yes, Mother knew what she was doing. You see, she was chaperoning your sister last night, but no one was chaperoning us. Your reputation is damaged far worse than Phillipa's. You've been hopelessly compromised with no chance of finding a respectable duenna for tonight either. That's what I meant about needing to be brave."

"What's bravery got to do with it? You could move in with one of your tenants for the night, or my maid and I could go to an inn."

"What, on Christmas?" He pried the little ring from her stiff fingers. "You've got the ring, I've got the license. Shall we?"

"Shall we what, Merle?"

"Get married, of course. That was Mother's intention all along, naturally, befriending you, having you take over the household, leaving us in the lurch like this so you are hopelessly compromised past redemption."

"That's fustian! You're forgetting that my name is already so tarnished my own mother wouldn't receive me. I can go on home tomorrow with no one the wiser to this latest coil except for your servants."

"And the thirty or so guests coming for dinner in three hours."

"Oh no! I have to leave, now!" Johna made a dash for the doorway, but Selcrest grabbed for her hand.

"What, and leave me to face all of them? Besides, where would you go? There's an easier way, Jo. Would it be so bad, being the new Lady Selcrest?"

"You don't wish to marry me, Merle. I cannot let your sense of duty force you into such an impossible situation."

He let go of her hand. "You're refusing me, then?"

There hadn't been a single word of love. Not even affection. "I have to."

Selcrest was studying his fingertips. "Old Lady Wilburham is coming to dinner. I'll ask her to spend the night. She's half-deaf, but will satisfy the conventions. Everyone will be too busy exclaiming over Mother and Denton to notice any irregularity. We can talk more about this later, after the guests leave."

But the guests never came.

9.

"It's me, I know it. They aren't coming because of me." Johna was wearing out the velvet of her new crimson gown, rubbing it between nervous fingers. The goose was hot, the wine was cool, and no one was there except her and the viscount. Not even old Lady Wilburham. Her sister leaving, the love of her life offering a marriage of convenience, now this fiasco of a holiday feast—this had to be the worst Christmas ever, if one discounted last Christmas and Sir Otis's demise. No, this was worse. "You see, marriage to me would cost you all your friends. We're not even married and they won't come to dinner. You'd be throwing out food every day."

Selcrest poured her a glass of sherry. "Don't be a peagoose. You have nothing to do with it."

"What then? Are your neighbors staying away because they disapprove so strongly of your mother's elopement?"

Merle drank the glass himself. "That's even more foolish. Mother's friends knew about her and Higbee for years. They'd come to laugh and drink a toast to her happiness."

"Then it's me. They're all afraid I did the cooking!

I told you word would reach Suffolk. Now you see I was right: I would ruin your life too. You wouldn't dare show your face in London."

Merle put his arm around her, but she didn't relax against him. "And that's not going to work either."

"Silly goose, I only want to show you the view." With his arm still on her shoulder, he turned her to the window and pulled the heavy drapes open. "I bet you've been too busy all day to look outside."

Johna looked, and saw nothing but white. The trees were covered, the lawns, everything.

"It's been snowing all day, a regular blizzard. I hope Mother and Denton made it to their ship before the roads became impassable. But that's why no one is going to come out on such a night, especially when they all have to travel at least three or four miles."

"You said it was going to snow."

"I said a lot of foolish things. But come, get your coat and boots and a heavy muffler. We're going for a ride to see your Christmas surprise. I meant to take you earlier, but there was too much upset and confusion."

"But it's nearly dark, and you said carriages couldn't get through."

"Carriages can't, but sleighs can. And it's not so far away, on Selcrest lands. Besides, you wouldn't want all that food to go to waste, would you?"

So they bundled up in their warmest hats and Lady Selcrest's new mittens, with hot bricks at their feet and heavy blankets over their laps. The rest of the sleigh was filled with baskets and boxes of roast goose and ham, a baron of beef, pies and punch and marzipan angels. The sturdy farm horses pulled the sleigh effortlessly, bells jingling, ribbons streaming from their harnesses.

The countryside was like a Christmas painting. No, Johna thought, it was like a magical glass snow globe that someone had shaken, with swirls and shadows and stars peeking through the clouds. She was sorry when they arrived so soon at a stone building set off the path. The structure was small but solidly built, with lights pouring from all three stories and an enormous wreath on the door.

"What is this place, Merle?"

"I'm not quite certain yet," he said, lifting her out of the sleigh. "The Otis Ogden Home for Unwed Mothers? Hutchison Hospital? You'll have to decide. I was hoping you'd select Lady Selcrest's Girls' School."

The door was opened and Johna could see Lorraine and Kitty and a much expanded Mimi shepherding a flock of nightgowned moppets up the stairs, laughing and singing Christmas carols.

"You did this, for me?" she asked, standing in the hallway.

"Don't you know I would do anything for you, my lady?" He unwrapped the muffler from around her neck. "But I did have help. Do you remember those gambling chits you were going to burn? Those chaps were so pleased to be out of Sir Otis's clutches that they all decided to contribute to the maintenance of this place."

"With a little persuasion?" Her heart was so full, Johna could have wept, if she weren't surrounded by the children and the women. They were all talking at once, exclaiming over the baskets of food, explaining how they were learning to sew and cook and read— with real teachers, too. They could go into service or make good housewives, Mimi said, eyeing the viscount's tiger, who was helping unpack the sleigh.

"So you better let him make an honest woman out of you, my lady," Lorraine teased with a wink and a nod. "We're counting on you for references, don't you know."

"One more surprise," Merle told her when they were back at his home. By chance and by Merle's maneuvering, she was standing under the mistletoe bough. So he kissed her. It was but a moment's work to warm their cold lips, faster than the wassail could have done.

Johna's thoughts went flying like the snow in the glass globe; they always did when he kissed her. And her toes were tingling. Eventually she recalled herself enough to say, "No, you've done enough. Truly, that house for the girls is the best present I could ever receive."

"Then this one is for me." He left, to return in a minute with a silver tray on which reposed a magnificent Christmas pudding.

"Oh, no, I never want to taste another spoonful of pudding!"

"You'll like this one, I swear. I didn't cook it but I prepared it myself, just for you." Merle was having trouble cutting the pudding. The knife kept hitting things.

"What in the world did you put in that pudding?"

He handed her the knife. "Here, you try slicing it."

So Johna pressed down with the blade, and a ring fell out, then another. With her next cut, more tumbled onto the plate or rolled to the floor with the nuts and candied fruits. Rings and tiny keys and little boats and coins and crumbs—but mostly rings.

"And this one goes with them." Merle reached in his pocket for a velvet pouch, and removed a diamond-and-ruby ring. "Will you marry me, my dearest Johna, and make me the happiest of men? I'm not asking out of duty or to fulfill any notion of propriety. You've given me the gift of knowing there are so many things that are more important than maintaining my dignity. Your love is the most important of all, the finest Christmas present I can imagine."

Her hands full of rings and raisins, Johna couldn't reach out for him, but she could say, "Then Merry Christmas, Merle, for I have loved you for ages, ever since I saved you from choking to death."

Selcrest didn't care how sticky she was, or how she still persisted in her rattle-pated rescue. He took her in his arms, crumbs and all. "I do love you, Jo. More than I can ever say." And he placed the ring—the ruby-and-diamond one—on her finger. "According to your sister, tradition says that the girl who finds the ring in her pudding will marry within the year. What would you say to within the week?"

"I'll marry you tomorrow, Merle, on one condition."

"Anything, my love."

"Tell me why Kitty called you Silky."

"Now that, my precious, I can only show you." He picked her up and headed for the stairs. "What was that little key for anyway? A grand opportunity, was it?"

The Wassail Bowl

❄

Mary Balogh

The great hall of Wyndham Park, with its vast two-story height and its marble pillars, its tiled floors and massive double doors, was not by any means the warmest room in the house. The twin fireplaces, facing each other across the width of the hall, were both blazing with heaped logs, but there was a great deal of space for the fires to heat and they were woefully inadequate to the task. It was the evening before Christmas Eve, a cloudy, chilly night that threatened snow.

But the Earl of Wyndham and large numbers of his family and friends and house guests were gathered in the hall rather than in the cozier drawing room abovestairs. Maids had been sent scurrying for shawls for the ladies, and chairs close to the fires had been found for the elderly. Most of the people gathered there were imbibing warm, spicy punch from the large wassail bowl set on a table facing the doors. Indeed, the contents of the bowl were already severely depleted despite the fact that those for whom it had ostensibly been prepared had not yet arrived. But another bowl was being kept warm in the kitchen belowstairs.

The village carolers were expected at any moment.

WASSAIL

There were many recipes for the punch that was served from the wassail bowl. This is one authentic recipe. It certainly sounds both sticky enough and spicy enough to have been the very one with which the Earl of Wycherly had an unfortunate encounter.

2 lemons	1 blade mace
6 cloves	6 allspice berries
1 bottle port wine	3 slices ginger root
1 cup water	⅓ cup (2 oz.) sugar cubes
1 cinnamon stick	Roasted apples (optional)

Press the cloves into one lemon and bake at 375 degrees 20 minutes. Bring to a boil port, water, and the remaining spices. Cover and let stand for 20 minutes. Return to a boil with the baked lemon and let stand for 5 minutes. Rub the sugar cubes over the rind of the other lemon and put them at the bottom of a large wassail bowl. Squeeze about half the juice of the lemon over them. Pour in the spiced port and serve while still warm with hot roasted apples floating on it, if desired.

They were to come, as they came every year on this particular evening, to cheer the company with song, to remind the earl and his guests of the joy of the season, to partake of the wassail bowl and of the mince pies and fruitcake that would be carried up by footmen when the allotted half hour of singing had been completed.

Very few of those gathered in the hall resented the fact that they were chilly. There was tradition to be observed, after all, and when all was said and done, as Horace, Lord Petersford, the earl's maternal uncle, remarked every year in his loud and jovial voice, it was in a good cause. No one had ever thought to ask the obvious question—*what* cause?

Except perhaps the Earl of Wyndham himself, though he did not do so aloud. If he had his way, he thought, hovering near the wassail bowl and smiling politely at the conversation that was flowing about him, he would listen to the carolers from the drawing room and merely send down his compliments while the servants fed them their cake and wassail. If he had his way, the carolers would not even come to Wyndham. Neither would his family and friends and guests. If he had his way, Christmas would be ignored.

He could not have his way, of course. Not that he had ever tried. Not that he had ever even voiced his preference. Christmas at Wyndham with family, friends, and assorted other guests in attendance was a tradition beyond the power of a mere earl, owner of the property, to break.

This year would be a little different from the last three, of course. The earl felt somewhat cheered at the thought. He had been disappointed today, restlessly watching the driveway all afternoon while pretending to be occupied with all sorts of other activities with his guests. He had watched until darkness fell. But only two carriages had arrived, both bringing late guests. Neither had been his own carriage, bringing his son and the boy's governess. But then, he had not really been expecting them today. He had summoned the boy, stating in his letter that he expected him to arrive no later than Christmas Eve. It had been too much to hope that they would arrive early.

Tomorrow he would come. The earl took an empty glass from the timid young companion of his great-aunt and filled it again with punch. It was Aunt Edith's fourth glass. Fortunately, as past experience had proved, Aunt Edith merely nodded quietly asleep whenever she became inebriated. And—as Uncle Horace was fond of saying with hearty good cheer—it was only once a year.

The Earl of Wyndham had seen his son only three times in the last three and a half years. Each time he had had the boy brought to London during the late spring—for a mere week each time. But this year, he had decided months before, he was going to have his son with him at Wyndham for Christmas. He was going to indulge himself. He was going to be selfish—but then he had every right to be selfish. It was time the boy came home. It was time he came home to stay. He was after all heir to all this. He was the Viscount Hedley.

And then, above the hubbub of voices and laughter, his lordship heard quite distinctly the sound of the brass knocker banging against one of the huge doors from the outside. The carolers had arrived! The slight swell of sound that followed the knock subsided into an expectant quietness and all eyes turned in the direction of the doors, both of which two footmen opened wide despite the fact that doing so admitted twice the amount of chill winter air into the already inadequately warmed hall.

But the expected crowd of singers with their lanterns and music books and flautist did not spill into the hall. Instead three people stepped inside—a young boy holding the hand of a plump and neatly dressed young woman, and behind them a slim young lady wearing a fur-trimmed green cloak and hood and carrying a blanket-bound bundle, which appeared to be another young child.

Quietness surged into delighted sound when the boy appeared, but the incipient greetings faltered again when the cloaked woman and her bundle appeared. The earl too, whose heart had leaped with sudden gladness, for whom Christmas suddenly and gloriously arrived, felt the sudden checking of his joy. It was replaced, all within a matter of seconds, by cold fury— if it was possible for fury also to be cold.

A pathway had cleared, as if by magic, from the doors to the wassail table, beside which the earl still stood. The plump young woman—the governess—released the hand of her young charge and urged him forward. He came a little uncertainly, looking very small and even younger than his six years, swathed as he was in coat and muffler and cap. Eyes as blue as his own regarded the earl warily.

The moment was ruined. His lordship had not expected his son's arrival to be such a very public affair, although everyone knew that the boy was coming. He had pictured himself seeing the carriage arrive and running down the steps outside the house to open the carriage doors himself and to lift his son out and straight into his arms. He had pictured an unabashedly fond and sentimental greeting.

Even now, with all his family and guests looking on, he might have gone down on one knee to meet his son on his own level. He might have put his arms about him and hugged him. But the moment was totally ruined. He stood where he was, his hands clasped behind him.

"Jeffrey," he said rather stiffly. "Welcome home, my son."

"Happy Christmas, sir," his son said, gazing at him with apprehensive eyes.

Belatedly, the earl thought to extend his hand to the boy, who put his small mittened hand into it. Such a small hand. His son! He looked up at the governess, who instantly bobbed him a curtsy.

"Miss Matthews?" he said.

"Yes, my lord." She bobbed another curtsy.

"I must thank you for bringing Viscount Hedley safely to Wyndham Park," he said. "I did not expect you today once darkness fell."

She glanced over her shoulder. But he was looking directly at her. It was at her his words had been directed. "We were that close, my lord," she said. "And it is not a dark night."

"I am thankful that you kept coming, then," he said. "Welcome to my home. If you step forward, my butler will be delighted to serve you with a glass from the wassail bowl."

She curtsied once more and moved ahead somewhat hesitantly. The stillness and silence in the hall had become almost a palpable thing. It was the worst of all possible situations, the earl thought as his eyes finally focused on the green-cloaked lady, who still stood with her bundle just inside the door, her chin lifted proudly, her eyes on him.

"And you, my lady," he said, his voice coldly formal. "May I offer you some wassail?" He indicated the bowl with one hand, though he did not pick up either a glass or one of the ladles.

She moved toward him then, her eyes on him the whole while, and he was half aware of a murmuring from those gathered in the hall, as if some crisis had been averted. He had been marginally polite, and she was about to accept a glass of wassail from his hands.

She stopped before the bowl. "Miss Matthews?" she said, and when the governess turned, she handed her sleeping bundle into her arms and turned back to look at the earl. He knew her well enough to recognize the tight look of anger in her face. She had been snubbed and she knew it—she could not fail to have noticed. He felt a cold triumph as he lifted the ladle from the bowl.

"Thank you," she said, "but you may have it all yourself, my lord."

It was a large and heavy bowl, difficult to lift even when empty. Two servants were required to carry it when it was full. Now it was not by any means full. Neither was it quite empty. She succeeded in lifting it. He found himself watching in foolish puzzlement and curiosity. He was facing her fully, his eyes wide open, when she dashed the contents of the bowl into his face.

Oh no, it had not by any means been empty. One of the bobbing apples caught him a smart blow on one eyebrow before bouncing off his shoulder and landing with a thud on the floor.

A gasp and a swell of sound was succeeded by renewed silence. No one wanted to miss the earl's response to such an act of gross incivility.

His eyes had closed instinctively. But he opened them without raising his hands to clear them. He clasped those at his back. His eyes stung from the spices. His head felt suddenly cold as the warm punch cooled instantly and ran in rivulets down his face and dripped from his chin onto his already soaked neck-cloth and from his hair down his neck beneath his collar. He felt cold and wet and sticky. And murderous.

She had replaced the empty bowl on the table and was rubbing her gloved hands together. Obviously they had not escaped quite unscathed from the encounter.

"Watkins," he said to his butler, not taking his stinging eyes from her—his voice was still calm and chilly, "you will have her ladyship and Miss Matthews conducted to guest rooms and Viscount Hedley to the nursery, if you please."

One corner of her mouth lifted in the suggestion of a smile before she turned to take the infant from the governess's arms into her own once more. She had not failed to notice, of course, that his instructions had made no provision for the child.

He watched them leave, a quiet little procession, before moving to take the towel one of his cousins was thrusting with a nervous flutter at his hand. He tried to wipe the sticky mess from his face. There had been a rush of sound again, but all eyes were on him, he saw when he glanced about him, and everyone fell silent again when it was obvious he was about to speak.

"The carolers will be here at any moment," he said. "I shall withdraw for a few minutes to don dry clothes. The wassail bowl will be filled again within minutes. Do please replenish your glasses. I shall rejoin you within a short while. I seriously doubt that *my wife* will do likewise."

With which speech, delivered while he dripped

sweet and sticky wassail onto the tiled floor, he made his unhurried departure for his rooms. If she were but wise enough to keep her neck out of reach of his hands for the rest of the night, he thought grimly as he took the stairs two at a time, perhaps—just perhaps—she would survive this night's insolence.

Jeffrey, ever timid, ever anxious, had eaten scarcely any supper though some had been sent up to the nursery and though he had complained of hunger during the last hour of the journey. The nursery was deserted, the other children having already been put to bed. Jane, quiet and self-contained as she usually was, had eaten all the food set on her plate. It was long past her bedtime, as it was past Jeffrey's, but she had slept in the carriage and remained awake now, though her big eyes told of her tiredness.

They were put to bed in twin beds in the same room, at their mother's insistence, despite a nurse's obvious disapproval. They were not going to be separated when they were in a strange house and among strangers. And all the guests really were strangers to the children despite the fact that their mother knew most of them and many of them were relatives.

"Mama." Jeffrey was in tears. He asked the question he had asked a number of times already, though he added something else this time. "Why did you do it? Now he will hate me."

"Oh no." She sat on the edge of his bed and smoothed a hand over his straight dark hair—her hair texture, *his* dark coloring. "No, he will never hate you, dear. He loves you. He is your papa."

"But he never comes to *see* me," the child wailed.

"He would if he could," she said, smiling warmly

at him. "He loves you dearly. Has he not sent for you now to spend Christmas here with him and with your cousins? He does not hate you, Jeffrey."

"He did not even *look* at Jane," he said.

No, he had not looked at Jane. He had behaved as if she was not there, as if she did not exist. "Jane was sleeping," she said gently. "Tomorrow he will look at her and talk to her. And to you. He loves you, dear. Both of you."

She knew she lied. He loved Jeffrey. She had never doubted that and she had never given in to the temptation of withholding the fact from their son, of trying to turn the boy against the man she hated. But he had no love at all for Jane. She doubted he would ever acknowledge her existence—except in the one way.

"Promise?" Jeffrey said now, sniffing and sounding quite pathetic.

"I promise," she said, bending to kiss him. "Sleep now. It is very late and tomorrow there will be a great deal to do. So many cousins to meet. So much fun to have."

He was settled at last. She turned to Jane, who was still awake, still quietly looking up. She had her cheek against the rather battered porcelain head of her favorite doll, an old one of her mother's she had steadfastly refused to abandon for the new doll that had been given her for her birthday.

"You will sleep, sweetheart?" She smiled at her and touched a hand to the child's auburn curls.

Jane nodded.

"Jeffrey will be close by," her mother said. "And the nurse will take care of you and keep you safe. Mama will not be far away. I will see you in the morning. Good night, sweetheart."

Large hazel eyes gazed back at her. She bent and kissed her daughter before turning reluctantly to the door.

"Mama," Jane said, "you forgot Pamela."

"And so I did," she said, turning back to kiss the doll on one cracked cheek. "Good night, Pamela."

The Countess of Wyndham closed the door softly behind her and felt her spirits drop to lodge very firmly in the soles of her slippers. But then they had been there ever since she had opened his letter one month ago, her stomach fluttering as it always did on the rare occasions when she saw his bold handwriting on the outside of a letter. He was inviting Jeffrey to spend Christmas at Wyndham Park. Though it was not really an invitation. It was an imperious summons. And it applied only to Jeffrey. She had considered defying him. She could not do without her son at Christmas of all times. But she had known such defiance would be useless.

And so she had devised a different defiance. Perhaps she could manage without Jeffrey for Christmas. She would be able to manage by pretending that it was not Christmas at all, by living for the day of his return. But Jane could not manage without her brother—or without Christmas. If Jeffrey must go to Wyndham, then Jane would go too. And if Jane was going, then of course her mother would have to go with her.

It was a decision that had terrified her, though she had not wavered from it in the days and weeks since. He had never seen Jane, never inquired after her, never sent her gifts. Well, now Jane would be beneath his roof. Perhaps he would contrive still not to see her, but beneath his roof she would remain for as long as Jeffrey stayed there. They were brother and sister and there was a close bond of affection between them.

She had not seen him in over three years, the countess thought as she made her way from the nursery wing to the apartments that had been allotted her— her old rooms beside *his*. She wondered briefly if he would have her removed to a more distant part of the house when he realized that she had been put there.

He had changed since she last saw him. Oh, he was as handsome and as elegant as he had ever been. More so, perhaps. She had never seen him dressed in black evening clothes, as he had been tonight. They suited his dark good looks and lean physique to perfection, she was forced to admit. But his face was harsher, more cynical than it had used to be, his blue eyes harder, flatter.

She had hated him with a new intensity as she had watched him surrounded by all the members of his extended family, by all the friends who had once been hers too. She had hated him for the cool haughtiness of his reception of Jeffrey, for his total ignoring of Jane. She had hated the way he had kept her waiting, the way his eyes had raked over her, the way he had called her *my lady*, the way he had offered her a glass from the wassail bowl, just as if she were one of his precious carolers.

She was glad—oh, how glad she was!—that the bowl had been more than half empty. Only now did she consider the humiliation she would have felt if she had been unable after all to hoist it and chuck its contents in his face.

She smiled. And then she laughed. She entered her bedchamber and stood with her back to the door, unable to control her laughter. She held her nose and tried to suppress the sounds. One never knew when someone might be listening. And sound carried in this house. While eating her supper in the nursery with the children, she had been able to listen to the music of the carolers two stories below.

Oh, it was Christmas, she thought, sobering and setting her head back against the door. She closed her eyes. The last three Christmases had been bad enough, but this one was going to be intolerable. It was *Christmas,* yet for her and for her children there would be no peace or goodwill. No tidings of comfort or of joy.

He had asked the question with great reluctance only because he was afraid he might know the answer. He should have given more specific instructions, he thought when it was too late. But at the time he had been wet and uncomfortable and humiliated and furious. He had been fighting an inward battle for dignity and control.

The evening festivities went on forever, or so it seemed, first in the hall and later in the greater comfort of the drawing room. Everyone appeared to be in merry mood. Partly, he guessed, they were trying to comfort him, or trying to cover their own embarrassment at having been witnesses to that encounter between him and his estranged wife. No one mentioned her. And no one mentioned Jeffrey either, since doing so would inevitably lead to mention of her. Instead, everyone was determinedly merry.

And so it was not until very late, after midnight, as he followed the last of his guests upstairs to bed that he asked the question of his butler. He might have spared himself the breath. The answer was the one he fully expected.

"Her ladyship is in her own apartments, my lord," Watkins said, a look of momentary surprise on his face. Perhaps it had not struck either him or the housekeeper as possible that he would not want her there in apartments that adjoined his own.

"Thank you, Watkins," his lordship said. "Good night."

He never had found the key to the door between their dressing rooms. It had been a joke between them in the years before they were estranged that there was no key, that neither could lock the other out. He had been through that door more times than he could count . . .

He felt something like fury now as he entered his dressing room, where his valet waited, and glanced toward the door, almost as if he expected it to burst open at any moment. Could she not have demanded to be lodged somewhere else in the house? Or had she made the assumption that because they were still legally married she had every right to be treated in this house with the deference due to his countess? He wondered if the child was with her or if she had left it in the nursery. It! The child was a girl. Jane. He knew that much. Nothing else. He knew nothing else about her and fully intended to keep it that way.

He lay down in his darkened bedchamber after he had dismissed his valet for the night. He had had a busy day, entertaining his guests—pleasure, he found, was often more wearying than business—and a long day. Tomorrow would be worse. And after that there would be Christmas Day. He needed a good night's sleep. But sleep eluded him, Totally.

He threw back the covers impatiently at last and walked on bare feet through to his dressing room.

Without benefit of light he found and donned his brocaded dressing gown. He shivered. There was no fire in the dressing room. He glanced to where he knew, even without the benefit of sight, that offending door stood shut but unlocked. The door that had been keeping him awake. Almost as if it acted of its own volition, his hand reached out and turned the handle slowly, so as to make no noise. Her dressing room was in darkness, but there was a thin thread of light beneath the door opposite.

Either she slept with a candle burning or with a bright fire burning, or else she was not in bed at all.

He stood for long moments in the doorway between their dressing rooms before striding across hers and opening the other door. He made no attempt at stealth this time.

The bed was unmade. She had obviously been lying down on it. But she was standing now beside it, her eyes on the door as he came through it. She must have heard him opening the first door. She was wearing a long white nightgown, which covered her from neck to wrists to ankles. But it was not the nightgown he noticed first. She had grown her hair, he thought. She had always worn it fashionably short. Now it reached halfway down her back, heavy and shining in the candlelight, and dark auburn in color.

There was no sign of the child in the bed behind her.

He closed the door, looking at her as he did so. She was smaller than he remembered, more slender, more fragile looking. More beautiful. He felt a return of the cold fury he had felt on his first sight of her earlier.

"On whose authority did you bring yourself to Wyndham Park, my lady?" he asked her.

"You think to tongue-tie me with such a question," she said quite calmly after a few moments of silence. "There can be only one answer. A good wife recognizes the authority of only one person in her life—of only one *man*. She may not lift a finger except with the permission of her husband, of her lord and master. I believe it has been long established between us, John, that I am not a good wife and that I do not recognize your authority over me. You forfeited my respect a long time ago."

He felt a wave of hatred that shook him with its intensity. He thought it had muted to mere dislike. But his feelings had never been tested. He had not seen her for longer than three years, not since he had banished her to one of his smaller homes.

"I believe," he said, "that one of the conditions for my further support of you, ma'am, was that you remain at Lanting for the rest of your life."

"Well, then," she said, "you still have power over me, John. That will be a pleasant feeling for you. All men need to feel that they have power over someone, I know, preferably a woman. Why are you here? Why have you come to my room? To exercise your conjugal rights? I suppose that being in the country, hemmed in by the propriety of family and other house guests, must be a severe trial for you. You are deprived of the services of your whores and mistresses."

They had lived together for four years without **any** serious quarrel. They had lived in a make-believe world of harmony and love and passion. He had not known until close to the end how barbed her tongue could be, how scornful her face. He had not known how fragile was their accord. He had done something remarkably stupid and she had retaliated by outdoing

him a thousandfold. She had torn their marriage asun-
der and in the process had ripped into his very being,
leaving wounds that were still tender to the touch,
wounds that would perhaps never fully heal.

"Yes indeed," he said. "But I believe I will wait for
their superior services when I return to town rather
than disappoint myself with inferior goods before
then." He could not quite believe that those words
had come from his mouth, but there they were, spo-
ken, beyond recall.

She surprised and infuriated him by laughing and
looking genuinely amused. "I came, John," she said,
"because I would not be deprived of my son at Christ-
mas and because I would not deprive my daughter of
her brother."

"You had no business," he said, "bringing the child
here, Antonia. Have you no decency?"

"Fool!" she said contemptuously. "Obviously I have
not. I like to have my children close to me. I like to
have them close to each other. Most indecent of me.
We will not offend your sensibilities for long, my lord.
As soon as you have tired of Jeffrey, I shall take them
both home again to Lanting. Your duty will be done
for another year or so."

It seemed impossible that she still had the power to
hurt him. But some of those inner wounds of his were
opening up. "As soon as I tire of Jeffrey?" he said in
little more than a whisper.

She had the grace to look slightly disconcerted.

"Jeffrey is my *son*," he said, his voice still very
quiet. "He is my reason for living. It has broken my
heart to be without him for the past three and a half
years. I have endured his absence only because he

has needed his mother—even such a mother—during those years."

Her head went back almost as if she had been struck on the chin.

He wanted to hurt her because she had hurt him. He had been toying with an idea for a long time, though he had not intended to implement it just yet. But now it became a weapon more than an idea and he hurled it at her without stopping to consider that it was late at night, that they were both tired, that seeing each other again had frayed both their nerves.

"You may stay," he said, "until the day after New Year's Day. You and the child, provided you keep her out of my sight. In company I will even give you the deference due my countess. Then you will return to Lanting, Antonia, you and the child. Jeffrey will stay here. It is time he was with his father and learned about his future inheritance. It is time he had a tutor rather than a governess."

He felt a moment's pang of regret when she paled noticeably even in the candlelight and swayed on her feet. Regret and triumph.

"No." He saw her lips form the word though he scarcely heard it. "No. No, John. No. No." She could seem to say only the one word over and over again. He could see that he had wounded her far more deeply than he had expected.

"It is my turn," he said, the triumph of his words feeling remarkably hollow.

They had been standing well apart, she beside the bed, he just inside the door. But she came rushing toward him now and grabbed the silk lapels of his dressing gown. "No," she said. "He is only six, John.

He is a baby. He still needs me. Oh please, please. You cannot do this."

"Cannot, my lady?" She had backed him against the door. Her body was pressed against his from bosom to knees. He wondered if she realized it. There was a familiar smell, a soap fragrance he had not smelled in three years.

"You are doing it to punish me," she said. "Oh, cruel, cruel. My children are all I have to live for. You must not take them from me. Oh, you used not to be cruel, John. Don't take them from me."

"Them?" he said. "*Them*, my lady? I have one child, a son. He will remain here with me. You may keep your daughter."

"John." She was gasping, as if there was not enough air in the room. "John." Her face was in shadow, but he could see the unnatural brightness of her eyes.

Triumph was an evil thing, more like a knife twisting in his stomach than the joy he might have expected. He had her where he wanted her—at last. She had looked at him only with scornful dignity and the peculiar half smile that was new to her when he had pronounced the sentence of banishment on her. And this evening she had dashed the contents of the wassail bowl in his face for all his family and friends to see.

He did something very stupid. Incredibly stupid. He spread one hand over the back of her head and set the other beneath her chin. And he kissed her—open-mouthed, angry, frustrated, upset, hungry. Ravenous. He thrust his tongue hard and deep into her mouth. She sucked on it so that he moaned. Her arms, he realized, had come tightly about his waist.

He lifted his head and looked down at her. His

thoughts were paralyzed. He did not know what to say.

"John," she whispered, "you were once kind. You once loved me, or so I thought. I loved you. Please not yet. Give me another year or two with him. Perhaps when he is eight—or ten. Please. In memory of the tenderness there once was between us. In memory of the day he was born."

Contrary to custom, and to the eternal shock of physician and midwife, he had witnessed the birth of his son and the agony of his wife. He remembered that agony now and the discomfort she had suffered during the last few months of her confinement. She had borne his son in pain. The intensity of his love for her on that day had been an agony of its own.

"I can see that you remember," she said. "John, give me one more year. One more? Please? What can I do to persuade you?"

Those last words were a mistake. He had felt himself weakening. "You would buy a year with our son," he said, looking down into her eyes, "with your body?"

She did not hesitate. "Yes," she said.

"My son," he said, "is not for sale, my lady."

Her arms fell away from him and she took a step back. The look of panic and pleading had gone from her face. She stared at him, chin up, expression unreadable. He turned without a word, opened the door, and closed it behind him after stepping into her dressing room. His hand, he realized, withdrawing it from the door handle, was shaking.

It was snowing. Thick flakes were falling, almost obscuring the view from her window. It must have snowed through most of the night. Already a thick blanket of white made it impossible to know where lawns and flower beds ended and where paths or driveway began. Tree branches, bare and brown just yesterday, were loaded with snow.

Of course it had snowed through the night. It was the imminence of the snow that had persuaded them to push on after dark last evening. They had known that they might have been marooned at some country inn this morning if they had stopped. And all through an almost sleepless night she had seen the darkness almost as bright as daylight beyond her window.

It was a magical sight. It was a rare treat to have snow for Christmas and such fresh and such thick snow. The children would be ecstatic, and some of the adults too. There would be trudges and games in the snow. There would be sleigh rides. And the greenery would be gathered in the snow. It was traditional at Wycherly that the greenery with which the house was to be decorated was gathered on the morning of Christmas Eve by everyone who was fit to step out-doors. And everyone decorated during the afternoon. It was rather late to decorate, perhaps, but Christmas always came suddenly and with a burst of glory to Wycherly. It started with the carolers and the wassail bowl on the evening before Christmas Eve . . .

She rested her forehead against the glass of the window and closed her eyes. She felt physically sick. She had been unwilling to part with Jeffrey for the one week of Christmas and so had defied John and come with him. She and Jane. And now, as a punishment, Jeffrey was going to be taken from her forever. She was sure it was punishment—for coming and for the childish gesture of contempt she had made with the wassail bowl. He had not said anything in his letter summoning Jeffrey about not sending him back again after Christmas.

There was a buzzing in her ears. She thought she might faint.

I have one child, a son.

He had not believed her, then. She had always known it, of course. He had not acknowledged Jane's birth. He had never made mention of her in his infrequent letters. And he had never revoked the banishment. But hearing him speak those words last night had been a shock anyway. *I have one child ... You may keep your daughter.*

It was Christmas, she thought, lifting her forehead away from the glass and turning toward her dressing room. For the children's sake she must silence the terrible panic she was feeling. She could imagine the excitement that must be reigning in the nursery as the children realized what day it was and noticed what was beyond the windows. She must make sure that Jeffrey and Jane were part of that excitement.

They were both in the main room of the nursery, she discovered a short time later, with a whole horde of other, incredibly noisy children. Antonia looked at them all and recognized a few, but not many. Children could change beyond all recognition in three and a half years. Two little boys were talking to a wary-looking Jeffrey. Jane was standing close to her brother, half hidden by him, her doll clasped in one arm.

"My Christopher, and Penelope and George's Wilfred," a voice said from beside Antonia and she turned, startled, to look at the lady who had ap-

proached her unseen and was nodding in the direction
of the two children with Jeffrey.

"Margot," she said to Lady Sugden, her husband's
sister, "how are you?"

"The better for seeing you here this year with the
children," her sister-in-law said, taking her arm. "I do
not know what happened, Tony. John's lips have been
very tightly buttoned, but Vernon and I—indeed the
whole family—were more shocked that I can possibly
say. If you two of all people could break up, what
hope was there for anyone's marriage, we all thought.
But you are back. Jeffrey has grown from babyhood
to boyhood and is going to be every bit as good-
looking as John. Jane is just adorable—those eyes and
those curls!"

Antonia smiled uncertainly. John had said nothing?
No one—not even his sister—knew why their marriage
had fallen apart? Somehow she had imagined that she
would be a pariah here. She had imagined that he
would have severely blackened her name. But of
course, pride would have kept him from doing that.
No man would openly admit to being a cuckold. No
man would want to admit to having acknowledged in
name, if nothing else, the bastard child his wife had
borne. She had John's pride to thank for the fact that
her daughter was Lady Jane Beattie. And that every-
one believed she had every right to that name—except
for John Beattie, Earl of Wyndham, of course.

"Come," Margot said, "and introduce me to your
children. I will reintroduce you to mine. Doubtless
they will all look very different to you. You have
grown your hair, Tony. How long is it when it is
down?"

Antonia spent half an hour in the nursery, though

very little of it was with her children. The temptation was to snatch them away, to be private with them, to enjoy every moment with them that was left—but that was a thought she did not care to pursue. She realized, though, the necessity of leaving them alone to make the acquaintance of their cousins and of the other children. They had enough of solitude at Lanting House. Jane was going to be unbearably lonely . . .

After half an hour Margot bore her off downstairs to breakfast. It was something Antonia would have preferred not to do. But it had been her choice to come to Wycherly. Having done so, it would be foolish to cower in her rooms or in the nursery. He had said last night that in public he would accord her the deference due his countess. Besides, if Margot was to be believed, no one knew the truth behind their estrangement—or the perceived truth. Despite the opening scene last evening, to which Margot had tactfully made no reference, perhaps everyone would believe that she had been invited. Perhaps she would not be snubbed.

She overcame her dismay at finding the breakfast room full of people by concentrating on the relief of finding that *he* at least was not present. She looked about the table and smiled.

Miss Matthews was in the nursery, talking with the nurse the earl had hired for Christmas to help the others who would come with the various children. Jeffrey was in one corner with Margot's Christopher and a few other children. They were playing with a spinning top, he could see. He summoned the governess to him with a lift of his eyebrows. She came hurrying toward him and curtsied.

"You will show me which is my son's bedchamber,"

he said to her, "and then send him to me there, if you please."

"Yes, my lord," she said. "This way."

He might have guessed, of course, that the room that had been his as a child was now his son's.

"Miss Matthews," he said, before the governess returned to the nursery, "the children at Wycherly need very little supervision over the holiday. They entertain one another and there are always parents and other relatives to keep an eye on them. Be sure to enjoy the holiday yourself belowstairs."

"Thank you, my lord," She made him another curtsy and looked openly surprised. Doubtless Antonia had prepared her to meet an ogre.

He was being selfish, he realized. Jeffrey was playing with other children. He was just getting to know them. He should have been left to continue doing so. But soon it would be time to go out to gather the Christmas greenery and although the rest of the day would be full of activities to involve the children as well as the adults, there would be precious little chance for private moments. He yearned to be alone with his son.

The boy came a minute or so later. He was a small child, slender, good-looking. His eyes were very blue, his hair dark. There was no mistaking his paternity at least. He had lost some of his baby looks since the last time. He came to stand before the chair on which the earl had seated himself. He stood quietly and he looked steadily into his father's eyes. But he was afraid. The earl pushed aside annoyance. His annoyance was not for the boy anyway.

"Jeffrey," he said, "did you sleep well?"

"Yes, thank you, sir," his son replied.

Sir. It was difficult not to be formal. It was difficult not to feel awkward and tongue-tied. He leaned forward and set a hand lightly on the boy's head. "Jeffrey," he said, "how are you, my son?" But even that would not do. He picked the boy up and set him on one of his knees.

"Well, thank you, sir," his son said, sitting stiffly there, his eyes downcast.

"Has your mother instructed you to call me *sir?*" he asked.

"N-no," Jeffrey said. "Mama always calls you Papa."

Papa? Always? Did she talk about him sometimes, then? He felt a strange ache in his throat.

"That is who I am," he said. "Papa. You are my son, my little boy, and I love you. As your mother— as Mama loves you. Tell me about yourself. Do you read and write?"

He was hungry—hungrier than he had realized—to know his son, to know all the small, unimportant details of his life that he would have known intimately if the boy had always lived with him. He ached with unspent love.

His son answered all his questions. He even began to relax after a few minutes and sometimes raised his head to look into his father's face. This was Christmas, the earl thought. Just this. This was the gift of all gifts, this son given at Christmas. Or *taken* at Christmas. He had tried to take the boy from his mother. He felt that ache again.

And then he became aware that the door was opening slowly. He raised his head and watched a small child enter, one he did not know. A tiny little girl in a pretty green dress and white pinafore. A little girl with hazel eyes far too large for her face and a halo of auburn curls about her head. She was clutching an old doll in one arm.

His stomach felt as if it dropped several inches before doing a complete somersault and settling painfully into place again. He wanted to tell the child to go away. He wanted to tell her to go back to the nursery to the other children. Instead he watched her cross the room to stand a foot from his knees. She had watched Jeffrey the whole time, but when she stopped, she changed the direction of her gaze.

Oh God! There seemed not enough air in the room.

His son was looking at him, his eyes somewhat troubled. "Jane, Papa," he said.

Yes. Oh God. She looked very like Antonia except for the curls. "Yes," he said. He closed his eyes briefly, but he could still feel the child's gaze. And he realized something in a flash. She was a child. A real child. He had always absurdly thought of her as a thing—a child, *it*. She was a child, a little innocent, in no way to blame for the ugliness that had given her existence.

"Come," he said, reaching out the arm that was not about his son. He hoped desperately that she would be frightened away, that she would go scurrying back to the nursery. He had not wanted to see her. He did not want to know of her existence.

She took the extra few steps forward and climbed onto his unoccupied knee. She sat there very upright and turned her head to gaze into his face. She weighed nothing at all, he thought. She was like a little piece of air—of fragrant air. She smelled of the same soap as Antonia used.

"That is a pretty doll," he said, noticing the chipped

paint of the doll's hair and the crack across its face, cutting directly through one of its staring eyes.

"Pamela," a sweet and tiny voice told him. She had not shifted her gaze from his face.

"That is her name?" He said. "Pamela is a pretty doll."

But he did not want to talk to her. He did not want her there. He did not want those big eyes gazing into his face. He returned his attention to his son and continued asking questions about his life. How did he best like to spend his time? Did he like the outdoors better than the indoors? Did he have friends? What made him laugh? What made him cry? No, he assured his son, it was not unmanly to cry if the occasion warranted tears.

He held the other child and tried to pretend that she was not there. But he was relieved when she looked down at last in order to lay her doll very carefully across her knees.

"Sh," she whispered. "Go sleep."

And then her face turned in toward his chest, and a quick glance showed him only the shining curls on top of her head. Her hands were working at the long row of buttons down the front of his embroidered waistcoat, opening them laboriously one at a time. He ignored her and went on talking to his son. She opened every single button and then started to do them up again with just as deep a concentration. She was halfway through the task when the door opened again, rather more hurriedly this time.

His wife stopped short. Her eyes closed and her mouth opened before she lifted both hands and pressed them to it.

The child wriggled off his lap and crossed the room

to her mother. She lifted both arms, her doll clutched in one hand. Antonia swept her up and held her close, her cheek pressing against those shining curls. She closed her eyes again for a moment.

"Mama," Jeffrey said, "I have been telling Papa about how we go on picnics in the summer. And I met Christopher and Wilfred and Simon this morning and they let me play. They let Jane play too, but I had to spin the top for her. You should see all the colors when it spins. Simon is having soldiers for Christmas. We are going to play with them tomorrow."

Her eyes were on his half-buttoned waistcoat. His eyes were noticing that she really was slimmer. Thinner, paler, though just as beautiful. Madonna and child, he thought—a thoroughly irreverent thought under the circumstances.

"And today," he said, lifting Jeffrey off his knee and standing up, "there is work to be done. Lots of it, and we need every available hand, from the smallest to the largest. There is holly to be gathered and ivy and mistletoe and pine boughs. There is a house to be decked out for Christmas. And there is snow outside to be waded in and rolled in, snow to be thrown at the unwary and to be built into snowmen. If we do not hurry, we will be left behind and will miss all the fun."

He felt happy suddenly, for no reason he could fathom. He grabbed his son impulsively and swung him up to toss him toward the ceiling. For the first time he heard the boy laugh. He laughed with him. He tossed him once more.

"And Jane too," his son cried excitedly. "Jane too, Papa."

The child had turned in Antonia's arms and was watching, big-eyed. She reached out her arms now. His wife frowned and turned hurriedly toward the door, but he stepped forward and took the child from her. She was an innocent baby. He tossed her upward, not as high as he had thrown Jeffrey. She looked frightened and clung to his neck when she had come down again.

"More," she whispered in his ear.

The second time she giggled. A sweet sound of innocence and happiness and trust. He handed her to Antonia.

"Get them ready," he said gruffly, not meeting her eyes. "Everyone will be meeting down in the hall within the next half hour or so."

He left the room without another word and hurried in the direction of his own apartments. *Them,* he had said. *Get them ready.* Well, she was only a baby. Why should she be punished for her mother's sins?

Madonna and child. He thought unwillingly of a man who during this season they were celebrating had accepted a child who was not of his own seed. A man named Joseph. But the comparison seemed hardly appropriate.

Everyone appeared to have forgotten the task at hand. They had stepped outside, a footman told Antonia with an almost exaggeratedly deferential bow when she went downstairs with the children. She was afraid they had been left behind and would not know what direction the others had taken. For herself and for Jane she would not have minded. But Jeffrey would have been disappointed.

However, there was nothing to fear. There were

masses of people both visible and audible as soon as the doors were opened. A group of young people, shrieking and laughing, were hurling snowballs at one another. A few small children, helped by mothers and one father, were building a snowman. A group of little girls was making angels in the snow. Most of the boys, several of the men, and a few of the bolder girls were making a long slide down the path that sloped to the sunken garden. Other men and a group of women watched and laughed and called encouragement.

John was among them, looking tall and distinguished in his many-caped greatcoat and his beaver hat and topboots. But his attention obviously was on the door. He came striding toward them as soon as they appeared on the steps. He was looking tense again and rather morose. She was glad of it. She had been shaken by the sight of him this morning, looking relaxed and paternal with both Jeffrey and Jane on his knees—*Jane had been opening the buttons of his waistcoat.* She had been even more disturbed by the sight and sound of his laughter as he had tossed Jeffrey toward the ceiling. He had looked younger. He had looked like—like the man she had once loved.

"We will be going to the lake soon," he said, his eyes sweeping over her but not quite meeting her own. "We will find all we need there for decorating the house. There will be a bonfire after we have finished and chocolate to drink."

As usual. Everything was traditional about Christmas at Wycherly. The young people in particular enjoyed the search for greenery among the trees surrounding the lake. There were any number of chances for a brief tête-à-tête, and good excuses for a little more if mistletoe had been found. She could remember John kissing her hotly against the trunk of a tree one year, his hand holding a sprig of mistletoe above their heads. The year of their betrothal.

I want you, he had whispered against her lips, shocking and thrilling her. *God, I want you.*

"That will be pleasant," she said now.

"But first the children have to be allowed to play," he said. "The children of all ages, that is. Come and slide, Jeffrey." He held out a hand for his son's. He did not glance at Jane.

She watched them for a while, zooming dangerously down the path made slick with hard-packed snow. The men were enjoying themselves as much as the children and fell just as often. Jeffrey was soon one of the group. She had worried about him. He was a quiet, somewhat timid child. She had hoped he would mingle well with his cousins. He appeared to be doing so. He needed a man's influence in his life. She had known that. He needed a father. And now he had a father and would be without a mother's influence. She shivered.

But she was being hailed by Margot and Penelope and took Jane to see the snowman and to make a tiny snow angel. Margot taught her how.

"Oh, what a darling you are," she said after dusting Jane off and catching her up in a close hug. "And how fortunate your mama and papa are to have a little girl. All I have is four boys. Four!" She pulled a face so that Jane chuckled and Antonia smiled.

But the smile faded quickly. John was standing just behind her shoulder.

"It is time to work," he said, raising his voice. "We are going to the lake."

There was a loud groan followed by laughter as the

snowman's head rolled off its shoulders and landed with a thud in the snow.

"Take my arm, my lady," he said, looking stony-faced at Antonia. She knew he had heard what Margot had just said. She knew too that he was doing what he had promised to do—he was treating her with the courtesy due his countess for all to see. "Jeffrey is with the other boys. It is where he belongs."

She took his arm and reached down her free hand for Jane's. She smiled at her. They walked in silence, surrounded by noise and laughter and darting children. Forever had lasted such a short time, she thought.

I love you, he had said against her mouth on their wedding night, after he had finished consummating their marriage. *I love you so much it hurts. I am going to love you forever. Be warned.* He had laughed softly. *Forever and ever, amen.*

Forever had lasted for four years. Then he had started amusing himself with whores.

They separated at the lake. He took Jeffrey and Margot's eldest, a lanky lad of sixteen, and several other smaller boys and girls in search of mistletoe while she went trudging off with Jane and Vernon and George and several others to gather holly. It was not a disciplined work party. Several times snowball fights broke out and Vernon had to whistle everyone back to business. George, plumper and ruddier of complexion than he had been three years before, spotted an auburn curl peeping out from beneath Jane's hood and threatened to cut if off to wear on his fob chain. He came toward her with his gloved fingers working like scissors and Jane hid behind her mother, giggling. George laughed heartily.

"She is fortunate enough to have her mother's coloring, but those are her father's curls right enough," he said.

None of them knew why the marriage had broken up. John really had kept his mouth shut. George was one of his favorite cousins, the brother he had never had.

"It is good to see you back home, Tony," George said, smiling kindly before turning and bellowing in feigned wrath at a small group of lads and girls who were slacking off.

They were all chilled by the time they gathered about the fire, built and kept bright and hot by a couple of the gardeners. It was the part of the morning everyone always enjoyed most. The greenery was piled in a great circle behind them, ready to be hauled back to the house, while they all basked in the glorious warmth of the fire and the blessed heat of the chocolate in their mouths and stomachs. They always tended to stand in family groups about the fire. The earl came to stand by his wife, bringing their son with him. Inevitably, Uncle Horace began the carol singing—because someone had to do the dirty job of being leader, as he always said—and they all joined in with varying degrees of musicality.

Jane gazed big-eyed into the fire and held her cup with both hands. Jeffrey was happy and excited and looked about at all the playmates who were already making this the best Christmas ever for him. Antonia felt a pang at the realization. She had tried so hard to be everything to her children. But when all was said and done, she could be only a mother.

Jane had wandered away, she realized when the fire was beginning to die down and the chocolate had all been drunk and the trek back to the house was about to begin. And John had moved from her side. She turned in sudden anxiety. There were so many trees among which to get lost.

But the child had not gone far. She was standing beside a pile of holly, gazing down at one white woolen glove and at the red stain on one forefinger. Her lower lip was wobbling. John was in the process of going down on one knee in the snow and taking the little hand in his. He eased off the glove. Antonia stood where she was, unconsciously holding her breath.

"Wicked holly," he said. "It loves to do that." He reached into a pocket of his greatcoat and came out with a large white handkerchief. He dabbed it gently at the little bead of blood on the tiny forefinger while Jane looked up into his face, her lip still trembling. It took a great deal to make Jane actually cry.

"Kiss it better," she said.

Antonia closed her eyes and bit her lip. When she looked again, he was holding the finger against his lips.

"It will stop bleeding in no time at all," he said. "We will just wrap the handkerchief about the finger like this and then about the hand. By the time you get back to the house it will be all better. The kiss will have done the trick."

Jane gazed into his face.

"You are cold," he said, holding her bandaged hand between both of his. He looked at her rosy cheeks and red nose.

Antonia took one step forward, but then she stopped again. He was unbuttoning his greatcoat. Before she fully realized why, he had opened it up, drawn the child against his chest, wrapped the heavy folds of the coat about her, and stood up with her. His eyes met his wife's, hard and bleak.

"I suppose there are enough people here to carry the loads," he said. "She is chilled." And he strode off through the trees, Antonia beside him, while the others made a great noisy to-do about scooping up the greenery.

Antonia felt very much like crying. He was holding Jane. He had her cradled against him, warm against his chest and beneath the bulk of his greatcoat. Because she was cold and tired and because she had pricked a finger. She fought her tears. How foolish he would think her. How foolish she was. In three years he had shown the child no kindness at all.

Jane was sleeping by the time they arrived back at the house. Antonia held out her arms to take her when they were inside the hall.

"No," he said. "Where is her bedchamber?"

"Jeffrey's," she said. "They are in the same room. They are strangers here and far from me. They need to be able to see each other and talk to each other."

"You do not need to justify yourself to me," he said and turned to lead the way to the stairs.

No, she had never been able to do so anyway. He had always believed what he wanted to believe of her. She was sorry she had felt the necessity of explaining.

He set the child gently down on her bed while Antonia eased off her boots and then set her doll on the pillow beside her. She had expected him to stride from the room as soon as he had set down his burden, but she was aware of him standing quietly behind her as she folded a quilt over her sleeping daughter.

"She is a beautiful child, Antonia," he said.

The tears came then, much as she despised them,

and she bit hard on her upper lip. She could say nothing. He had left the room before it became necessary to turn to face him.

The two sleighs had been prepared and hitched to horses. They had been in constant use all afternoon while at the same time the hall and staircase, the dining room and the drawing room were being transformed into a Christmas wonderland with greenery and bells and silk bows and kissing boughs. Suddenly there were all the sights and smells of Christmas, the distinctive smell of the pine boughs vying with the aroma of puddings and mince pies escaping upward from the kitchen.

And finally dusk came and then darkness. The children, who had been loose in the house and the outdoors all day, were herded back to the nursery after tea, where there would be games and supper before bedtime. None of the children were ever reluctant to go to bed on Christmas Eve. Tomorrow there would be church followed by the presents. The children all knew that going to bed and to sleep was the fastest way of bringing on that supreme moment of the year.

The Earl of Wycherly had had a busy day, with no time at all for relaxation. During the afternoon he had supervised and helped with the decorating, slipped away to the town five miles away and back again all within two hours, and played some energetic games with the children just before tea. It was time he took a short while just for himself. He wandered down to the hall, where his head groom had been organizing the sleigh rides all afternoon and ensuring that the horses were changed frequently. The earl had a word with him and went to find his wife in the drawing room, where she was being entertained to one of Great-Aunt Edith's interminable monologues. He waited politely for her to stop to draw breath.

"I will take you for a sleigh ride, Antonia," he said. "One of the sleighs should be back within ten minutes. Wear something warm."

It was hard not to be abrupt with her. He felt as if he had been on stage all day. He had been fully aware of the avidly curious glances of his family and friends. Perhaps he should have asked her to ride with him, he thought, instead of telling her. He was glad there was no wassail bowl within easy reach. But she got up quietly enough after looking at him in open surprise, and left the room.

He had been coming to a decision all day. He had no idea if it was the right one. He did not know if he would feel the same way tomorrow or the day after. Christmas had a damnable way of distorting one's vision and making the impossible seem altogether possible. Perhaps he should wait out the week. He had told her, after all, that he would send her back to Lanting House on the day after New Year's Day. It was even longer than a week.

She was waiting for him in the hall when he went down again. She was wearing the green, fur-trimmed cloak she had worn the night before, with brown half boots and leather gloves. He looked deliberately to see if she carried a muff, but she did not. A muff would have made the sleigh ride cozier for her.

"The sleigh is waiting, my lord," his groom said with a bow.

The snow had stopped falling hours before though the temperature was low enough to prevent it from melting. The air was still. The sky was bright with starlight. It was a perfect evening for sleighing. Far more magical than the afternoon.

They sat side by side in the sleigh after he had handed her in and covered her legs with a warm rug, listening to the muted thuds of the horses' hooves on the snow, the metallic squeak of the sleigh's runners, the jingling of the harness bells. Neither of them spoke for a long time. He could remember bringing her out like this the year of their betrothal. He had stopped the sleigh beside the lake in order to kiss her. He could remember slipping his hand beneath her cloak after first removing his glove, and cupping her breast through the wool of her dress and rubbing his thumb over her hardening nipple. He could remember fighting for decency and control. He could remember realizing that she did not fully understand the danger. He had felt very protective of her.

God, he had loved her.

"John?" She broke the silence at last. Her voice was tense and breathless.

"Yes?" He turned his head to look at her. She was staring straight ahead, her chin lifted, her hands twisting in her lap.

"I have been a good mother," she said. "I spend time with them, I listen to them, I make sure that they learn manners and morals and that Jeffrey learns his lessons. I make sure that when necessary they are disciplined. I tell Jeffrey about his father and about this place and about the life he will live and the duties that will face him when he grows up. I take them to church. I—I have been a good mother. I have tried."

"I do not doubt it," he said. "You were a devoted mother to Jeffrey when he was very young."

"I know he cannot stay with me forever," she said.

"I know that more is demanded of his education as a gentleman and as your son than I can provide. But he is only six."

"He is no longer a baby," he said.

Her voice was shaking almost beyond control when she spoke next. "Just two or three years," she said. "Even one. He can come to you now and then for a few days. Perhaps more often than he has done in the past. But let him come home with me. Please. I—Please."

"He will not be leaving here," he said quietly.

She was very still. He saw when he glanced at her that her eyes were closed. "How can you be so cruel?" she said as quietly as he had spoken. "How could I have been so deceived in you? I thought you were not only my husband and my lover. I thought you were my dearest friend. You took from me all my happiness and all my dreams. Will you now take my son too?"

"It seems to me, ma'am," he said, and he could hear the deadly chill of his own voice, "that you dashed your fair share of dreams—most of them mine. You have a devastating way of effecting revenge."

She did not retaliate. They moved on in silence for a while, the beauty of the scenery on the far side of the lake lost on them, the gaiety of the bells mocking their dark, bruised thoughts. No, he thought at last, he would not wait another week. He did not believe he would change his mind. Everything had changed since last night, when his heart had leaped with gladness at the sight of his son and then he had seen her too. Nothing could change back again.

"You will be staying here too," he said abruptly. "My son needs both a mother and a father. And we have established that you are a good mother. You have also pointed out that he is still young. You will remain here. I shall send to Lanting House to have your possessions brought."

For a long time she was silent. "And Jane?" she whispered at last.

Did she think him a total monster? He felt thoroughly irritated. Now that the words were out, he was not at all sure that he was doing the rational thing. How could they live together in the same house? How could he look at her day after day, picturing another man ...

"Your daughter will stay here too, of course," he said. "She has my name. She always has been under my protection, has she not?"

"Why have you never believed me?" she whispered. "John—"

But they had returned to the house, and his youngest cousin was out on the terrace with the young lady on whom he had fixed his interest this year, the daughter of one of the earl's older friends. They were both laughing and stamping their feet and impatiently awaiting their turn in the sleigh. Parents were always remarkably indulgent about chaperonage at Christmastime, the earl thought as he jumped down into the snow and reached up his arms to lift his wife down. Anything could happen despite the half-hour limit his rules imposed for each ride and despite the coldness of the night. Everything had almost happened between him and Antonia, after all, during that long ago year of their innocence.

The cousin and his young lady drove off into the darkness, their shoulders touching.

"Well?" The earl turned back to his wife and paused with her on the lowest step before going inside.

"Does it please you that you will be staying here? Or would you prefer that I send you back to Lanting?"

"Do I have a choice?" she asked.

He had not given her a choice three and a half years ago. "Yes," he said.

She looked steadily at him for several seconds. "My daughter and I will stay here with her brother and my son," she said at last and turned to climb the steps alone.

He stood looking after her. He felt rather as if she had thrown spiced wine in his face again.

She had scarcely slept at all the night before. For the two nights before that she had been on the road. Inn beds were never conducive to sleep. And for many nights before that she had slept fitfully, terrified by her decision to go with Jeffrey to Wycherly.

She stood at her bedroom window for all of half an hour after coming to bed, looking at the bright sky. The Christmas sky. She could not decide whether it felt like Christmas or not. Certainly there was limitless joy in the knowledge that after all she was not to be separated from her son, that her children were not to be separated from each other. But somehow there was the same loneliness that had made bleak memories of the past three Christmases. Loneliness amid the crowds.

But she was too weary to be kept awake by loneliness or anything else. She lay down and was fast asleep within minutes.

His mouth was warm and gentle on hers with the faint taste of wine. She loved his gentle kisses. But then she loved his passionate kisses too. She sighed with contentment.

"Antonia," he was saying. He had never called her Tony, as her parents had always done and almost everyone else who was on a first-name basis with her. He would never call her Tony, he had told her once. He loved her full name better. It was beautiful and feminine. "Antonia."

"Mm," she said. She wanted his mouth back on hers. And she was aware, as she so often was when he kissed her and caressed her and spoke soft words of love, that she dreamed. She willed the dream to go on. She fought not to wake up and not to fall more deeply asleep. In her dreams he never went beyond kisses and mild caresses. She wished dreams could be shaped into the form one wished them to take.

"Antonia," he said, his breath warm and wine-scented. "Don't say no." He kissed her with the same light gentleness. "Don't say no."

He was sitting on the side of her bed, wearing a white nightshirt. He was leaning over her, his hands on either side of her pillow. She was not—she tested the thought warily—she was not dreaming.

"Don't say no," he said again.

Would he go away if she did? She had never said no to him until that dreadful night after all the terrible bitterness had started. He had gone away then. He had never come back. Yes, the choice was hers just as the choice of staying or going back to Lanting House had been hers.

"Let me come into your bed," he said.

She watched her hand reach up in the semidarkness to touch one of his dark curls. Perhaps she was not awake after all. Perhaps she could pretend she was still asleep, still dreaming. All responsibility for what happened would be taken away from her if she could convince herself. She wanted him. Deep in her womb she could feel the throbbing she had had to fight over and over again during the past three years and longer. But she was awake.

"Yes," she whispered.

He pulled his nightshirt off over his head before drawing back the bedclothes and lying down beside her. He had always slept naked with her, even the very first time. She had been shocked and frightened, and her reaction to what he had proceeded to do to her had been violent and uncontrolled and wonderful beyond imagining.

She had forgotten so much, she thought, shocked again now as his hands and his mouth went to work on her. Oh no, she had not forgotten exactly. With her mind she had remembered. She had relived his lovemaking more times than she cared to admit during the lonely years. She had remembered clearly what he did. But she had forgotten quite how it felt. She had forgotten the stark carnality of it—the feel of him, the taste of him, the smell of him, the sounds of his breathing and her own.

He worked on her with skilled patience until her body was humming with desire, until she was taut and wet with need, until her breath came in gasps. She did not even notice the moment at which she finally lost her nightgown and was flesh to flesh with him. She throbbed for him with deep pulsings of anticipation. Not with emptiness, as she had throbbed so often over the past years, but with the knowledge that soon she would be filled.

He was coming over her, lowering his weight onto her, pressing her legs wide with his own. His hands slid beneath her to hold her steady. But she struggled to clear her mind, and set her hands against his already damp chest. He paused and looked down into her eyes.

"I will not share you," she said, gasping to control her breathing. "I will not share you."

"And I," he said, "will not share *you*. Not ever again. This is mine for the rest of our lives. And this is yours." He penetrated her body with one deep, hard thrust while they still looked into each other's eyes.

Ah, she had forgotten the sheer physicalness of it. And yet it was achingly familiar.

He held deep in her while he slid his hands from beneath her and found her own hands. He twined his fingers with hers, palm to palm, and stretched her arms wide on either side of her head. She lay spread-eagled beneath him, helpless against the pleasure he began to give and take. Slowly as he had always conducted their foreplay, he had always taken even longer over the union of their bodies. He did so now, pumping firmly and deeply into her with a steady rhythm that suggested strength and control and an infinite power to prolong pleasure and take it to its utmost limits.

She reached the heights before he did, clenching tightly and convulsively about him with inner muscles, tautening in every muscle in her body until the final stabbing of erotic pain sent her shattering downward toward formless, mindless relaxation. She felt him thrusting against her pain, against her fall, until that most exquisite moment of all, when she felt the heat burst at her core and all his relaxed weight bore down on her.

She wondered, somewhere far back in her mind, if she would be ashamed of herself when rationality finally returned. It was one thing to grant him his conjugal rights. It was another thing altogether . . . But she would think of that later. His mouth was on hers, open, warm, relaxed.

"My love." It was the warm, throaty voice she remembered. The one that came during or following lovemaking. "My beloved."

It was a strange, almost theatrical word. But it had always been spoken from the depths of his being. He had used it often after a particularly powerful uniting. She did not believe now that he was using it for deliberate effect.

She was lying on her side then, snugly fitted to his body, his arm beneath her head, the bedclothes up about them. She must have fallen asleep, she thought. She wondered how long she had slept. She had been unaware of his disengaging from her body and lifting himself off her. She felt comfortable from the roots of her hair down to her toenails. She could hear his heart beating steadily against her ear. She wondered if it was the stamp of ownership he had been placing on her tonight. She wondered if he was gloating over her obvious and ravenous pleasure. She wondered— Oh, she did not want to wonder. She wanted merely to feel. She turned her head farther in toward his chest. She could smell his sweat. She wondered why it was always such a pleasant smell after a sexual encounter.

"The Christmas star," he said.

She turned her head again. Some stars were visible through the window, one brighter than the others. It was Christmas Day. She was in bed with her husband. They had just made love. She was going to be staying with him. They were going to be a family again. Perhaps. She did not know exactly what he intended.

" 'Over where the young child was,' " he said so softly that she knew he was merely speaking his thoughts aloud. He was quoting words from the Bible. He breathed in deeply and let the air out slowly. "You are exhausted, Antonia. Sleep now. The children will need all your attention in the morning."

The children, he had said. Not just Jeffrey. *The children.*

She turned her face back in against his chest and obeyed him.

She was one of the last down to breakfast. She hesitated after she had stepped through the doors of the breakfast parlor, clearly daunted by the numbers. He got to his feet from his place at one end of the table and extended a hand in her direction. He had kept the seat beside him empty.

She turned her head and looked at him—and blushed. She looked delicate and fragile in her simple high-waisted dress of pale yellow. She looked very like her daughter at that moment—all big hazel eyes. How could he ever have convinced himself, he wondered as she came toward him, dealing with a chorus of greetings as she did so, that she was no longer everything in the world to him? She set her hand in his and he carried it to his lips.

"Happy Christmas, Antonia," he said.

"Happy Christmas, John." For one brief moment her eyes met his and her blush deepened.

He had left her bed while she was still sleeping, edging away from her so that she would not awake. And he had stood looking down at her for a while before covering her with the blankets again. The new slenderness made her look more vulnerable. He found her infinitely desirable—as he had done since his very first sight of her dancing at her come-out ball in London during the Season, dressed in virginal white and looking as if her eyes would fall out of her head with the wonder of it all. He had fallen in love with her before he had even been presented to her, before he had danced with her himself.

His butler was putting food on her plate at her direction. Precious little of it. He had just eaten a very hearty breakfast himself. But it had always been thus, he remembered. He had used to tease her about it. Sex had always made him ravenously hungry while it had seemed to leave all her appetites satiated. If he grew portly with age, he had told her, she would have herself to blame. And if she grew to be reed-thin, she had said in retaliation ... But no, he had told her, he was planning to make her deliciously plump and portly at regular intervals over the next ten years or so.

The memory brought a jolt of unbearable pain with it. He returned his attention to the table at large.

But no one lingered over breakfast. It was Christmas Day and there was a great deal to do. There was church to attend within the hour. And after that the gift giving and all the serious business of feasting and enjoying the day. The earl watched his wife leave the breakfast parlor with his sister and some of the other ladies who had children in the nursery.

This was the day he had come to hate more than any other in the year. This year he looked forward to it with almost painful eagerness. He tried to tell himself that nothing really had changed except that he had put an end to his wife's banishment and had exercised his conjugal rights with her the night before. He tried to remind himself that she was still an adulteress with a child born of that adultery. And that he was still the man whose stupidity—one stupidity piled upon another—had undoubtedly driven her to it. But this morning, try as he would, he could not quell hope.

She had lived an exemplary life for longer than three years—he could have no real doubt about that though he had never appointed anyone to spy on her. And he—well, he had missed her far more than he had realized until she had stood in his hall again two evenings before, quietly dignified, holding the child of her sin. She was home again, and he was going to keep her at home with him. He loved her.

He watched them come through the arched doorway from the stairs, all warmly bundled up for the outdoors, and strode across the hall toward them. His son, he could see, was full of the suppressed excitement of Christmas. He was holding one of his mother's hands while the child held the other.

"The carriages can get through to the church today," the earl said. "Several have left already. Do you wish to wait for one, Antonia, or shall we walk?"

"I would prefer to walk," she said.

They had always walked to church on Christmas morning, leaving the carriages for the more elderly of his relatives. He had carried the baby, Jeffrey, on two of those occasions. On this particular morning, after seeing to it that everything was organized before leaving the house, making sure that there would be carriages for all those who still lingered in the hall, he took his son's hand in his and they fell into step behind his wife and her daughter.

"Church first," he said, smiling down at Jeffrey, "to remember why we are celebrating this day, and then back home to open the gifts. I wonder if any of them will be for you."

"Mama brought some parcels with our baggage and would not tell us what they were," Jeffrey said. "I think maybe they were our gifts, sir."

His father chuckled. "And why are we going to church this morning?" he asked. "Has Mama explained to you?"

"It is Baby Jesus' birthday," his son said. "There was a stable and shepherds and wise men and angels. And a star. Mama told us the story. And Miss Matthews had me draw pictures."

Ah yes, the star. And the stable. And the man who had kept and protected the woman who had given birth to a child who was not his. And had taken the child for his own. The parallels had persisted in his mind, and they no longer seemed so irreverent to him. He was, he admitted fully to himself for perhaps the first time, as flawed as she. Perhaps more so. If he had not been so stupid to start with and had not compounded the stupidity by lying to her ...

"Are we going to live with you here for always, sir?" Jeffrey asked him.

"Would you like to?" he asked.

"Mama and Jane too?" His son was frowning and looking wary.

"Yes," he said. "You and Mama and Papa and your sister. Would you like that?"

"Do you really want us?" The boy was still frowning. "Do you love us? Do you love me?"

"Yes." He nodded. "I love you very dearly, and I want you here with me all the time. All of you. Do you ride? Swim? Play cricket? I want to do all those things with you. All the things papas do with their boys."

"And help be the man of the house, like Mama says?" his son asked him.

"And that too." He smiled. "You and I together, my son."

"Then I think I would like to stay, sir," Jeffrey said. "I love cricket more than anything else in the whole wide world."

The church was full, half of its pews filled with family and friends and guests from Wycherly. The Earl of Wycherly took his place in the family pew with his wife and his family and looked at the carved Nativity scene before the altar and listened to the church bells pealing out the glad news of a child born into the world eighteen hundred years before and newly born again each year. His son was seated between him and his wife. The child was at her far side. He turned his head to look at his wife. They had exchanged scarcely a dozen words today. He wondered if she regretted last night, if she had said yes while still only half awake, if she was disgusted with herself and with him this morning. She turned to look back at him and he smiled at her. She half smiled in return—and blushed.

It was only for the past three years that he had hated Christmas, he thought during the following hour. Before that he had always liked it, even loved it, for various reasons. But never as much, perhaps, as this year. As now, this morning, in the village church at Wycherly. Never before had he felt so poignantly that Christmas was all about family and commitment and acceptance and total, unconditional, self-giving love. That it was about love for one's woman and the children of her body and about giving her and them the protection, not only of one's name, but also of one's strength and one's love and one's trust.

"And he arose, and took the young child and his mother, and came into the land of Israel. . . . And he came and dwelt in a city called Nazareth."

Joseph had protected his woman and her child and guarded them and had taken them home with him so that he might nurture them down the years.

There was a great deal of talking and laughing and handshaking in the porch and on the church path after the service was over and the church bells began to peal again. But the children were impatient to be gone. Their exuberance at knowing what part of the day came next was no longer to be contained. Jeffrey ran on ahead with some of his cousins. A whole noisy group from the house trudged homeward through the snow, stepping off the driveway whenever a carriage passed them by.

The earl walked silently beside his wife. But she stopped after a while and he could see that the child had released her hand and was holding both arms up to her. Before she could respond, he leaned across her and swung the child up into his own arms. They walked on.

He was aware as he walked of feather lightness and of a warmth about his heart—and of the child's face turned to his from only a few inches away. She had a disconcerting habit of silently gazing. She lifted her hand after a while and set it against one of his cheeks. But something did not satisfy her. She pulled off her glove with her teeth and patted her bare hand against his face. She drew it downward along his jaw to his chin and then pushed it back up again, pressing a little harder. He realized that she was fascinated by the slight roughness of the stubble there, though he had shaved earlier. Possibly, he thought—no, probably—she had never been this close to a man's face before.

"Jane—" his wife said, sounding embarrassed and even a little alarmed.

"Let her be," he said. "She is just a baby."

A baby who was somehow twining herself about his heartstrings.

They walked on in silence, surrounded by noise and laughter and the occasional flung snowball.

Soon enough the children would want to be out in the main room of the nursery, she knew. Especially Jeffrey, who was finding the lure of other children to play with quite irresistible. They would want to be out there comparing gifts with the other children, playing with them, sharing one another's new toys.

But for now she had them all to herself in the privacy of their bedchamber. She had all the wonder to hug to herself of their expressions as they unpacked their gifts. Her children were all she had had to live for in more than three years. She knew that she had come to cling too tightly, even if only emotionally. She knew that it was good for them to have other children about them for the next week. She knew that it would be good for Jeffrey to have a father with him even beyond that.

Perhaps, she thought, she would be able to learn to let go a little, with Jeffrey anyway. She would have a husband with her for the next week and even beyond that. He had promised that she would never have to share him again. She hugged secretly to herself the memories of last night and the physical reminder, the slight soreness inside. It had been so long.

Both children stopped short on the threshold of the room. There were parcels on each of their beds, put there by Miss Matthews after they had left for church and before she had followed them there. And beside Jane's bed, the gift that had been too large to wrap. Antonia watched her daughter's face. Her eyes grew even larger than usual and her mouth formed a silent oh as she gazed at her new doll's cradle, beautifully carved by the gardener at Lanting, whose talent the countess had encouraged and who was now developing a quite impressive clientele. Jane walked toward it and touched the wood, smoothing her hand almost reverently over it.

"Oh, I say," Jeffrey said, "now you have a bed for Pamela, Jane."

By day, perhaps. Their mother could not quite imagine Pamela being spared from sharing Jane's pillow by night. She smiled. Jane had just discovered that the cradle rocked.

Antonia sat in the large chair and watched her children alternately open their gifts—a set of building bricks, carved by the gardener, brightly painted by herself, for Jeffrey, as well as a cricket bat and ball, a new muffler, and some books, and frilled and embroidered pillows and blanket and comforter and mattress for Jane's cradle as well as mittens and picture books, and paints for both of them from Miss Matthews.

Jeffrey hurled himself onto her lap when they were finished and clung tightly to her neck. "Thank you, Mama," he said. "Thank you. You are the best mama in the whole world. I am going to build a castle with my bricks and Simon can defend it with his soldiers. Jane can wrap Pamela in her new blanket and come and watch. She can help build a tower." He spoke in an excited yell.

Jane was patting the pillow into place in the cradle.

And then the door opened. Antonia had been half expecting him. But she had been hoping to leave before he came, to take Jane with her. It was Jeffrey who had been summoned here for Christmas, Jeffrey whom he wanted more than anyone else in his life. She was under no illusions about his main motive for allowing her to stay. His son still needed his mother. She did not fail to notice now that he set three parcels down on Jeffrey's bed and smiled at the boy as he scrambled from her lap.

"I have a new cricket bat," Jeffrey told John in a voice that would have reached his father if he had been three rooms away. "I can hardly wait for summer to come. I am going to hit a mile with it."

"And in the meantime," John said, "I can see that you will be able to build me a fort."

Antonia got to her feet. "Come, sweetheart," she said to Jane, "we will go out and find some other children. Shall we wrap Pamela in the new blanket and take her too?"

"Do sit down," her husband said. "The child has a new cradle to play with here."

Antonia sat. Some of the joy had gone from the day. Jane—ah, Jane. She was watching as John handed one of the parcels to Jeffrey, who whooped with delight and tore off the paper. He was bounding around then, yelling with exuberance.

"Soldiers!" he yelled. "A whole army of them. Oh, wait till I show Simon. And Christopher. I will be able to put my own soldiers into my castle. Oh, *thank* you, Papa."

His father ruffled his hair and picked up the second parcel. Antonia put her head back against the chair. She felt rather like crying.

"And for you," John was saying, holding it out toward Jane.

Antonia frowned and bit her upper lip. And held her breath. She could not remember a moment more sweetly painful. He had bought a gift for Jane?

Jane took it, wide-eyed, and undid the ribbon with painstaking slowness before unfolding the paper. Her mouth formed that silent oh again and she lifted from the folds of the paper with infinite care a porcelain doll that looked for all the world like a newborn baby.

Antonia swallowed convulsively.

"A baby sister for Pamela," John said, his voice gentle. "And I see you have a cradle for her to sleep in. I daresay Pamela is too big a girl for a cradle. She needs to share your bed."

Jane stared at her doll for a long time before raising her eyes and gazing unblinkingly upward. "Are you P'pa?" she asked.

He went down on his haunches in front of her and rested one hand lightly on her curls. "I am," he said. "Jeffrey's papa and your papa. You are my little Jane. My treasure."

Antonia could no longer see. She tasted blood from her upper lip.

When she had finally succeeded in blinking away her silent tears, she saw that the third parcel was being held out to her. Her eyes snapped up to his. "Oh no," she said. "But I have nothing for you."

"Oh yes," he said, his eyes smiling at her, "you do, Antonia. Believe me, you do."

She took the parcel and opened it slowly. It was a fur muff. It matched the fur on her green cloak. She slid her hands inside it and lowered her nose into its softness. She closed her eyes.

"Thank you," she whispered. "Oh, John, thank you." She believed that he understood she was thanking him not just for the muff. Though it seemed to her at that moment that it was the most precious gift he had ever given her. "But you did not know we were coming."

"I went into town yesterday afternoon," he said.

To buy gifts for her and for Jane? Jane had seated Pamela beside her on the bed and was quietly rocking her new baby. Jeffrey was standing his soldiers in a row. John was smiling at her.

"The servants will be waiting for their Christmas boxes," he said, "and for their mince pies and wassail. We had better go down and fulfill our duties."

"You want me to come?" she asked.

"You are my countess, are you not?" he said. "The Countesses of Wycherly have always waited on the servants in the drawing room for this one hour of Christmas Day. You know that from experience. Come then."

She set her hand in his and got to her feet. Was it possible that life could resume almost where it had left off more than three years ago? Could they possibly just close the book on the past and move on into the future? Was there after all a future for them?

"Out into the nursery, then," he said, turning to look at Jeffrey and chuckling at his obvious impatience, "to see if you can yell louder than the other children. Away you go, son." He looked in the other direction. "Ah, baby is snugly wrapped. Take her out to show the other children, Jane. Is she sleeping?"

"And Pamela too," Jane said. "Bring her, P'pa."

He picked up Pamela with his free hand and carried her through into the incredibly noisy nursery to set her down on a chair as a silent spectator of the proceedings there. Jane bent forward and kissed her on the cracked, painted lips, careful not to wake her baby.

"John," Antonia said as they descended the stairs together, "how clever of you to buy her a *baby* doll. I gave her a splendid doll for her birthday, a doll that far outshines the shabby Pam. She sits in solitary splendor in one corner of the schoolroom at Lanting and hardly earns a glance in a week."

"Perhaps," he said, "with tortoise-like speed, I am learning some wisdom in my dealings with the women in my life, Antonia."

There was no opportunity to explore the meaning of his enigmatic words. They had reached the drawing room, and the butler had been sent on the formal mission of summoning the servants to join them there.

The day proceeded at its usual hectic pace. There was the Christmas dinner, after which it was imperative either to exercise or to fall asleep. Most of the older relatives nodded off beside the large fire in the drawing room or withdrew discreetly to their own rooms. Most of the younger people, including those who had children, went outdoors. There were to be organized games for the children, but inevitably the whole thing quickly degenerated into an energetic snowball fight.

The earl helped Jane mold snowballs and helped

her throw them at relatives who were kind enough to step within a foot of her and then pretend to be amazed and wrathful at being hit. Jane, he discovered, had a delightful and infectious giggle. He was soon laughing merrily with her. She was also, he noticed with interest, becoming a general favorite. His young cousin took her up on his slender shoulders and bore her off in pursuit of his young lady. The next time she came into sight she was riding, solemn and dignified, on George's broader shoulder.

And then there was tea in the drawing room with all the children present and everyone stuffing away platefuls of rich food while all the time protesting that they were about to *burst.* They could all fast for the next month, after all, Uncle Horace said, as he did every year. Inevitably someone suggested blindman's buff again as soon as all the tea things had been removed.

And so it would go on, the earl knew, until bedtime—a late bedtime—put an end to the day's frolicking. Any private moment on Christmas Day had to be quite ruthlessly stolen. When blindman's buff was moving into the third round, he removed himself to the only room where he could be almost sure of remaining undisturbed—his study. He sent his butler to ask his countess if she would wait on him there.

He was not really sure how he was going to proceed. He only knew that wonderful as everything seemed between them today, they could not drift on without some decisive moment marking the beginning of a new life. Once Christmas was over, once everyone else had gone back home or back to town or wherever they were going next, there would be an awkwardness between them, an invisible barrier.

He was standing staring into the newly lit fire, his hands clasped at his back, when she came. She was wearing green this afternoon, the color that looked best on her. But it was still a dress of simple design in contrast with the fussy creations many of the other ladies had donned for the occasion. Her beauty, of course, did not need artificial enhancing.

She stood close to the closed door, looking at him. The color was high in her cheeks. Her eyes were bright—and wary.

He was acting from instinct. He had no plans. He reached out one arm toward her. "Come," he said quietly.

She came. She hesitated for a moment when she was close, her eyes on his, but she came the rest of the way. Her mouth was open when it met his. He kissed her hungrily, his tongue licking into her mouth, tasting her. Through the barrier of his clothing he could feel her slender, very feminine curves arched in against him. He set his hands on her hips and pressed her close.

"I have never stopped desiring you," he said, lifting his head away from hers.

"Or I you," she said.

"We will continue with our marriage, then?" he said. "We will start anew, Antonia, as if this were the beginning? As if last night was our wedding night? We will put the past behind us as if it never were? Would that be best? Is it possible?"

She opened her mouth and drew breath as if she would speak, but she closed it again and shook her head and shrugged at the same time.

"You know I still love you," he said.

Her eyes filled with tears.

"Or should we talk about it?" he said. "Do we have to first go back if we are ever to go forward? I am afraid that if we go back, if we talk about it, we will find that after all we cannot move ahead. I cannot bear to lose you again. I have been so very lonely without you."

He had not thought of loneliness as his main problem in the past three and a half years. But he knew that he had spoken the truth. He had been lonely without her. Unbearably lonely.

"Why did you not believe me?" she asked, lifting one hand to wipe at a single tear that had spilled over and rolled down her cheek. She moved back just far enough that they were no longer touching. "You still do not, do you, even though you have been kind to her today. You want Jeffrey here and you want me here and you have decided that if Jane is to stay too, she cannot be ignored. I think you have even begun to love her a little. But you still do not believe me."

"Why did I not believe you?" He frowned. "When? Over what?"

"When I wrote to you," she said. "You never answered the letter though I know very well that you received it. You never acknowledged her birth. You never sent for me to come home. I took such care with the letter. Why did you not believe me?"

"The letter." He was still frowning. But he was blanching too. There was a buzzing in his ears. "The one you wrote just after her birth?"

"The day after," she said. "I felt so guilty and so bleak. I remembered how you had watched Jeffrey's birth. I was so very sorry for withholding the truth. And so I wrote to you as soon as I was able to sit up. But my punishment only became worse. You would not forgive me or believe me. Worse even than either—you ignored me. Can you understand the full horror of that punishment, John? Can you even imagine what it was like waiting day after day, watching day after day for the delivery of the post? Or perhaps for the arrival of your carriage? I expected you to be angry. I was prepared to deal with that, even to accept that you had more reason to be angry with me than I had to be angry with you. I was even prepared for things to be strained between us for a while. I was prepared to work very hard at our marriage. But you ignored me."

"You asked forgiveness," he said, his voice troubled, "and I did not grant it. Perhaps I would have if I had read the letter, Antonia. And perhaps I would have asked forgiveness too. I am sorry now. We have wasted more than three years of the lives we have together. I was very deeply hurt, but that was no real excuse. I had hurt you too. Let us forgive each other now. You have done well with her. She is a sweet and an irresistibly lovable child. From this day on she will be my child too—my daughter. I will never think of her otherwise."

But she was staring at him with wide eyes of disbelief. "If you had read the letter?" she said. "If ... *You did not read the letter?*"

"Forgive me." He could picture her now the day after giving birth, pale and weary and lonely and troubled, writing to him, choosing her words with great care, begging his forgiveness, when he had never begged for hers. And waiting, endlessly waiting for his reply. "Ah, forgive me, Antonia. I had received word of the birth only hours before your letter arrived. I cannot imagine living again through more wretched hours and coming through them sane. It somehow seemed worse that the child was a girl. I had so wanted a daughter of my own. I tossed your letter onto the fire without even breaking the seal. By the time I managed to retrieve it with the fire tongs, it was burned to ashes. I never did it again. I read every letter that came from you. I read the words and read between the lines and—"

He lunged for her then as she swayed on her feet, one hand pressed against her closed eyes.

"Forgive me," he said, lowering her into the chair that was behind her, going down on one knee and chafing her cold hands with his own. "I am so very sorry. Forgive me."

She had her head against the back of the chair. Her eyes were closed. "John," she said, "I have never lain with any man but you."

His hands stilled on hers. There was that buzzing sound again. "What?" His voice came out as a hoarse whisper.

"It all went too far," she said. "It became a nightmare. Suddenly I had power. I was delirious with it. And frightened by it. And tempted by it. I gave in to it."

"Antonia—" he said.

She had not opened her eyes. Her hands lay limp in his. "I was shattered," she said, "totally, utterly shattered when I found out about what you—when I found out about you. I wanted to die. And I wanted you to die. And then I wanted to hurt you—very, very badly. I did not think it would be possible. I thought you did not care for me at all any longer. But I tried anyway. I .."

"Started to collect a court of admirers about you,"

he said when she hesitated. "Started to accept escorts to every *ton* event of the Season. Started to look glitteringly happy. Started to have no time to spare for your husband."

"It was all unexceptionable," she said. "It was little more than wives are expected to do. Wives are not expected to hang on their husbands' coattails. I was very careful not to be a subject for gossip, not to disgrace you. All I wanted to do was hurt you—if it was possible. I wanted so badly to hurt you."

"I was hurt," he said softly.

"And then I found I was with child again," she said. "I suppose I had known for some time. But for a while I thought it was merely that I was very unhappy, very upset."

"Antonia—" The pain was coming back in all its rawness. "The child was born a month early."

"No," she said. "She was two weeks late."

He surged to his feet suddenly, dropping her hands, and turned to stare sightlessly into the fire. He dared not believe. He dared not. He would come all to pieces. He had had no marital relations with her during the last three months they had been together. The child could not possibly—

"When I told you," she said, "I was going to tell you too how unhappy I was, how much I wanted to patch up our marriage. I was going to tell you that I forgave you but that I desperately hoped there would be no more—no more *women*. I was going to ask if we could have a marriage again, a real marriage, not a typical *ton* marriage. I had planned so carefully what I was going to say. I got no farther than telling you I was increasing."

Who? He had turned to a block of ice with a furnace at his core ready to erupt. He could almost hear again the words he had said to her. *Who is he? Give me his name. He is going to die.*

"I begged you to listen to me," she said.

Whore! he had said. *Who is he? Who has fathered his bastard on you?* Over the years, he realized now, he had blocked the memory of those words. He could hardly believe he had spoken them.

"You called me something terrible," she said. "You called me a whore. That changed everything. I thought of the unfairness of it—of what you had done and of what I had not done. I was furious at your moral outrage. Again I wanted only to hurt you. I wanted revenge."

She had smiled at him. *You will never know, John,* she had said coolly, *unless the child has the misfortune to physically resemble his father.*

"And so I let you believe it," she said. "I do not suppose I intended for you to go on thinking it. When you left me alone in that room, I thought of Jeffrey and the unborn child and the ruin of what we had once known together. But then you came back."

Stand up, he had told her, rather like a sergeant talking to his rawest recruit. *Your belongings are being packed, my lady. You will be taken to Lanting House tomorrow. You will be leaving at first light. You will live out the remainder of your life there. You will continue as my wife in name and I will continue to support you provided I never see your face again. Do you have anything to say?*

Jeffrey? she had whispered.

Jeffrey will go with you, he had said, *and remain with you while he is in his infancy. Then I will take him back.*

He held out his hands to the flames now. He was shivering.

"I held onto my anger," she said, "until Jane was born. The labor was even longer and harder than it had been with Jeffrey. I knew that she would have your name. By sending me away you had proclaimed your decision to allow no scandal. But she was a tiny innocent, far more real after she was born than before. I could not bear the thought that in your eyes she would always be a bastard. I wrote to you." There was a lengthy silence. "And you burned the letter."

Something was trying to get through to his consciousness. He reached up one arm and rested his wrist against the high mantel. He bowed his head and gazed into the very center of one of the flames.

"She is mine," he said at last. "Jane is my daughter." He turned his head to look over his shoulder. But he could not see her clearly. "She is ours. We have a daughter, Antonia."

"Yes." He had not seen her get to her feet. He felt her fingers brush lightly against one of his cheeks and was aware of the wetness of his own tears. He wrapped both arms about the slender form of his wife, drew her close against him, and wept against the side of her head.

Yes, it had been necessary to talk. It had been tempting to agree with his first suggestion, that they put the past behind them, that they start afresh today with last night as a new wedding night. But there had been more than just themselves to think about. There had been Jane.

It had been right to talk. He had believed her after all. He had never read the letter. She had never even considered that possibility. She had sent it by personal messenger and had been assured that it had arrived and had been placed in his own hands. She had never thought that perhaps he had not read it.

He released her a long time after he had stopped sobbing and turned his back on her while he drew a handkerchief from a pocket and firmly blew his nose. When he turned back his eyes were red and watery—and smiling. He cupped her face with both hands.

"And you said you had no gift for me!" he said. He laughed softly and looked so happy that her heart turned over. "A daughter is not a gift, Antonia? Jane is not the most precious gift the world has to offer?"

She had time only to smile back before he kissed her firmly and warmly.

"Thank you," he said against her lips. "Thank you. She is beautiful. Dainty and pretty. Eyes as soulful as her mother's. You must know that she had enslaved me even before we came to this room."

"She has her father's curls," she said.

She could see him accepting the truth of it—that his daughter was half him. He laughed again. "We have a son and a daughter," he said. "A family."

His conversation had been anything but profound during the past minute or so. She laughed with him.

"*Now* we can go forward," she said. "*Now* we can put the past behind us once and for all, John. We can, can we not? I know I will blush because I always did when talking of such matters, did I not? But I will say it anyway. Last night's wedding night was every bit as wonderful as the first." She could feel the heat in her cheeks. He had used to tease her because she was never comfortable talking about—she had never even been able to get her mouth around the word, short as it was. About sex.

But he had stopped smiling. He was gazing into her eyes, the warmth and the happiness gone. His arms dropped away from her and he stepped back. He turned toward the fire again.

"Antonia," he said, "I have been unfaithful to you."

She did not want to go back to the past yet again. She had lived through that pain already. She had forgiven him.

"It is the present and the future I want," she said. "I want to forget the past. It will not happen again, John. I know it. You love me. You see? I believe it now. I would not believe it then, would I, though you said it over and over again. I did not believe it was possible that you could do—*that* with someone else and yet still love me. But it is over. I believe that you love me and that it will not happen again. I trust you."

"Once," he said. "I was unfaithful once. A little less than a year ago."

Her mind had stopped functioning. She could not seem to calculate times and dates.

"She was a dancer," he said. "I was planning to set her up as my—as my mistress. I had decided that I could not live celibate for the rest of my life. Just once it happened. Once too many times. It was horrible. Horrible." His hand, resting by the wrist against the mantel, clenched and unclenched. "She was not you." He drew a deep and audible breath.

Less than a year ago. Had they not been separated for longer than that? She searched the confusion of her mind. Jane was almost three years old.

"John?" she said.

"That other time," he said, "when I went to London

ahead of you and Jeffrey, I— A few of my former
university friends organized a sort of reunion. A din-
ner, involving a great deal of reminiscing and laughing
and drinking. We all regressed several years. Almost
inevitably we ended up at that brothel."

There were always women—ladies—who heard
about such exploits, secret as men always believed
they kept them. One of those ladies had been eager
enough to tell Antonia about it as soon as she arrived
in town with her son.

"They teased me," he said. "I was the only married
one among them. They teased me about being in love
like a girl, about being tied to my wife's apron strings.
It seemed the thing to do to go along with them and
hire a girl. It was the way to prove my manhood, to
prove that I was master of my own life. To show that
I was still the devil of a dashing fellow. Until I got
there and realized how stupidly immature it was to try
to prove those things in such a juvenile way. I loved
you. I wanted only you. And even if I had not, I had
vowed to keep myself only for you for the rest of my
life. I sat in the lounge with her, talking, while the
others were upstairs. I made the strange discovery that
she was a person." He laughed softly. "Poor girl. And
then when the others returned, one by one, I boasted
about having had more practice than they, about need-
ing less time— No, the rest does not need to be said."

"Why did you not *tell* me?" she said, staring wide-
eyed at his profile. But she knew the foolishness of
the question even as she asked it.

He turned his head to look at her. "I did," he said.
"Over and over. But you were furious, Antonia, dis-
traught. You did not at all behave as a wife of good
ton is supposed to behave. You did not pretend that

you did not know. And I was unable to deny that I
had been to the brothel."

Yes, he had told her. He had told her that he had
sat with one of the prostitutes, doing nothing but talk-
ing to her. She had treated his lies with loud scorn.
At least have the decency to admit the truth, she had
yelled at him. She had done a great deal of yelling
that day. And throwing. She had hurled and smashed
several costly ornaments. And so eventually he had—
admitted the truth.

Have it your own way, he had said at last, his voice
raised to match hers in volume. *I took her upstairs
and I rutted with her. I made rare sport with her. I
went back the next night to try out one of the other
girls and the next night to ride yet another. Are you
satisfied now?* He had stalked from the room, and they
had exchanged scarcely a word over the three months
following—until she had gone to him to tell him she
was increasing.

"We were a pair of jealous fools," he said. "We
had had things too easy. We fell in love at first sight
and we loved our way through a betrothal and four
years of marriage just as if we fully believed that
happily-ever-afters were possible. We lived in a fairy
tale. And then came the inevitable test. We failed it
miserably. But it was all my fault. I did not sleep with
her, but I went there fully intending to do so. And
then I allowed hurt and anger to rule me. I lied to
you. And forced you into everything that came after."

"A pair of jealous, *lying* fools," she said. "How
could we possibly have made each other suffer so
much for nothing at all, John? Are we savages? I am
frightened by what we were both capable of. Are we
still capable of it?"

"Yes," he said, looking at her. "I think civilization must be fought for every single day—just as love has to be fought for and a marriage. We can be sorry creatures when we give up the fight."

She swallowed awkwardly.

"Perhaps that is why we have Christmas every year," he said, "and then Easter so soon after. To remind us. And to assure us that love and decency can prevail despite the odds."

"John." She shivered. "Hold me."

"I have been unfaithful to you," he said, misery in his eyes.

She shook her head and forced herself to smile. Strangely, it was not difficult after all. She even found there was some merriment in her smile. "But it was horrible," she said. "She was not me. This is me." She opened her arms to him.

He was in them then and hugging her to him as if he would make her a part of his own body. She felt all the breath whoosh out of her lungs, but she wrapped her arms about his neck and made no protest. Even when his mouth was hard on hers and his tongue deep inside and she found it even more difficult to draw breath, she did not protest. She clung as if her very life depended upon clinging.

It was a very good thing, he thought, sitting reclined and relaxed on the most comfortable chair in the room, his wife curled on his lap, that no one ever disturbed him when he was in his study. He had taken her on the carpet before the fire with voracious hunger and without any thought whatsoever to where they were or to the fact that the door was unlocked. The realization could make the hairs prickle at the back of his neck when he thought of it now, but they were respectable again if a little disheveled. He laughed softly.

She turned her head and kissed the underside of his jaw. "It must be almost time to change for dinner," she said. "You would not want to be late."

"To the devil with dinner," he said, "if you will excuse my language."

"I suppose," she said, "if one is to judge from the sounds of distant merriment, there is still time. No one else seems to have retired yet."

"Then stay where you are and let me enjoy Christmas," he said. "I am glad after all that we went back, Antonia, though it was excruciatingly painful, was it not? Now we have an unclouded future ahead."

"But not a happily-ever-after," she said. "We are wiser than to make that mistake again."

"Mm," he said. "And no more hurled wassail bowls either if it is all the same to you."

She chuckled and then laughed outright. "You looked like a drowned rat," she said. "And you should have seen your face."

He joined in her laughter despite himself. "It was not so much the wetness that was bothersome," he said. "It was the stickiness. It was horrible punishment, Antonia."

They subsided into a comfortable quietness again until a slight creaking had him turning his head sharply toward the door. It was opening slowly. Thank heaven, he thought, this had not happened just ten minutes earlier. Whoever it was had not even knocked. A little mop of auburn curls appeared about the door.

"Come on inside, Jane," he said.

She came, her baby firmly tucked into one bent elbow, Pamela dangling from the other hand. She came toward them, placed her dolls carefully on Antonia's lap, and then climbed onto his, squeezing between her mother and the arm of the chair. She set her head against his chest and yawned.

"Tired?" he asked.

She nodded.

"Have you had a happy day, sweetheart?" Antonia asked.

Jane nodded again.

"Oh, I say," another voice said from the doorway. "You are not supposed to be in here, Jane. Uncle George said Mama and Papa needed to be alone. I will take her up to the nursery, sir. Come along, Jane. I will help you put the baby to bed."

But the earl smiled at his son. "Come on inside," he said, "and close the door. Come and sit here." He patted the arm of the chair. "Mama and I want to be alone with our children. Jane is falling asleep, I do believe. Come and tell us if you are enjoying Christmas."

Jeffrey looked from one to another of them as he obeyed his father. "I am enjoying it," he said. "I like having a mama and a papa both at the same time. Will it be like this next Christmas too?"

"Next Christmas and every day between now and then," the earl said. "I have Mama in one arm and my son in the other and my daughter against my chest—not to mention Pamela and the new baby. Why would I be foolish enough not to make every day Christmas Day?"

Jeffrey reached out one arm to set about Antonia's neck—she was smiling warmly at him. He tipped his head onto his father's shoulder and sighed. "This is the best Christmas in all the world," he said.

"Yes," his father agreed, "you are right there, my son. They do not come any better than this one. Ah, I thought as much. Jane is asleep."

He bent his head and kissed his wife softly on the lips. They smiled at each other with warm affection.